ADVANCED

Language LEADER

COURSEBOOK
and CD-ROM

PEARSON
Longman

David Cotton   David Falvey   Simon Kent

Ian Lebeau   Gareth Rees

Language Reference and Extra Practice by Diane Hall

CONTENTS

LANGUAGE LEADER ADVANCED

Listening	Speaking	Scenario	Study and writing Skills
Radio phone-in Job interview	Discussing differences in education Discussing the key to a successful life Talking about job hunting	**Choosing an intern** **Key Language:** stating requirements; saying what is essential and desirable **Task:** choosing an intern	Self-awareness A covering letter
Dr Graham Watkins interview about tourism and conservation	Talking about different types of tourism Discussing different ways of protecting nature	**Granville Island** **Key Language:** stating your position, clarifying **Task:** participating in an informal meeting	Planning and organising essays Analysing the questions Brainstorming A problem-solution essay
Radio interview – ambassador's life	Discussing national characteristics Talking about international organisations Solving crisis in a diplomatic way	**The oil spill crisis** **Key language:** stating objectives, giving strong advice **Task:** devising an action plan	Active listening A speech
Film review of *Sicko* Speech at a graduation ceremony	Talking about health and fitness Discussing healthcare systems in different countries Talking about nurses and nursing	**Change your ways** **Key language:** Justifying your opinions **Task:** choosing and planning a publicity campaign	Analysing visual information Describing visual information
Radio programme on consumerism Radio programme on fashion and social responsibility	Discussing consumerism and materialism Talking about luxuries in life Discussing controversial practices in the fashion world	**Retail revamp** **Key language:** discussing hypothetical ideas **Task:** developing a recovery strategy	Reading complex text effectively Building an overview Reading for detail Summarising Identifying main points Avoiding plagiarism
A dialogue with a career advisor	Discussing the effects of technological changes Talking about technological innovation	**A radio debate** **Key language:** using persuasive language, giving examples, conceding criticism **Task:** participating in a debate	Advanced dictionary skills A sales leaflet

CONTENTS

Listening	Speaking	Scenario	Study and writing Skills
Lecture on creativity Radio programme on rediscovered people	Discussing creativity Talking about national/local famous people Sharing good ideas	**Camomila** **Key language:** approving ideas, expressing doubt/objections **Task:** a new plan for Camomila	Critical thinking An opinion-led essay Essay planning Essay writing
People in the media talking about their jobs A talk on journalism	Discussing the future of newspapers Talking about the importance of journalism Discussing new channels for media	**Sailing close to the wind** **Key language:** being cautious **Task:** resolving ethical dilemmas	Research skills Features article for a magazine or newspaper
Extracts from a radio serialisation of a book Talk on youth crime and punishment A talk about immigration	Talking about different behaviour and unwritten rules (in a society) Discussing juvenile justice Talking about immigration	**Law makers** **Key language:** balancing an argument **Task:** amending and modifying the law	Synthesising information A literature review
Interviews; performance reviews Webcast – benefits of the Internet	Discussing art and entertainment Talking about music Discussing digital development	**Reality Island** **Key language:** an informal talk **Task:** auditioning	Seminar / discussion skills Creative writing (a screenplay)
A banker talking about redundancy	Planning the distribution of public spending budget Discussing the reasons for the global financial crisis Role play: negotiation	**Ariel capital** **Key language:** setting the agenda, responding to offers **Task:** negotiating a contract	Making a business presentation Introduction Body of the presentation Conclusion A tactful business email Paraphrasing
Descriptions of films/novels Video blog on 'plastic'	Discussing science fiction books/films Talking about consumption of plastic Discussing the importance of bees to nature and human life	**Ask the panel** **Key language:** referring to what other people have said **Task:** taking part in a panel discussion	Examination skills Exam vocabulary Exam culture Preparation A personal statement

Audioscripts (p170–191)

1 Education and employment

1.1 ISSUES IN EDUCATION

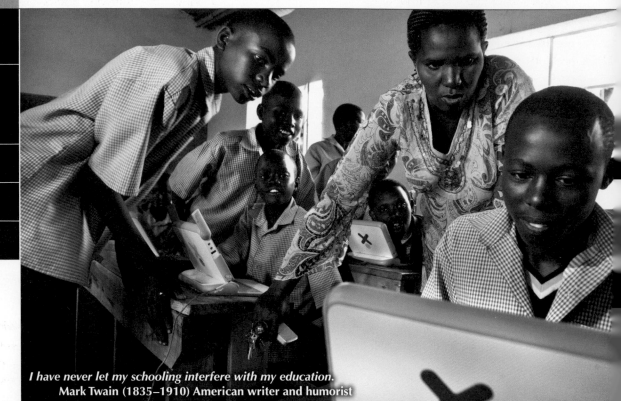

I have never let my schooling interfere with my education.
Mark Twain (1835–1910) American writer and humorist

SPEAKING

1a Use the words in the box to complete the opinions below.

> assessment   curriculum   dumbing down   elitism   interpersonal skills   plagiarism   streaming

1 'Education is not about developing your _____ but about learning facts.'

2 'Frequent examinations are a much more reliable and useful way of measuring performance than continuous _____ .'

3 '_____ is an excellent idea because it enables students with a similar ability to work at the same pace.'

4 'The most important aspect of education is the _____ , or subjects which are taught.'

5 'Private education creates _____ and encourages inequality in society, which is absolutely disgusting.'

6 'Copying someone else's ideas, _____ , cheating in exams, and buying qualifications is sometimes necessary.'

7 'It's easier to get good grades nowadays because education is _____ . Qualifications are worth less than in the past.'

1b Which opinions do you agree or disagree with? Discuss your ideas with a partner.

2 In pairs talk about:
1 your country's education system
2 your own educational experiences

READING

3 Which of the following are important to learn at school do you think?
1 important dates in history e.g. battles
2 the names of capital cities
3 times tables e.g. 4x 7=28
4 scientific formulae e.g. $E=mc^2$
5 spelling
6 mental arithmetic e.g. adding up numbers in your head
7 poems and excerpts from literature

4 What techniques do you have for learning any of these? Tell a partner.

5 What do you understand by the term 'rote learning'? Scan the article to check your answer.

6 According to the article are the statements below true, false or not given?

1 Teachers are no longer important.

2 Learning new things is not essential.

3 The British education system is old-fashioned.

4 Student autonomy is becoming more common in British schools.

5 Many people agree with Tapscott's views.

7 Do you agree with Tapscott's views? Why / Why not?

LISTENING

8 **1.2** Listen to three people on a radio phone-in programme talking about the purpose of education. Answer the following questions.

1 Where are they from and what do they do?

2 How do their opinions differ?

3 Which is closest to Tapscott's view do you think?

4 What is your reaction to the views you heard? How common do you think they are?

VOCABULARY: idioms

9 Match the following idioms (1–6) that describe people and their abilities/characteristics with the definitions a–f below.

1 Whiz-kid   4 Dark horse
2 High-flier   5 Team player
3 Know-all   6 All-rounder

Someone who:

a) has many different skills and abilities.

b) is very successful in a job or at school.

c) works well in a group especially at work/ in business.

d) behaves as if they know everything.

e) is quiet but who surprises with their hidden talents.

f) is a skilled or successful young person.

SPEAKING

10 In groups, talk about the following questions.

1 What is the main role of education for you?

2 'You get what you pay for.' Do you think this statement is true for education in your country?

3 What was missing from your own education?

Google generation has no need for rote learning

Memorising facts and figures is a waste of time for most school children because such information is readily available a mere mouse click away, a leading commentator has said.

The existence of Google, Wikipedia and online libraries means that there is no useful place in school for old-fashioned rote learning, according to Don Tapscott, author of the bestselling book *Wikinomics* and a champion of the 'net generation'.

A far better approach would be to teach children to think creatively so that they could learn to interpret and apply the knowledge available online. 'Teachers are no longer the fountain of knowledge; the Internet is,' Tapscott said. 'Kids should learn about history to understand the world and why things are the way they are.' But they don't need to

know all the dates. 'They can look that up and position it in history with a click on Google,' he said.

Tapscott denies that his approach is anti-learning. He argues that the ability to learn new things is more important than ever 'in a world where you have to process new information at lightning speed.' He said: 'Children are going to have to reinvent their knowledge base multiple times. So for them memorising facts and figures is a waste of time.'

His observations chime with a trend in British classrooms to cut back on traditional teaching and to personalise learning.

Schools are increasingly moving towards more independent study and so-called enrichment activities, with pupils learning at their own pace and focusing on what interests them most. At Wellington College in

Berkshire, for example, teenagers are not taught from the front of the class, but instead sit around a large oval table for seminar-style discussions.

Tapscott believes that the model of education that prevails today in most classrooms was designed for the industrial age. He suggests that the brains of young people today work differently from those of their parents. He argues that digital immersion, in which children may be texting while surfing the internet and listening to their MP3 player, can help them to develop critical thinking skills.

His views are unlikely to be universally welcomed. Richard Cairns, Headmaster of Brighton College, one of the country's top-performing independent schools, said that a core level of knowledge was essential: 'It's important that children learn facts. If you have no store of knowledge in your head to draw from, you cannot easily engage in discussions or make informed decisions.'

SPEAKING

1a Think of three successful people in the following fields: business, the arts or science. Why do you think they are successful? Tell your partner about them.

1b Which qualities do the people you have described share?

READING

2 Read the profiles of three successful people quickly and say in what way they are successful.

3 Look at the characteristics commonly used to describe successful people. Which of them apply to the people you read about?

a) hard-working   d) creative

b) innovative   e) business-minded

c) highly educated   f) self-disciplined

4 Read the profiles again and answer the following questions.

1 How do you think Kim and Simenon's earlier careers could have helped them achieve their later success?

2 What do you think of Nooyi's management style?

3 Which of the three people are you most impressed by? Tell a partner.

VOCABULARY: suffixes (adjectives)

5a Find adjectives in the profiles which are formed from the nouns below.

passion, allergy, power, success, persuasion, superstition, fiction, psychology

5b What suffixes are used to form these adjectives?

passion – passionate

6a Make adjectives from the following nouns using the suffixes.

education, affection, speculation, logic, ambition, empathy

6b Answer the following questions.

1 Who is the most successful person you know? Give your reasons.

2 Who is your favourite fictional character? Why?

3 What is the most powerful piece of art or film that you have seen?

4 Are you superstitious about anything? If so, give an example.

Indra Nooyi

In 2006, Indra Nooyi was appointed Chairperson and Chief Executive Officer of PepsiCo. She has been named as the most powerful business woman in the world by Fortune magazine. Born in India, she has a Bachelor of Science degree, an MBA from the Indian Institute of Management and a Masters degree in Public and Private Management from Yale University.

Nooyi has a reputation for being very persuasive and she has the ability to rouse an audience. She also has a very informal style in meetings and openly solicits the opinions of her staff. At one investors' conference, Nooyi sat down with the delegates and conducted the business equivalent of a fireside chat.

Nooyi is constantly reinventing her business model. 'The minute you've decided a new business model, it's extinct, because somebody is going to copy it.' For years she's been talking about the importance of healthier products and nutrition education. She works 18–20 hours a day and is currently serving on the boards of several organisations.

GRAMMAR: the continuous aspect

7a Read the profiles of Angela Jia Kim and Indra Nooyi again. Underline examples of the:

1 present continuous

2 past continuous

3 present perfect continuous

7b Which of the tenses you found are used to talk about:

a) actions that were in progress at an earlier time?

b) actions that are currently in progress?

c) an action which began in the past and is still continuing, or has just finished?

➡ **Language reference and extra practice, pages 134–135**

Georges Simenon

Georges Simenon was one of the most successful and prolific authors of the 20th century. Simenon had extraordinary energy as a writer and in one year, 1928, he wrote 44 novels. He was born in Liège in Belgium on Friday, 13 February, 1903, but his superstitious mother registered his birth as being a day earlier.

His success was not down to his education. He left school at the age of 15 and worked in numerous short-term jobs until he took a job as a journalist a year later. (Eventually, he even interviewed the Emperor of Japan.)

His first novel was published in 1921. He is best known for his psychological thrillers and in particular for the character of Inspector Jules Maigret, who, after Sherlock Holmes, is the world's most famous fictional detective. Maigret used psychological intuition to understand the criminal's motives.

Simenon wrote 75 Maigret novels which have inspired 55 films and 279 TV adaptations. For the last 40 years of his life he was probably the best-selling novelist in the world.

Angela Jia Kim

Angela Jia Kim is a successful entrepreneur – having already founded two companies.

Her first piano teacher was her mother and later she graduated from the Eastman School of Music. Her classical refinement and passionate performances have delighted audiences worldwide.

One day just as she was about to perform on stage she had an allergic reaction to a body lotion. As a result of this she decided to develop her own line of skincare products. 'I was paying attention to what I was eating,' she says. 'Shouldn't I pay attention to what I was putting on my body?' She started experimenting to find non-toxic creams and eventually launched *Om Aroma & co*, an organic skincare line.

Her degree was in music, not business, so she sought advice from respected businesswomen who were going through similar experiences. She went on to create *Savor the Success*, an online community for female entrepreneurs. She says her success in business is due to her training as a concert pianist and, of course, hard work.

8a Look at the pairs of sentences below. Explain the difference in meaning between them.

1 a) I work in Madrid, but I live in a village 40km away.

   b) I'm working in Madrid at the moment, but I'm moving to Barcelona next year.

2 a) I've worked in London, Paris and Rome, but now I work in Tokyo.

   b) I've been working in Tokyo for a year and expect to continue to do so for some time.

3 a) I worked in Oslo in 2006.

   b) I was working in Oslo when my father fell ill.

4 a) I'll work when you get home, if you look after the children.

   b) I'll be working when you get home, so please try to keep quiet.

8b Which of the actions in the sentences above are:

a) incomplete?

b) temporary?

c) happening around a point of time?

d) already in progress when something else happened?

9 Correct the errors in the use of tenses in this text.

I really respect my best friend. He *is coming* [comes] from Poland and is speaking four languages. He is living in London since 1998 and I've been knowing him for ten years. We met on holiday when we hitchhike through Spain. One day while we walk through the Cantabrian mountains he told me that even though he had been leaving school at 15 he was going to be very successful. He joined his company when it is having difficulties. He was working his way up to the top. He has only been working there for seven years and he is already being the Managing Director.

WRITING

10 Write a short paragraph giving your opinion on one of the following statements.

1 'A good education is the key to a successful life.'

2 'Luck and family connections are more important than a good education.'

1 In small groups, discuss the following questions.

1 How do you find out about jobs in your country?

2 What jobs have you had?

3 Have you ever written a CV/résumé? When?

4 Is there a standard format for CVs/résumés in your country?

READING

2 Which of the following do you think are essential to mention in your CV?

1 Website addresses of companies you have worked for

2 Details of pre-university qualifications

3 A photograph

4 Date of Birth

5 Mail address

6 Telephone number and email address

7 Names of referees

8 Internships / work placements

9 Computer programmes and software used

10 Charity work

11 Interests

12 Positions of responsibility

13 Title, e.g. Mr / Miss / Ms

3a Read the CV of Vadim Kufenko quickly. In your opinion, has he left out any essential information?

3b Read the CV again and answer the following questions.

1 What do you notice about the way the profile is written?

2 Which exchange programme might he have found the most difficult? Why?

3 What kind of jobs do you think he might be suitable for?

4 Vadim is applying for a job in the marketing department of a British company that exports British products to Russia. They require a fluent Russian speaker, with advanced English and experience in finance and marketing. Rewrite Vadim's profile to help him get this job.

Curriculum Vitae

Name: Vadim Kufenko
Date of birth: 8 May 1986
Address: 58 Suvorovsky pr., apt. 52,
St Petersburg 191015, Russia
Telephone: +7-812-264 69 22
Email address: v_kufenko@online.ru

PROFILE

An enthusiastic and dedicated professional with excellent analytical abilities in the field of finance. High levels of numerical capability. Quick to grasp new ideas and concepts and able to work on his own initiative. Has a logical approach to challenges and is able to meet tight deadlines. Strong project management skills. A good team player with good interpersonal skills.

WORK EXPERIENCE

December 2008 – present
    Financial Analyst at the Bank of Foreign Trade, St Petersburg. Responsibilities: daily financial analysis, preparing financial statements, data processing, and marketing surveys

EDUCATION

September 2007–July 2008
    MA Degree in Economics specialising in Finance and Credit, St Petersburg State University of Economics and Finance
September 2003–June 2007
    BA Degree in Economics, St Petersburg State University of Economics and Finance
1998–1999
    Southwest Junior High School, Lawrence, Kansas, USA
1993–2003
    School #157, St. Petersburg

VOCABULARY: abbreviations

5 In groups, match the education abbreviations with the descriptions below.

1 PhD	3 MBA	5 BEC	7 IELTS
2 MSc	4 BA	6 UCLES	8 TOEFL

a) A first degree in the humanities.

b) A postgraduate degree in a science subject.

c) A postgraduate degree, which entitles the holder to the title Dr.

d) A postgraduate business qualification.

e) A qualification in Business English.

f) A British examining board for exams in English as a Foreign Language.

g) A test of reading, writing, listening and speaking often used by British and Australian universities.

h) A test of comprehension in written and spoken English, often used by American universities.

1.3

INTERNSHIPS AND EXCHANGE PROGRAMMES

September – December, 2007
  Exchange Program at the University of Jyväskylä, Finland. Programmes: Finance, Business Networks, Family Business, Marketing (in English), Finnish language
April 2007
  Short internship at the Bank of Foreign Trade, St Petersburg
April – July 2006
  Exchange programme at the Berlin School of Economics, Germany, Programmes (in German): International Economic Relations; International Marketing; German language.

ADDITIONAL SKILLS

  Languages: English (advanced IELTS 8.0, BEC Higher (awarded by UCLES))
            German (intermediate)
            Finnish (elementary)

HOBBIES

  Trading in stocks and shares, swimming and jogging

REFERENCES

  Available on request

LISTENING

6a ▪**1.3** **Listen to part of Vadim's job interview. Answer the following questions.**

1 Why does the interviewer mention when the interview will finish?
2 What regret does Vadim mention?
3 What advice does the interviewer give Vadim?
4 How does Vadim turn a possible weakness into a strength?
5 Why does Vadim want the advertised job?
6 What mistake does the interviewer make?

6b **Listen again and evaluate the interview.**

1 Do you think what Vadim said highlights his strengths?
2 How would you describe the interviewer's attitude towards Vadim?
3 How do you think the interview is going (so far)?

GRAMMAR: the perfect aspect

7 **Look at Track 1.3 on page 170 and find an example of the following (there may be more than one answer):**

1 present perfect   4 perfect infinitive
2 past perfect   5 perfect -ing
3 future perfect

8 **In sentences 1–5 below, which action:**

a) is completed?
b) looks back from now to a time before now?
c) was completed before another action took place?
d) is expected to be completed by a particular time in the future?

1 Hopefully, we'll have finished the interview by 3 p.m.
2 I'd applied for a number of work placements before I got the one in the bank.
3 I've been on two exchange programmes: one in Finland and one in Germany.
4 Having read your CV, we'd like to know more about your internship and exchange programmes.
5 I seem to have lost your references.

➡ Language reference and extra practice, pages 134–135

9 **Fill in the blanks with present, past or future perfect.**

1 I intended to come for just a couple of months, but next September, I _____ (be) here for five years.
2 When I interviewed him he _____ (already/be) out of work for over a year.
3 My sister _____ (be) the head of a PR company for the last ten years.
4 We _____ (interview) five people since 9 a.m. but I don't think any of them meet the requirements.
5 It's no use sending your CV now. They _____ (choose) a candidate by the end of today.
6 I was hoping _____ (finish) by now.
7 _____ (complete) my training, I'm now looking for a job in finance.

WRITING

10a **Choose a job that you would like to be interviewed for and write a short CV to help you get that job.**

10b **In pairs, tell each other which job you would like to be interviewed for, give your partner your CV and take it in turns to interview each other.**

SITUATION

Anderson University is a private university in the United Kingdom. Many of its students want to do internships of three to six months with companies or international organisations. They generally pay a fee and use the services of Morton Associates, a firm that specialises in arranging internships.

Morton Associates is looking for a suitable candidate for an internship with the international organisation UNESCO.

United Nations
Educational, Scientific and
Cultural Organization

UNESCO Activities

UNESCO promotes international co-operation among its 193 Member States and six Associate Members in the fields of education, science, culture and communication. It has a wide range of programmes, which will appeal to students from diverse disciplines.

AIMS
- to halve the proportion of people living in extreme poverty in developing countries by 2015
- to achieve universal primary education in all countries by 2015
- to eliminate gender disparity in primary and secondary education by 2015
- to help countries implement a national strategy for sustainable development

1a Read the situation, the description of UNESCO and the duties of the intern.

1b In pairs/small groups, discuss what kind of person would be suitable for this internship. Think about the candidate's educational qualifications, personal qualities, experience, skills and interests.

2 Discuss your profile of the ideal candidate with another group.

DUTIES OF THE INTERN

- to assist in administrative duties as assigned by the director
- to assist in the research and writing of department publications
- to assist with desktop publishing
- to help to coordinate special events and conferences
- to take part in the development of student educational programmes

3 **1.4** In pairs listen to Lisa and Howard, (two members of Morton Associates) talking about the requirements for candidates applying for an internship at UNESCO. Make notes under the following headings.

- Qualifications
- Languages
- Work experience
- Computer skills
- Interests
- Duration of internship

KEY LANGUAGE: stating requirements; saying what is essential and desirable

---

4 **1.5** Listen to part of the conversation and complete the following extracts. Use a maximum of two words for each gap.

1 L: It's _____ that candidates are doing a postgraduate degree …

2 H: What about languages?

   L: They _____ an excellent knowledge of one of the working languages of the organisation …

   H: Right, so that's _____ .

3 H: How about work experience?

   L: They don't mention that specifically, but it's obviously _____ to have some work experience …

4 H: You haven't mentioned computer skills.

   L: Well, candidates _____ to be able to use office-related software.

5 H: Anything else?

   L: No, but we'll be _____ some evidence of a special cultural or scientific interest.

5 Look at Track 1.4 on page 170. Underline all the phrases which are used to *state requirements* and say whether each one is *essential* or *desirable*.

| TASK: choosing an intern |

6a Work in groups of three. You are members of Morton Associates. You are going to recommend one intern for an internship at UNESCO. There is only one vacancy at the moment.

Student A: read the profile of Carla Dias

Student B: read the profile of Stefan Muller

Student C: read the profile of Hiroko Watanabe

Underline the strong points of each candidate. Make a note of any points you think the candidate lacks.

6b In your groups, discuss the candidates. Talk about their strengths and weaknesses and why they should/shouldn't get the internship.

6c Rank the candidates in order of their suitability for the internship (1 = most suitable, 3 = least suitable).

6d Choose the best candidate to recommend for the internship at UNESCO. Then, compare your choice with the other groups.

PROFILE

Qualifications
Final year PhD in Computer Science.

Languages
Bilingual German/English.

Computer skills
Extensive knowledge of computer program and software.

Attitude
Ambitious. Wants to work for a multinational company running its communications network. Has travelled widely in Asia during his vacations. Is studying French in evening classes.

Availability
Flexible.

Other information
Dressed casually for the interview. Quiet and thoughtful with a strong sense of social responsibility.

Stefan Muller

PROFILE

Qualifications
Final year Masters Degree in Architecture.

Languages
Good oral and written English. Fluent Portuguese, Spanish.

Computer skills
Competent in Word and Excel.

Attitude
Interested in current affairs. Previous one-month internship in International Labour Organisation (ILO) Geneva. Would like to pursue a career as a diplomat.

Availability
Is interested in a 4-month internship.

Other information Smart appearance. Very articulate and self-confident. Inquisitive. Under-16 tennis champion in her home town.

Carla Dias

PROFILE

Qualifications
Final year PhD in English literature.

Languages
Fluent oral and written Japanese, English and French.

Computer skills
Basic knowledge of office software. Claims to be a quick learner.

Attitude
Demonstrated a good knowledge of current affairs. Wants to represent Japan in an international organisation.

Availability
Would ideally prefer a longer internship (six months).

Other information
Well dressed. Spoke fluently using a wide range of vocabulary. Says she's a good team player. A member of the International Society at university. Seemed very nervous during the interview. Asked no questions.

Hiroko Watanabe

OTHER USEFUL PHRASES

Talking about strengths and weaknesses

One of his/her strongest points is …

His/her best quality is …

What impresses me about X is …

His/her biggest asset is …

One of his/her major weaknesses is …

I think he/she lacks …

I'm worried/concerned about his/her age/experience/qualifications …

What concerns me about the candidate is …

STUDY SKILLS: self-awareness

1a **1.6** Two students are being interviewed by a linguist who is researching the motivation of learners of English. Look at the descriptions of two types of motivation. Listen to the interviews with Jan and Marco. Then decide which type of motivation they have.

Instrumental motivation: The person is learning the language to achieve a definite goal, e.g. to get a better job, to be promoted, to pass an external examination, etc.

Integrative motivation: The person is learning the language to communicate with people from another culture that speak the language. The person wants to identify with the target language group and fit in with it.

1b Which student, Jan or Marco, expresses the following ideas? Listen again and check.

He …

- is a flexible person when travelling.
- will make more money by improving his English.
- wants to achieve native speaker proficiency.
- does not want to learn a lot about English culture.
- learned about English culture at an early age.
- is learning English in a company environment.
- wants to learn more about the literature of the country.
- needs to communicate better in English for work reasons.

2 In small groups, discuss the following questions.

1 What is your main motivation for improving your English?

2 What other things are motivating you to improve your English language proficiency?

3a Jan travels a lot and believes he has good cross-cultural skills. In groups, discuss some of the skills and qualities that people need when living or working in foreign countries. Make a list and show your ideas to the other groups.

3b Compare your list of cross-cultural skills with a list made by an expert in the field. See page 166.

3c Now discuss whether you think you have the qualities required to work in a foreign country. Give reasons for your answer.

4 **Learning style** It is important to be aware of your learning style, as this will indicate not only your strengths but also areas you need to develop. Read about four approaches to learning on page 166. Then, in groups, answer the questions below:

1 Which style do you think best describes you personally?

2 Are you a mix of the styles? If so, in what way?

3 Is one learning style predominant in your group?

4 What could each of you do to improve your learning style?

5 **Personal qualities and skills** Work in groups. First, note down the qualities and skills *you* have which would impress a potential employer. Then compare your list with those of other students in your group.

WRITING SKILLS: a covering letter

6 **When to use a covering letter** Complete the gaps in the text with the words in the box.

> convincing   motivate   speculative
> targeted   vacancy   vital

A covering letter should always be included when you send out a CV or an application form. It should create interest and ^{1}_____ the employer to get to know more about you. There are two types of covering letter. In a ^{2}_____ covering letter, the writer is responding to a specific advertised ^{3}_____ . However, in a ^{4}_____ covering letter, the writer aims at a specific employer or a number of companies or organisations he/she is interested in joining. A covering letter is ^{5}_____ if your application is speculative because the employer will only read it and look at your CV if your letter is really ^{6}_____ .

7 **How to structure a covering letter** Look at the information below and put it in the order it would probably appear in a covering letter.

1 Highlight your strong points, your understanding of the work, and why you are suited for it.

2 End the letter with an appropriate sentence.

3 Indicate your availability for interview.

4 Explain why you are interested in the job.

5 State what the vacancy is and how you heard about it. If the covering letter is speculative, say what kind of work you are interested in.

8 🔊 **1.7 What to do in a covering letter** Naomi Lloyd is a Communications Consultant. Listen to her talk, and make notes on what she says about the following:

- introduction
- your strengths
- length of the letter
- applying for different jobs
- ending the letter

9 Read Track 1.7 on page 171 and check your answers.

10a Vadim Kufenko is also applying for the position of Research Assistant with *Euronews Magazine*. The magazine provides readers with information on trends in international banking, foreign exchange investment and capital markets. Read the covering letter that Vadim includes with his CV. Do you think he has followed the rules of writing a covering letter? Discuss with a partner.

10b Look at the letter again. Each paragraph contains a *topic sentence* and one or more supporting ideas. With your partner, study the example, then analyse paragraphs 3 and 4 of Vadim's letter in the same way.

A topic sentence contains the main idea upon which a paragraph is developed. It often appears at the beginning of a paragraph, introducing the main idea.

Example: Paragraph 2

<u>Topic sentence:</u> *Having read your company literature, I am very interested in joining your organisation.*

<u>Supporting ideas</u>: *(The reasons why Vadim thinks he would be an asset to the company) He thinks the job suits his qualifications and experience and offers a suitable challenge.*

11 Certain phrases are common in covering letters. Find words/phrases in the letter which mean the following.

1 which I hope you will study carefully (paragraph 1)
2 descriptions of your organisation's activities (para. 2)
3 something that needs skill and energy to achieve (para. 2)
4 extremely useful (para. 3)
5 short and clear (para. 3)
6 getting work done very quickly and on time (para. 3)
7 have obtained (para. 4)
8 someone of value (para. 5)

Dear Ms Sommer,

Re: Research Assistant

(1) I am writing to apply for the above position advertised in the graduate section of *The Chronicle*, dated 5 June. I enclose my Curriculum Vitae for your consideration.

(2) Having read your company literature, I am very interested in joining your organisation. I am convinced that the position of Research Assistant would be well suited to my qualifications and experience. It would also provide me with an interesting challenge.

(3) My role as Financial Analyst in the Bank of Foreign Trade in St Petersburg has given me invaluable experience of working in teams on research projects. It has also enabled me to develop key skills such as analysing financial statements, undertaking marketing surveys and writing concise reports, which are all relevant to this position. Of course, I am used to working to tight deadlines.

(4) During my vacations, I have travelled widely in Europe and have gained useful cross-cultural skills. As a result, I feel I would be able to fit comfortably into the multinational teams which I know are an important feature of your organisation.

(5) If I am fortunate enough to be selected for the position, you will be employing an enthusiastic, highly motivated and loyal member of staff, who will be an asset to your organisation.

I am available for interview at any time and look forward to hearing from you.

Yours sincerely,

Vadim Kufenko

12 You have already written a CV. Now write an impressive covering letter for the job advertisement below, so that you will be called for an interview.

Volunteers WANTED

We are looking for volunteers with a wide range of skills and experience to participate in projects (such as building a school) in more than 30 of the world's poorest countries.

You can make a difference.

Send your CV to …

MOTIVATION

INSPIRATION

2 Tourism and conservation

In this unit

Grammar
- articles
- modal verbs

Vocabulary
- travel collocations
- multi-word verbs
- conservation

Scenario
- Granville Island

Study skills
- planning and organising essays

Writing skills
- a problem-solution essay

2.1 WISH YOU WERE HERE?

No travel writer I have ever known has written about the importance of parking.
J.G.Ballard (1930–2009) British Novelist

SPEAKING

1 In pairs, discuss the points below and put them in order of importance for you as a tourist.

- weather
- accommodation
- cost
- sights
- food
- activities
- ease of travel
- environmental considerations

2 What are popular holiday destinations for people from your country and how have these changed in the last ten years?

VOCABULARY: travel collocations

3a Match the following.

budget airline

1	ancient	a)	deal
2	boutique	b)	delights
3	carbon	c)	~~airline~~
4	last-minute	d)	footprint
5	gastronomic	e)	monuments
6	~~budget~~	f)	temperatures
7	organised	g)	hotel
8	baking	h)	excursions

3b Now match collocations 1–8 to the correct category in Exercise 1.

3c What other collocations can you add to each category?

accommodation ⟶ *luxury hotel*

READING

4a Read the holiday brochure extracts on page 17. Which of the holidays listed would be suitable for the people below? Discuss your ideas in pairs.

1 A wealthy older couple looking for a relaxing holiday.
2 An adventurous student of ecology with a limited budget.
3 A sporty group of friends in their 20s looking for fun and excitement.
4 A young professional couple who want peace and quiet.
5 A cultured holiday-maker interested in the environment.

4b Which holiday would you like? Why?

5a Match the brochure entries to one of the holiday types below. Some of the choices are not needed.

an adventure holiday, a city break, a cruise, a resort holiday, a sightseeing tour, a working holiday, a safari, a self-catering holiday, backpacking

5b Can you add any other types of holiday to the list?

VOCABULARY: multi-word verbs

6 Some tourists are talking about what they like to do on holiday. Complete the gaps in the sentences with the words in the box.

around	away	back	down	in
of	off (x2)	up (x2)		

1 'A holiday is all about getting _____ from it all.'

2 'I just want time away from work when I feel I can really let my hair _____ .'

3 'I just love going somewhere new and soaking _____ the atmosphere.'

4 'We live in a big city, although I grew up in the country, so getting _____ to nature is important.'

5 'I love to blow a lot of money and really live it _____ when I go on holiday–no expense spared.'

6 'We're keen on finding unusual places– going _____ the beaten track.'

7 'Steering clear _____ the tourist traps is our main priority when booking a holiday.'

8 'I don't really like to do very much on holiday. Just lounging _____ by the pool is enough.'

9 'The main thing is to avoid getting ripped _____ , so I try not to look like a tourist.'

10 'I love seeing new things and taking _____ the sights.'

SPEAKING AND WRITING

7 What do you know about some of the specialised types of tourism below? How do you feel about them? In small groups, discuss your ideas.

battlefield, culinary, eco, disaster, celebrity, health/medical (including 'surgery safaris') volunteer, space

8 Choose one of the types of tourism above and write your opinion of it in a short paragraph.

A *Spend seven nights exploring the Caribbean aboard a state-of-the-art vessel:* The Palladium. Offering the ultimate in five-star indulgence and boasting 11 decks, it still retains a unique and intimate atmosphere. Select a stateroom with balcony for awe-inspiring ocean views. With five restaurants to choose from, each meal is a gastronomic delight. In the evenings, choose from a comprehensive range of entertainment options. Pamper yourself with the wide variety of treatments available in the Palm Court Spa. Fully escorted excursions are available at each port of call. This is an experience not to be missed. Call now on …

Last minute package deals

B *Valentine's Day special:* Weekends for two in Paris. Explore the famous sights of the city of love – the Eiffel Tower, the Louvre, Montmartre – and then sample the culinary skills of renowned Parisian chefs. Stylish boutique hotel in the heart of this chic, bustling capital. Unbeatable prices. For more info go to **Earlybird.com**.

C *Feeling restless? Itchy feet?* An active two weeks in New Zealand, including a week of escorted trekking with breathtaking views, the opportunity to bungee jump and try paragliding. Experience a variety of exotic landscapes with a visit to a volcano, glacier hiking and white-water rafting. Local specialities and hospitality as you've never experienced before. All flights and internal transfers included. **DownUnder.com**

D *Sri Lankan Odyssey.* Fully guided holidays to explore the spectacular ancient monuments of an island rich in history. Enjoy baking temperatures, superb beaches and indulge in mouth-watering local delicacies prepared by top chefs. Our 'Green' hotels encourage visitors to calculate carbon emissions and will arrange for guests to plant trees if they want to offset their carbon footprint. Luxury holidays for the discerning and sophisticated traveller with an interest in sustainable development. An experience to savour. Flights not included. Single supplements apply. For further details go to **Exped.com**.

E *7 nights on the picturesque Greek island of Kefalonia* (as seen in the film *Captain Corelli's Mandolin*) in an isolated, restored cottage. Experience the stunning views and secluded beaches and unwind in this off the beaten track location, far from the stresses and strains of the rat race. Steer clear of the tourist traps, recharge your batteries and return completely refreshed. All-inclusive deal. Special offer price includes flight (budget airline), accommodation, Jeep hire. **Athena travel**

F *The holiday of a lifetime. Ten nights in the Badumbas National Park.* See the big game and get back to nature. Staying at the exclusive Masai Game Lodge with three-star facilities, you will also spend two nights under canvas out in the bush. Stunning flora and fauna. A visual feast of wildlife all experienced at close quarters, including lions, elephants and rhinos. All travel is in air-conditioned off-road vehicles. No single-room supplement. **ZebraTourZ**

READING

1 Look at the photos below and quickly read the description of the Galapagos Islands. Choose one or more photo(s) for the webpage.

2 Read the website and answer the questions below.

1 Where are the islands?
2 How many islands are there?
3 What area is covered by the islands?
4 Why are they so special?
5 What can you see there?
6 What is the tour company's attitude to tourism?

3 Read the website again. Answer the following questions.

1 What words does the writer use to encourage you to visit the Galapagos Islands?
2 What sort of people would be attracted to the islands?
3 What kind of problems might the Galapagos have?
4 Would you like to go there? Why / Why not?
5 What might you expect to do as an 'environmental ambassador'?

LISTENING

4a **1.8** Dr Graham Watkins is the Executive Director of a conservation charity and is an expert on the Galapagos Islands. Listen and say whether the following statements about him are true or false. Correct the false information.

1 His father was a conservationist.
2 He studied biology at Oxford University.
3 He worked as a guide in the Galapagos Islands.
4 He studied zoology and evolution at the University of Pennsylvania.
5 His first job after the University of Pennsylvania was in the field of conservation biology.

---

http://www.galapagosinspirations.com/

HOME
GALAPAGOS TRAVEL
, OPTIONS
INFORMATION
WHEN TO GO
WHICH BOAT?
HOW TO HELP
SPECIAL OFFERS
MAP

GALAPAGOS
INSPIRATIONS

Cruise Galapagos

Located 600 miles off the coast of Ecuador in the Pacific Ocean and just a short flight from Quito, the capital, the Galapagos archipelago consists of thirteen large islands and more than 100 smaller islands and islets and has a total land area of about 5,000 square miles. About 28,000 people live on the four inhabited islands.

The Galapagos Islands are truly unique. They are among the most scientifically important and biologically outstanding places on the planet. Zoologists, botanists, ecologists and geologists from all over the world have been inspired by them since their discovery in 1535.

However, the islands are not just for scientists. Anyone interested in nature and wildlife will find a visit to these extraordinary islands a life-changing experience. Nowhere else in the world will you get closer to the wildlife and be able to see Giant Galapagos tortoises, land and marine iguanas, flightless cormorants, Galapagos penguins and boobies roaming freely.

For those who want to get away from it all to truly deserted beaches where you can watch birds, playful sea-lions, humpback whales, exotic plant life and volcanoes, this will be an unforgettable cruise.

Our company tours responsibly and you can return home as an environmental ambassador for the area.

4b 🔊**1.9** Now listen to Part 2 of his interview and answer the following questions:

1 Does Graham think tourism is a bad thing? Why / Why not?

2 Give examples of negative consequences of tourism that are a) direct and b) hidden

3 What are 'invasive species'?

5a In Part 3 Graham is asked whether we should stay away from conservation areas. Predict what he will say.

5b 🔊**1.10** Now listen to Part 3 and check your predictions. Then answer the following questions.

1 How can the impact of tourism be minimised?

2 What are the best forms of tourism?

3 What is 'sustainable development'?

VOCABULARY: conservation

6 Complete the gaps in the sentences below with the words in the box.

biodiversity emissions endangered irreversible renewable sprawl

1 This charity is working to preserve the amazing _____ of tropical rainforests.

2 Many animals are becoming _____ because of the destruction of their natural habitats.

3 The government has set the goal of cutting carbon _____ by 15 per cent by 2020.

4 Urban _____ is the spreading of a town or city into the rural area around it.

5 The report says that humans have already done _____ damage to the planet.

6 Examples of _____ energy are sunlight, rain and geothermal heat.

GRAMMAR: articles

7 Which of the rules a–k below explain the use of the articles underlined in the travel company website?

1 Definite article:

a) common knowledge – we know we can tell from the context what is being referred to

b) repetition – this is not the first mention of the person or thing

c) uniqueness – the only one of its kind the world, or in this context

d) with a superlative phrase

e) with the names of countries or groups of islands which are plural

f) with names of rivers, oceans and seas

2 Zero article:

g) with uncountable nouns when speaking about the noun in general

h) with the names of most cities, streets, countries and continents

i) with plural countable nouns

j) with most numbers (except a half, a hundred, a thousand)

3 Indefinite article:

k) with a singular countable noun mentioned for the first time

➡ Language reference and extra practice, pages 136–137

8 Read extracts from the interview a–c. Some articles are missing. Write in the articles where appropriate.

Graham:

a) I became ⁄ᴬ conservationist, in part, because of my family background. My father was agricultural scientist and travelled throughout world. One of my brothers was born in Africa. I was born in British Guiana.

b) I went to University of Oxford to study zoology. I finished my first degree there. After that, I was lucky enough to become guide in Galapagos Islands. I did that for about 18 months and as a result of that experience, which was really quite life-changing experience, I went to University of Pennsylvania to study ecology and evolution.

c) I think the first thing to say about tourism is that in many situations it's very positive thing. It can help conservation quite substantially but there are also many examples in world, for example in Caribbean, where tourism also causes problems and has direct impacts on environment. Many of reefs in Caribbean have serious problems as result of pollution.

SPEAKING

9 In groups, choose one of the following in your country that you would like to protect. Discuss how you would protect it.

1 a natural feature

2 a historical building

3 an endangered species

READING

1 In groups, discuss the advantages of going to:

a) an isolated, unspoilt beach with no amenities

b) a resort beach with sun-loungers, waiter service and full water sports facilities.

2 Read the article quickly and choose the best headline:

THE BEACH THAT TURNED BACK THE COMMERCIAL TIDE

MEXICAN COMMUNITY STOPS DEVELOPERS

3 Complete the subheading below with a possible ending.

Robert L. White reports on how a determined group of locals in Mexico …

4 In which paragraphs are the following topics mentioned?

1 resorts for the wealthy

2 the campaign to save the beach

3 an unspoilt beach

4 the fate of other beaches

5 Compare paragraphs A and B of the article. What do you notice about the author's language?

6 Find two-word phrases in the text which mean the following:

1 a series of actions by ordinary people intended to achieve a result

2 a long, hard fight

3 an official organisation that has power to make decisions for a particular area

4 a group of companies working together

5 a problem concerning the people and things around you

6 a fact relating to human society that you think about

7 Read the article again and answer the questions.

1 Do you agree that the destruction of many of the world's idyllic places is really inevitable? Why / Why not?

2 In which ways do you think this story is an example of a significant or general change in attitude towards tourism development?

A Picture a perfect beach. From an expanse of flawless white sand, implausibly turquoise water shelves out over a stoneless seabed to a clear horizon. Overhead, pelicans wheel lazily in search of fish. One suddenly folds its wings, like a prehistoric umbrella, and hurtles downward. The splashdown is the first sound you can remember hearing for several minutes.

B Now imagine a whacking great hotel plonked on all this; plus a golf course and a few jetskis, of course, just to keep the decibel levels up. This is the fate that has befallen so many of the world's idyllic places that there seems something almost inevitable about it. Thanks to a determined and organised grassroots campaign, however, it won't be happening on this particular Mexican strand.

C Balandra beach, outside the city of La Paz, state capital of Baja California Sur, has been spared from future development after residents, civil society groups and environmentalists organised themselves into a collective, amassing a petition of 18,440 signatures calling on the regional authorities to protect the area. On March 25, after a protracted struggle by the Colectivo Balandra, state officials finally designated a total of 2,131 hectares of land and sea a Natural Protected Area, in a move that could signal a shift in Mexico's approach to tourism and conservation.

GRAMMAR: modal verbs

8 Which modals (*can, could, may, might, must, will, would, should, have to, ought to*) do we use to talk about …

1 likelihood / possibility / probability?

2 ability?

3 permission / requests?

4 obligation / necessity?

5 deduction?

9 Look at part of a leaflet encouraging people to sign a petition to save Balandra beach. Which modals express the following meanings/functions?

a) lack of obligation

b) obligation not to do something

c) advice

d) refusal

e) ability

f) future possibility

g) obligation

D   Environmental issues were, naturally, one of the main planks of the collective's campaign. As the group warned on its website: 'The landscapes of the rest of the beaches of La Paz have already been modified with various types of constructions and installations; Balandra is the only one that remains to us.'

E   But there were social considerations at stake here, too, because Balandra is essentially a beach for the people of La Paz, where tourism is of the unobtrusive variety. In stark contrast to the super-rich celebrity playground of Cabo San Lucas, just down the road, this is not a place that exists to service the appetites of deck shoe-wearing management consultants from LA.

F   The threat came, specifically, from a business consortium headed by the son of a former state governor of Veracruz, whose family own land in the area. Miguel Alemán Magnani's hotel-and-golf vision involved international capital, according to the Mexican newspaper *El Universal*, and the group had been trying since at least 2005 to get the go-ahead for the project.

G   Development of Balandra would surely have brought jobs: margaritas would have had to be served, tour parties guided and pets pampered. But the people of La Paz have looked into that particular future and dared to choose another path. They have shown that it is possible to take on the inevitable – and win.

GRAMMAR TIP

Must often expresses an obligation which comes from the speaker:

I must write to my mother.

Have to often expresses a more impersonal obligation:

You have to have a visa to enter the country.

➡ **Language reference and extra practice, pages 136–137**

10   **Underline the correct modal verb.**

1   I'm afraid that's absolutely impossible.
It *mustn't / can't / may not* be true.

2   That *mustn't / may not / can't* be Peter.
He's in Beijing.

3   I *can / must / might* have to go to Miami tomorrow.

4   We *mustn't / might not / don't have to* leave yet.
We've got lots of time.

5   It looks like it could snow, but it *can / could / might* not

6   You *may / would / will* sit down if you like.

7   You *don't have to / mustn't / might not* touch that button. It will delete everything.

8   I can't meet you tomorrow. I *have to / would / could* work.

9   Sorry, but I *can't / might not / may not* come to the meeting. I'm too busy then.

SPEAKING AND WRITING

11a   **Work in groups. You are responsible for looking after a local beach. Talk about the rules that users of the beach will have to follow.**

11b   **Write a notice with your list of rules to be placed at the entrance to the beach.**

SAVE OUR BEACH

We mustn't let the developers destroy our beach.

We don't have to let them win.

It might mean fewer tourists in the short term but, with your help, we can win this campaign and we may be able to change the government's attitude to the environment.

You should sign the petition on the back now. Your signature could help us make a difference. You have to be 18 to sign this petition.

We won't stop until the developers stop.

SITUATION

Granville Island is a fairly large island in the Caribbean with a population of 780,000. Its main sources of income are fruit, fish and tourism. Some five years ago, a hurricane devastated the capital city and towns, as well as the fruit plantations. As a result, the unemployment rate on the island has risen to 20 per cent. Now foreign property companies are coming into Granville Island to develop its economy and rebuild its tourist facilities. This has led local environmental groups to accuse the authorities of sacrificing Granville's natural habitats in order to develop a seaside resort.

Ricardo Hernandez

Born in Cuba, Hernandez entered the United States as a political refugee. He made a fortune in real estate in New York refurbishing old apartment buildings, then moved to Florida where he made another fortune constructing hotels. A billionaire, now of American nationality, he is thought to be in the top five of America's richest men.

1 Read the situation and the description of Granville Island and the information about Ricardo Hernandez. Then answer the questions below.

1 How might the authorities be sacrificing Granville's natural habitats?

2 What is special about Ricardo Hernandez?

2a 1.11 Listen to the excerpt from the local radio news. Make notes under the following headings.

• Reason for buying the Roberts Estate …

• Planned facilities …

• Possible problems …

2b In groups, discuss the possible advantages and disadvantages of Hernandez's project.

KEY LANGUAGE: stating your position, clarifying

3a 1.12 Listen to the conversation between Ricardo Hernandez and Louisa Bradshaw, who is the Mayor of the community where Hernandez would like to develop a golf course. Now answer the questions below.

1 What is Ricardo Hernandez's position concerning the length of the golf course?

2 What supporting arguments does he use to persuade the Mayor to accept his point of view?

3 What will Hernandez do if his project is not accepted?

3b Listen again. Complete the gaps in the extracts below with the language Ricardo Hernandez uses.

1 I'd like to make _____ about this.

2 The size of the course _____ , I'm afraid.

3 It _____ to shorten its length. It's my dream to build the _____ golf course in the world here on this island.

4 But I _____ if I have to build a shorter course.

5 You see, _____ a full-length 18-hole course if you want to _____ the top golfers in the world to play here.

6 I hope you _____ .

7 Exactly. A full-length course _____ . I couldn't go ahead _____ on that.

3c In pairs, practise saying the above extracts.

4 Look at Track 1.12 on page 172. Find examples of seeking and giving clarification.

Scale down? What do you mean exactly?

5 Paraphrase each of the examples you found in Track 1.12.

I can see that you really want to build this golf course.

TASK: participating in an informal meeting

The Mayor decides to hold an informal meeting to allow Ricardo Hernandez to talk about his project and for other group representatives to express their opinion and ask questions.

After the meeting, the Mayor will decide whether to recommend the project to the local council.

6 Work in groups.

Student A Mayor: turn to page 158 and study your role card.

Student B Ricardo Hernandez: turn to page 161 and study your role card.

Student C Head of the Wildlife Society: turn to page 162 and study your role card.

Student D Journalist (representing public opinion): turn to page 163 and study your role card.

Student E Chamber of Commerce representative: turn to page 163 and study your role card.

7a Hold the meeting.

7b The Mayor announces whether he/she will recommend that the local council approves the project.

OTHER USEFUL PHRASES

Supporting the project

There's no doubt it'll bring great benefits to our community.

The resort is clearly in everyone's interests.

This project will revitalise the area.

Rejecting the project

The project simply isn't feasible.

It's not the right thing for this area.

You haven't thought it through.

Asking polite questions

Could I (just) ask you, what else will you do for our community?

I'd like to ask you a question. How does this project help young people?

Expressing reservations

I'm not sure this is the right project for this area.

I think this needs further thought.

I don't know about this.

Let's think about the implications.

There could be several harmful effects. For example ...

Challenging an argument

I think there's a flaw in this argument.

I'm not totally convinced by what you say.

It sounds like a good idea but ...

STUDY SKILLS: planning and organising essays

1a There are some fundamental steps involved in writing academic essays. The order below is jumbled. Put the steps in the order you might do them.

a) Establish your argument or point of view.

b) Analyse the question and define key terms.

c) Brainstorm ideas.

d) Complete and check your references and bibliography.

e) Research and take notes on the topic, using books, journals, the Internet and other credible academic sources.

f) Write your plan and organise your ideas.

g) Write a first draft to include your introduction, main body and conclusion.

h) Prepare the final draft.

i) Redraft and edit your essay.

j) Have a friend or colleague read your final draft.

1b Now compare your order with a partner.

2 **Analysing the question** To answer an essay question effectively, it is essential to understand the verb which gives the key instruction. Look at the essay questions below. In pairs, decide what each of the verbs in italics means.

Example: Discuss the advantages and disadvantages of eco-tourism.

Discuss means you are being asked to write about the advantages and disadvantages of eco-tourism in detail, considering different ideas and opinions.

1 *Define* the term eco-tourism, giving examples.

2 *Account for* the decrease in the whale population during the last 20 years.

3 *Critically evaluate* the role of tourism in protecting the environment.

4 *Outline* the steps taken by your local community to recycle waste.

5 *Analyse* the threats to the world's coral reefs.

6 *Assess* the effects of illegal logging on wildlife in Mexico.

7 *Compare* the measures taken by Kenya and Uganda to protect wildlife.

3a **1.13** **Brainstorming** Brainstorming is an effective activity for generating new ideas about an essay topic. Listen to a university lecturer giving advice to a student, Erika, about three approaches to brainstorming. Make notes about the key points under the following headings:

- Free association
- Visual thinking
- Question and answer

3b Compare your notes with those of a partner. Which approach do you prefer?

WRITING SKILLS: a problem-solution essay

4a Study the following pattern of organisation, which is often found in academic texts presenting problems and exploring what can be done about them.

1 Situation

2 Problem(s)

3 Solution(s)

4 Implications

5 Evaluation (assessing the solution and implications)

4b Read the problem-solution essay about the Antarctic region on page 25. Match the paragraphs to the parts of the pattern given above.

5 Underline link words or phrases in the essay which:

a) add something

b) give an example

c) make a contrast

d) show cause and effect

e) indicate a good result

6 Work in groups. Read the essay question below. Brainstorm ideas for the topic using ONE of the techniques described by the lecturer in Track 1.13.

> The elephant is an endangered species. Discuss what actions can be taken to protect elephants and save them from extinction.

7a In small groups, discuss what information from your brainstorming could be put under each part of the pattern in Exercise 4a.

7b What do you think is the best way to deal with the problem? What are the implications of the solutions you propose? Assess the solutions and implications.

Discuss the reasons why the Antarctic is under threat and suggest how its environment can be protected.

The natural wilderness of the Antarctic is under threat because of the increasing number of tourists who are visiting the area. As many as 30,000 are expected to come to Antarctica this year to observe penguins, seals and seabirds.

1

Because of this, scientists worry that this curiosity to see the Antarctic area before the ice melts away will only hasten its deterioration. They believe that the growth in tourism could increase the risk to the marine environment and land eco-systems.

2

A major concern is that cruise ships are increasingly visiting the area and if there was an accident, they could cause major pollution. For instance, a Norwegian cruise ship recently ran aground on Antarctica's Deception Island, spilling diesel fuel.

3

Whatever the solutions, any action would be difficult to implement because, unlike in the Arctic region, there are no state or international laws governing tourism practices in the Antarctic. Moreover, the owners of the cruise ships do not seem to be able to agree on what sort of checks and controls are needed in the region.

4

Fortunately, the Norwegian ship was ice-strengthened, and it only spilled a small amount of fuel, which quickly dispersed in water. On the other hand, some bigger cruise ships use heavy fuel oil. This would be very difficult to clean up in the event of a serious accident and thousands of penguins and other marine life could become coated in oil.

5

As a result of the Norwegian accident, there have been several proposals for dealing with the problem. One idea is that there should be a ban on ships which have not been specially strengthened to deal with sea ice. Another suggestion is that there should be a buddy system for large ships so that if one gets into trouble, there would always be another vessel nearby, which it could call for help. A more radical suggestion is that only small research vessels should be allowed into the Antarctic area.

6

7c What are the implications of the solutions you propose? What do you think is the best way to deal with the problem? Assess the implications and solutions.

8 [1.14] Listen to a wildlife expert describing the situation of the elephant populations of Africa and Asia and make notes about the main points mentioned.

9a Write the first paragraph of the essay using a maximum of 70 words.

9b In pairs, read each other's first paragraph. Comment on its content and language.

10 Write a problem-solution essay, using the format above on one of the following topics.

1 An animal which is under threat of extinction, e.g. the elephant, rhinoceros, cheetah, gorilla, tiger or whale.

2 An environmental problem, e.g. the harmful effects of tourism.

International relations

3.1 NATIONAL TRAITS

READING

1 In small groups, discuss the questions below.

1 What do you think defines people from your country?

2 What is important to them? What do they value?

3 How do you think people from other countries see you?

2a Read the statements below about British people. Which do you think are true and which are false?

The British are …

1 serious

2 reluctant to express their feelings

3 extravagant shoppers

4 calm, patient drivers

5 home lovers

6 open and direct communicators

7 interested in social status

8 excessively polite

2b Compare your ideas with a partner and then read the article on page 27 and check.

To say nothing, especially when speaking, is half the art of diplomacy.
Will Durant (1885–1981) US writer

3 Which character traits of the British surprised you most? Why?

4 Which of the character traits listed are the same for your culture / nationality?

5 Scan the article and add the correct dependent preposition.

have an obsession   with

1 have a fascination _____

2 have a reluctance _____

3 have a passion _____

4 are proud _____

5 are great _____

6 have a love _____

7 have an ability _____

6 Make sentences about your own culture using the phrases above.

Telegraph.co.uk

SEARCH | ENHANCED BY Google

| Home | News | Sport | Finance | Lifestyle | Comment | Travel | Culture | Technology | Fashion | Jobs | Dating | Games | Offers |

HOT TOPICS Football | Royal Mail | China | The Dog Who Came In From The Cold

TRAITS OF THE NATION

Our top national characteristic is talking about the weather, just ahead of a passion for queuing, but other qualities in the top ten are not so endearing; sarcasm, a love of television soaps and curtain twitching were all identified as central to the British identity.

Obsession with class was also high on the list, along with more modern ills such as road rage.

Working long hours, fascination with property prices and the love of bargains also made it into the top 50.

But it was not all bad news. Stiff upper lip came out high in the poll, with respondents also choosing a reluctance to complain, a good sense of humour and the ability to laugh at ourselves.

The results were based on a study of 5,000 adults who were asked to pick out the things – good and bad – they believe makes us unique as a nation.

A spokesman for global research company OnePoll.com, which conducted the survey, said that despite some of the negative traits identified, Britons were still extremely proud of their country.

'This is a brilliant list of characteristics and some of the observations are absolutely spot on,' he said.

'You can't go anywhere or do anything in Britain without someone talking about the weather, and we're almost proud of the fact that we get more rain than anywhere else. What this poll demonstrates really well is how proud we are to be British – more than two-thirds of respondents said they felt honoured to be a part of this country.'

1 Talking about the weather
2 Great at queuing
3 Sarcasm
4 Watching soap operas
5 A love of bargains
6 A love of curtain twitching
7 Stiff upper lip
8 Moaning
9 Obsession with class
10 Inability to complain
11 Working long hours
12 Clever sense of humour
13 Obsession with property values
14 Road rage
15 Being proud of where we live
16 Not saying what we mean
17 The ability to laugh at ourselves
18 Jealousy of wealth and success
19 Being overly polite
20 An inability to express our emotions
21 Love of rambling through the countryside
22 Leaving things to the last minute
23 Keeping our homes neat and tidy
24 Achieving against all odds

VOCABULARY: adjectives of character

7 Choose adjectives from the box below which describe people who:

1 are unable to keep their feelings under control
2 rarely boast about themselves and play down their achievements
3 are knowledgeable about art, music and literature
4 approach problems in a rational, practical way
5 are always certain their beliefs are right
6 have a magnetic personality
7 are distant and unfriendly
8 are attentive to detail
9 use clever tricks and manipulation to get what they want
10 are welcoming and generous to visitors

aloof   charismatic   cultured   devious
dogmatic   emotional   hospitable
meticulous   pragmatic   self-effacing

8a Which of the adjectives in Exercise 7 are positive / negative / neutral?

8b Could any of the qualities be applied to your own nationality, do you think?

SPEAKING

9a In small groups, discuss the following in relation to your own culture.

1 greetings
2 silence
3 small talk
4 punctuality
5 personal space
6 gestures
7 etiquette and manners

9b What differences have you found when meeting people from other cultures?

SPEAKING

1a In groups, try to work out what these abbreviations for international organisations stand for.

IMF   IOC   UNESCO   CERN

1b **1.15** Listen and check your answers on page 173.

READING

2a Read the article on page 29 quickly. In pairs, discuss whether you agree with the heading. Give reasons for your answer.

2b Read the article again. According to the article, are the statements below true, false or not given?

1 CERN was originally a French laboratory.

2 One of the reasons it was set up was to make research into atomic physics more affordable.

3 CERN has four main aims.

4 The LHC is the most powerful particle accelerator because of its huge circumference.

5 Most of the scientists involved in experiments at CERN are not based there.

3 Find words and phrases in the article which mean the following.

1 on both sides of

2 shared undertakings

3 got bigger than

4 to provide financial support for

5 smash together

6 working groups of people in the same profession

4 Work in groups and discuss the following questions.

1 Can you think of other examples of successful international cooperation?

2 Do you think CERN is a huge waste of money?

3 Think of some examples of failed international cooperation. Why do you think they failed?

GRAMMAR: subordinate clauses

5a Look at this sentence, taken from the article, and answer the following questions.

(Part A) Once a research project has been reviewed and accepted by the committee (Part B) the scientists involved in the project collaborate.

Which part:

1 does not make sense on its own?

2 is a main clause?

3 is a subordinate clause?

5b In subordinate clauses we cannot usually change the order of the events in the clauses, because it changes the meaning. In the following sentences, which event comes first?

1 When the project was accepted by the committee, the scientists worked together.

2 When the scientists worked together, the project was accepted by the committee.

6 Find and underline other sentences in the article that contain subordinate clauses.

➡ Language reference and extra practice, pages 138–139

7a Combine the sentences below into one sentence using the words in brackets.

1 The scientists use videoconferencing facilities. The scientists work together from their labs all over the world. (in order to)

2 The main CERN site has a large computer centre. The computer centre contains very powerful data-processing facilities. (which)

3 CERN is currently famous for the Large Hadron Collider. CERN also gained prestige through its connection with the beginnings of the world wide web. (although)

4 In April 1993, CERN made an announcement. They said 'The web will be free to all'. (announced that)

5 The LHC is buried 100m below ground. The LHC has a circumference of 27km. (buried)

6 The system was shut down on 19 September 2008. A magnet was found to be faulty. (when)

7 I think the LHC is very dangerous. We don't know what will happen. (because)

8 The LHC experiment might work. Then it will revolutionise our understanding. (if)

7b Now classify the combined sentences from Exercise 7a according to the list below:

a) cause or reason   e) time

b) condition   f) reported speech

c) contrast   g) relative clause

d) purpose   h) non-finite verb phrase

CERN
A SHINING EXAMPLE OF INTERNATIONAL COOPERATION

*Science*Weekly

Situated about 10 kilometres north-west of Geneva and straddling the border between France and Switzerland, CERN is the world's largest laboratory for research into particle physics (the study of the elements of matter and how they interact with each other and with energy). It was originally established in 1954 as one of Europe's first joint ventures to bring together the best scientists in Europe and to allow member countries to share the significant costs of setting up and running an atomic physics laboratory. Today it has 20 member states, more than 2,500 full-time staff and provides the infrastructure and scientific instruments for the research projects of around 8,000 scientists and engineers who represent 80 nationalities and 580 universities and research facilities.

Although the organisation has long outgrown its original European dimensions and its focus on nuclear physics, its original aims have remained the same. These are to sponsor and help organise research projects that will lead to a better understanding of the universe, to push to the limit advances in different technologies, to educate the scientists of the future and to encourage international cooperation through science.

The main scientific instruments at CERN are particle accelerators and particle detectors. Scientists use the accelerators to send beams of particles towards each other at very high energy. They then cause the particles to collide with each other or with stationary targets and observe and record the results with the detectors. CERN is famously home to the Large Hadron Collider (LHC), which, with a circumference of 27km, is the largest and most powerful particle accelerator in the world.

While the smallest experiments at CERN may concern only a handful of scientists, the largest involve thousands. However, CERN itself employs comparatively few scientists and often only on a temporary basis. Most of the researchers remain based in their various universities and research institutes around the globe. Once a research project has been reviewed and accepted by peer committees, the scientists involved in that project collaborate, often simply via Internet-based conferencing facilities, to design, build and run their own experiments. All members of the team have free access to the data and share the results equally. It is a shining example of international cooperation.

VOCABULARY AND SPEAKING

8a In groups, combine words from the box to make the full titles of the organisations (1–8) below (each word may be used more than once).

Asian	association	Atlantic	committee		
countries	european	exporting	fund	health	
international	monetary	nations	north		
olympic	organisation	petroleum	southeast		
trade	treaty	union	wildlife	world	

1	WHO	3	ASEAN	5	EU	7	WTO
2	OPEC	4	NATO	6	IMF	8	IOC

8b What functions do the organisations (1–8) perform? Discuss your ideas in your groups.

8c Which of the names are acronyms?

WRITING

9 Write a short paragraph about one of the organisations listed in Exercise 1a or Exercise 8a. Try to include at least one subordinate clause.

AMBASSADORS

Ambassador Wang

SPEAKING AND READING

1 Choose three of the most/least desirable characteristics in an ambassador.

cultured   articulate   charming   pragmatic
persuasive   intuitive   aloof   analytical
observant   meticulous   good at solving problems
strong   energetic   modest   sensitive   eager
to learn   respectful   devious   provocative
impulsive

2 Read these extracts from interviews with serving ambassadors. Which of the personal characteristics from Exercise 1 are mentioned?

Ambassador Lavrov

A **Q:** _____

A: It's a tough job. In addition to promoting the interests of your country in a way that makes them understood by others, you have to also take into account the interests of your partners and work to forge a consensus that would embrace both.

B **Q:** _____

A: You have to be well versed in the history and culture of other countries and to be able to present your arguments clearly and persuasively. Any education which helps you to achieve these qualities would do.

C **Q:** _____

A: The hardest part of the job is to be woken up in the middle of a night to discuss a new crisis about which you don't have instructions. Then you have to go by your instincts and hope that they are right.

D **Q:** _____

A: My workday starts at 9.00 a.m. by reading cables from Moscow. Then I attend various UN meetings which last until late afternoon. After that, I have to write my reports and suggestions (hoping they will be accepted), which typically lasts until late night every day.

E **Q:** _____

A: Ambassadors are appointed by presidents. How they select ambassadors, I don't know. I never served as President!

F **Q:** _____

A: I'm a career diplomat. I had been engaged in diplomatic work for more than 20 years before becoming an ambassador. A rich diplomatic practice is an excellent way to prepare for being an ambassador. What you study in college does not matter much in determining whether you become an ambassador. The important thing is whether you can develop yourself and acquire certain necessary skills, such as thorough observation, in-depth thinking and analysis, and being good at discovering and solving problems.

G **Q:** _____

A: Being strong and healthy is very important as an ambassador. You must be able to endure the long-hour meetings and conferences at the United Nations and be energetic all the time. It is a great honour to be an ambassador. I'm very proud to represent a country that is the birthplace of a 5,000 year-old civilisation, now one-fifth of the world's population and whose economy has been developing at a rapid pace over the past two decades that is rarely seen in the world today.

H **Q:** _____

A: One's knowledge is always limited no matter how intelligent he or she is. There are 191 member states in the United Nations. Each country has its own different history and culture. So it is hard to know each culture very well. But I think the important thing is to be modest and eager to learn when you get along with people from a different culture. When you respect others and treat them as equals, you will surely be respected and find it easy to make friends.

3 Read the extracts again. Match the questions (1–7) below to the answers (A–H) in the interviews above.

What steps did it take to become an ambassador? F

1 Could you please tell me how ambassadors are selected?

2 What is the hardest part of your job?

3 How do you know what the proper etiquette is when dealing with different cultures?

4 What is the job of an ambassador?

5 What kind of education do you need to become an ambassador?

6 I would really be interested in knowing what it is like to be an ambassador. You must get very stressed out.

7 What is your workday like?

4 What do you think was most surprising about the ambassadors' answers?

5a Match words from column A with words from column B to make as many collocations from the world of diplomacy as possible.

A	B
diplomatic	meeting
overseas	conflict
summit	awareness
international	immunity
cultural	posting

5b Make your own sentences using some of the collocations.

LISTENING

6a **1.16** Elizabeth is the wife of an ambassador. She accompanies her husband on his overseas postings. Listen to an excerpt from a radio interview in which she talks about her life. How do you think she feels about being the wife of an ambassador?

6b Listen again and make notes under the following headings:

• Problems with overseas postings

• Regrets

GRAMMAR: modal perfect

7a **1.17** Listen to the following extracts from the interview and complete the gaps in the sentences.

1 I know I _____ some Russian before we went out there, but I didn't have time.

2 I suppose I _____ a local Russian to give me lessons, but I just didn't have the motivation at that point.

3 It _____ at least a year before I felt happy in Moscow.

7b Look at the three sentences in Exercise 7a (1–3) and at sentences (4–10) below. Match them with the functions a–h and say if they express:

4 He might have caused a diplomatic incident.

5 You didn't have to bring such an expensive gift, but thank you.

6 The ambassador didn't need to go through customs.

7 The ambassador needn't have gone through customs.

8 Our codes may have been broken.

9 You ought to have mentioned that earlier.

10 The ambassador can't have written this.

a) possibility   e) criticism

b) certainty   f) absence of necessity

c) impossibility   g) necessity

d) lack of obligation   h) regret

8 Answer the following questions about the sentences from Exercise 7a and 7b.

1 In sentence 1, did she learn some Russian before she left?

2 In sentence 5, did somebody bring an expensive gift?

3 In sentences 6 and 7, did the ambassador go through customs?

4 In sentence 10, did the ambassador write the letter?

➡ Language reference and extra practice, pages 138–139

9 Rewrite each sentence with an appropriate modal so it has a similar meaning.

I'm sure you left your passport on the plane.

You must have left your passport on the plane.

1 He was wrong not to pass on the information to the president.

2 I'm sure the ambassador didn't say that.

3 I finished the report by 5 p.m. but it wasn't necessary.

4 It wasn't necessary for me to tell the head of security.

5 Maybe the ambassador missed the plane.

6 It was a mistake for us to leave the ambassador's reception.

7 I'm sure the ambassador enjoyed the reception.

SPEAKING

10a Work in groups. You are all part of the organising committee for a diplomatic reception that was a disaster. Make a list of all the things that went wrong.

10b Criticise each other using *should have, should not have, ought to have, ought not to have.*

You should have sent out more invitations.

SITUATION

Four days ago, the oil tanker *Poseidon Marquis* was travelling a few kilometres off the coast of Libya when there was an unexpected explosion in its engine room. The tanker's hull was damaged and a huge amount of oil spilled into the sea. At present, the oil slick covers over 200 square kilometres and it is spreading all the time. The oil spill will have an immediate harmful impact on the coasts of Libya, Egypt and Algeria, and will in the longer term affect other Mediterranean countries unless swift action is taken.

1 Read the situation. Working with a partner, list some harmful impacts which will probably result from the oil spill.

2 Read some comments on the oil spill by various people who will be affected by it and answer the following questions.

1 Do the comments match the harmful effects that you listed in Exercise 1?

2 Which consequences of the oil spill do you think are most serious?

1 'It could take ten years for the coastline to recover. We'll need to bring in a number of international organisations to provide help, expertise and finance. We've no experience of dealing with this type of problem. Our countries do not have the capacity to deal with a disaster of this magnitude.'

(Minister of the Environment)

2 'There'll be no fishing along the coast for some time. There'll be no fish to catch. Many of us will lose our jobs.'

(local fisherman)

3 'The effect of the oil slick on marine life will be devastating.'

(Representative – International Wildlife Association)

5 'They could bankrupt the Poseidon Oil company.'

(a local resident)

4 'The spill could cause a dramatic increase in cancers and other diseases in the affected areas.'

(a local medical officer)

6 'Newspaper reporting of the oil slick will obviously have a negative impact on our tourism industry.'

(Minister for Tourism)

7 'It's probably the most beautiful beach on the coastline. Now it's covered with oil. I wouldn't dream of taking the children there. They'd probably start playing with it!'

(local resident)

8 'The spill will do irreparable damage to our reputation as an ethical oil company if we don't act quickly to clean up the sea'

(a director, Poseidon Oil Company)

9 'This will result in massive unemployment for workers who depend on coastal activities.'

(financial journalist)

10 'The international lawyers will be happy – they'll make a fortune from this disaster.'

(company director)

KEY LANGUAGE: stating objectives, giving strong advice

3a `1.18` Listen to the conversation between the chairman of the Poseidon Oil Company, Julian Leiterman, and a United Nations official. What major objectives does the chairman mention in the conversation?

3b Listen again. Tick the expressions for *stating objectives* that you hear in the conversation.

1 Our main objective now is to develop a strategy …

2 Your target must be to contain the oil spill.

3 So, one of our main goals will be to involve the international community.

4 That should be a key objective …

5 We would like to set up regular meetings.

3c Look at Track 1.18 on page 173 and find expressions for *advising strongly*. Underline the expressions in the text.

4 Work in groups. Make a list of all the actions (short and long-term) that must be taken to deal with the oil spill.

The company must raise money to finance the work of the clean-up operation.

TASK: devising an action plan

5a Form two new groups, A and B. Using your suggestions from Exercise 4, work out an action plan to deal with the oil spill. The action plan will be presented at a forthcoming press conference. The action plan should have three phases:

Phase 1 Actions to be taken in the next month

Phase 2 Actions to be taken in the next three months

Phase 3 Actions to be taken in the next year

Note: in Phase 1, you should include only those actions which you think should be prioritised (i.e. the company needs to take urgent action within a month).

5b Present your action plans to each other.

6 Now, as a single group, agree on a joint action plan which the chair will present at the press conference.

OTHER USEFUL PHRASES
Accepting
That sounds like a really good idea.
I think that's the right way to go.
Rejecting
I'm not sure it's the right thing to do.
(I'm afraid), I don't think it'll work.
I don't think it's feasible.

STUDY SKILLS: active listening

1 Complete the gaps in the text with words in the box.

careful	conscious	distracted	total

The best way to improve your listening skills is to practise active listening. Active listening requires you to make a ¹_____ effort to hear not only the words that someone speaks but also to try to understand the ²_____ message being sent. To do this, you must pay ³_____ attention to the speaker and not be ⁴_____ in any way.

2 Prepare a two-minute talk on the following topic:

In which overseas country would you like to spend a one-year study or work visit? Give reasons.

3 In pairs, listen to each other's talk. After listening, give an accurate oral summary of the talk you've just heard. Your partner should check your summary and correct any information which is not accurate.

4a Answer questions 1–5 below, and discuss your answers with your partner.

1 Was your oral summary
   a) very accurate?
   b) fairly accurate?
   c) not very accurate?

2 If it was not very accurate, what do you think was the reason?

3 What kind of verbal/non-verbal signals did you give to show you were listening (nodding your head, saying 'uh-huh', etc.)?

4 Did you interrupt at any time during the presentation? If so, why?

5 Did you concentrate on what your partner was saying throughout his/her talk?

4b Compare your answers with another pair.

5a 1.19 Listen to a trainer from a communication skills course. She is giving a short lecture on 'How to become an active listener'. Make notes under each of the following headings.

• Focus on the speaker's message
• Show that you are listening
• Give feedback
• Don't interrupt
• Respond positively

5b Compare your notes with a partner.

5c In small groups, discuss the ways in which you show that you are an active listener.

6a Now prepare a three-minute talk on one of the following topics.

1 An international leader, living or dead, that you particularly admire. Say what they have accomplished and explain why you admire them.

2 An international organisation that you particularly admire. Say what it has accomplished and explain why you admire it.

6b In pairs, listen to each other's talks.

7a How well do you think your partner listened to your talk? Was he or she listening actively? Did you get the impression that:

a) they understood your message?

b) they were keenly interested in what you were saying?

7b How would you evaluate your own active listening ability? Excellent? Very good? Good? Needs improvement?

WRITING SKILLS: a speech

8a To make an impressive speech, skilled speakers use stylistic devices to help make a speech more interesting, lively and memorable. Match the extracts (a–f) from some speeches to the descriptions (1–6) of the devices.

1 Three words or phrases which follow each other, so that they make an impact.

2 Comparing two things in a figurative sense.

3 Questions that a speaker asks but doesn't answer directly. Often used to persuade or emphasise.

4 Words or phrases that recur throughout a speech to emphasise facts or ideas.

5 Repetition of an initial consonant sound. The consonant is usually repeated in two words which come together, but sometimes in words that are not next to each other.

6 Emphasising the contrast between two ideas. Often a similar structure is used.

a) 'That's one small step for man, one giant leap for mankind.'

b) 'His steadfast belief in humanitarian values was a rock in a raging sea.'

c) 'Why do we support this misguided policy? What will future generations think of this fateful decision?'

d) 'Safety and security are of paramount importance. Therefore, we must take this action for the greater good of our country.'

e) 'A man touched down on the moon, a wall came down in Berlin, a world was connected by our own science and imagination.'

f) 'At a time when women's voices were silenced …

When there was despair in the dust bowl and depression across the land …

When the bombs fell on our harbour and tyranny threatened our world …'

8b Match each description (1–6) in Exercise 8a to one of the following rhetorical devices:

- alliteration
- metaphor
- antithesis
- rhetorical questions
- repetition
- tripling

8c Did you recognise any of the extracts?

9 Read the short, critical speech about the United Nations which will be made to a group of university students. Make notes about the speaker's main points.

10 In groups, think of arguments showing that the United Nations plays an effective role in international affairs. Note down your points. If you have time, research the topic on the Internet.

11 Use your notes and research to write a persuasive speech which presents the work of the United Nations in a positive light.

12 In pairs, take turns to deliver your speech. Imagine that your audience is a group of university undergraduates.

May I start by thanking the President of your society for inviting me to talk on the topic 'How effective is the United Nations in International Affairs?'

I'm afraid I'm going to disappoint many of you when I address this question since I believe the United Nations has been largely ineffective, unimaginative and powerless since it was set up in 1945.

What were the main aims of the United Nations Charter? Surely they were to create an organisation which would stop wars and create harmony among nations through cooperation, tolerance and fairness. Have they succeeded in those aims? The answer, in my view, is emphatically 'No'.

Since the United Nations was founded, there have been more, not fewer, wars than previously and its debates, resolutions and peacekeeping operations have not done nearly enough to prevent wars and conflicts. Let me give you some striking examples:

The United Nations failed to prevent the genocide of one million people in Rwanda in 1994. It failed also to prevent genocide in Darfur. It failed again to intervene in the Second Congo War. Are further examples necessary to illustrate the inability of the UN to deploy its forces where and when they are needed?

The Security Council, the organisation's main decision-making body is an undemocratic body and can be likened to a tiger without teeth and claws. It is composed of five members (Russia, China, the UK, the USA and France), all of whom have vested interests, and it excludes powerful nations such as India which has over a billion people. Because of the power of veto granted to its members, it is often powerless to take action in times of international crisis.

Likewise, in the area of disarmament, the UN has proved to be a toothless tiger. It has failed to stop the proliferation of arms trading around the world and it has been unable to stop powerful nations developing weapons of mass destruction.

The UN is an incredibly expensive institution to maintain and is extremely bureaucratic. Its staff live well, pay no taxes and have no incentive, therefore, to reform the inefficient organisation.

There is an urgent need to reform the United Nations if it is to be an effective organisation. The answer is probably to place less emphasis on its peace-keeping mission and to focus more on its humanitarian work. The UN can provide invaluable support when responding to natural and man-made disasters, such as droughts, earthquakes and food shortages.

I've presented the United Nations in a poor light to you, but I can assure you I'm simply reflecting many people's opinion. The United Nations, in its present form, is totally unable to achieve its objectives.

Teenage genius arrives in Cambridge

Most students arriving at Cambridge University have outdone their peers from their schooldays and gained an impressive number of 'A' levels (school-leaving qualifications). But while most students ¹_____ four or five, ²_____ has surpassed them all.

Ali Moeen Nawazish, a charming 18-year-old Pakistani from Rawalpindi has come to the prestigious university armed with not five, not ten, not 20, but 23 'A' levels. Considering that ³_____ prior to Ali's feat was 13, Ali ⁴_____ something remarkable. Yet the self-effacing teenager seems totally unaffected by his prowess.

He talks in a soft voice about his education in Rawalpindi. He says that he was not an exceptional student until he received a world-record mark for a computing exam, and it was at that point that he decided he ⁵_____ really aim higher. So Ali started with seven, passed those and went on to ten, then 14, and, ⁶_____ successful to this point and breaking the record, finally went on to his total of 23. By June 2008, when he took the last of his exams, Ali ⁷_____ ten hours a day consistently for over a year. Hard work had become his life.

Ali is clearly an impressive all-rounder: of the 23 'A' levels that he took, ranging from physics to critical thinking to travel and tourism, he gained the highest grade in all but two of them – chemistry and general further mathematics. ⁸_____ he feels bad about those two, Ali excuses himself by saying that he ⁹_____ 'a bit tired' when he took them – he'd been up since 8.00 a.m. on the morning of the exams and only finished the maths exam at 1.00 a.m. the following morning. He ¹⁰_____ about those two exams, however; he already had more than enough A grades to be sure of his place at Cambridge.

Ali has now settled into undergraduate life at Trinity College. He ¹¹_____ for a degree in ¹²_____, which means spending long hours in the computer laboratory – from 9.00 a.m. every morning, usually until 5.00 p.m. While for most first-year students this routine ¹³_____ particularly comfortable, for Ali it feels light in comparison with the hours he ¹⁴_____ before. And his plans now are no less ambitious – he intends to study Computer Science for three years, then go on to Medicine for four.

It has been said that Oxford and Cambridge Universities are the home for the naturally gifted. Ali proves that they're equally the home for those who are prepared to work hard!

GRAMMAR

1a Read the article above quickly, ignoring the gaps. Why is Ali Moeen Nawazish unusual?

1b Find words in the article that describe:
1 Ali's character
2 his achievements
3 what he has studied/is studying

2a Now read the article again, looking carefully at the gaps. Try to guess what might go in each gap.

1 – a verb phrase, probably in a perfect form

2b Now complete the gaps with the words below. In two places, two answers are possible.

1 a) can have taken b) might have taken
   c) must have taken
2 a) the student b) a student c) one student
3 a) the record b) record c) a record
4 a) achieved b) has achieved c) had achieved
5 a) must b) should c) might
6 a) having proved b) have proved
   c) to have proved
7 a) worked b) was working c) had been working
8 a) If b) Unless c) Although
9 a) was feeling b) had felt c) has felt
10 a) didn't worry b) didn't need to worry
   c) needn't have worried
11 a) studies b) 's studying c) has been studying
12 a) Computer Science b) a Computer Science
   c) the Computer Science
13 a) should not be b) might not be c) could not be
14 a) had been studying b) has been studying
   c) had studied

VOCABULARY

3 Complete the advertisement with words and phrases from the box.

> ability to   assessments   boutique hotel
> informed decisions   interpersonal skills
> knowledge base   organised excursions
> passion for

EVENTS ORGANISER

We run an exclusive ¹_____ on the Turquoise coast of Turkey and we are looking for a self-motivated person with excellent ²_____ to join our team. You will be responsible for organising events for our guests and for leading ³_____ in the area. For this reason, your ⁴_____ of the area, and of Turkey in general, should be outstanding. We expect the ideal candidate to be capable of making ⁵_____ about what events to arrange, and also of making quick ⁶_____ of any situation and to troubleshoot where necessary.
If you have the ⁷_____ get along with people and a ⁸_____ Turkey, we look forward to meeting you!

4a `1.20` Listen to two people from the hotel in the advertisement discussing three of the candidates they have interviewed. Make notes about the characters and abilities of the candidates.

4b Match four of the phrases and adjectives in the box with each candidate. Listen again if necessary.

> accomplished   all-rounder   cultured
> dark horse   devious   dogmatic   know-all
> over sensitive   pragmatic   self-effacing
> team player

Andrea McCartney: ——— ——— ——— ———

Will Davison: ——— ——— ——— ———

Kate Samson: ——— ——— ——— ———

KEY LANGUAGE

5a In groups of three, imagine you work for / study at a private language school. You consider that the school is not very 'green' and is wasteful of resources. Discuss in what ways the school could be made 'greener'. Make notes under the following headings:

- Use of paper
- Use of electricity (heating and lighting)
- Cars vs public transport

5b `1.21` Listen to a discussion at a language school and answer the questions.

1 Which issue from Exercise 5a do the teachers focus on most?

2 What do the teachers say should be done about each of the issues?

3 What is finally decided about the waste paper issue?

6 Match the halves of sentences 1–8 with a–h. Then listen again and check your answers.

1 It's essential that we consider
2 The paper issue
3 OK, if I understand you correctly,
4 I'd strongly advise you
5 It simply isn't possible
6 It would be helpful to have
7 It's an absolute priority to
8 So, it seems that

a) a bin in the café for waste food.

b) should be a key objective for us.

c) the number of teachers who come to the school in cars.

d) you'll take full responsibility for disposing of the paper?

e) you're saying that you think we should start recycling paper.

f) to provide bins for cans and organic waste too.

g) to think carefully about this.

h) work out who is going to be responsible for emptying them ...

7 In your groups choose one of the other two issues and role play a discussion about it. Use your notes from Exercise 5a and some of the phrases 1–8 from Exercise 6.

Student A: you are the head of the school.

Students B and C: you are teachers / students.

LANGUAGE CHECK

8 There is a missing or incorrect word in each of these sentences. Find and correct the mistake, then look at the pages to check your answers.

1 Will you finished that report by lunchtime? I need it for a meeting this afternoon. (page 11)

2 The builders plan have completed the main construction by July. (page 11)

3 Have already done some statistics, you should experience no problems with this course. (page 9)

4 What was the name of a lovely resort we stayed in on our holiday to Thailand last year? (page 19)

5 You have get a visa to travel to countries of the former Soviet Union. (page 21)

6 We decided to come on a later train the first one was so early. (page 28)

7 He shouldn't resigned from his job without having another one to go to. (page 31)

LOOK BACK

9 Find the exercises in Units 1–3 where you ...

- learn how to form adjectives from nouns (Unit 1)
- improve an applicant's CV (Unit 1)
- write a covering letter to go with your CV (Unit 1)
- talk about the future of tourism (Unit 2)
- read the rules of using articles in English (Unit 2)
- learn about subordinate clauses in English (Unit 3)
- listen to your partner giving a short talk (Unit 3)

4 Health and care

Grammar
- cohesion 1 (linkers)
- future forms with *to be*

Vocabulary
- health collocations
- health care
- the language of emotion

Scenario
- Change your ways!

Study skills
- analysing visual information

Writing skills
- describing visual information

I intend to live forever. So far, so good.
Stephen Wright (b1955) American comedian

SPEAKING

1 In pairs, discuss the following questions.

1 What do you do that is good or bad for your physical health?

2 What do you do that is good or bad for your mental health?

3 Rate your own fitness on a scale of 0–5 (0 = very bad, 5 = excellent). Are you happy with your level? Can/will you do anything to improve it?

4 Do you think there is a connection between health and happiness?

VOCABULARY: health collocations

2 Match the words in the box below with categories 1–8.

| blood pressure   chest pain   flu virus |
| heart attack   heart surgery |
| high salt intake   immune system |
| infant mortality   life expectancy |
| maternity ward   Omega 3 oils |
| premature ageing   tanning salon |

1 types of medical treatment
2 places
3 food
4 children
5 the body's defences against illness
6 health problems
7 causes of illness
8 ways of measuring health

READING

3 Read the article and answer the following questions.

1 Where do you think the article comes from?

2 What does it say about the connection between happiness and health?

3 Which phrases are used to show that the information in this article is based on serious scientific research – not just one individual's opinion?

4 Read the first sentence again. Why do you think that may be the case?

Your Health & Happiness

In the daily rush of life we don't always make our own happiness our number one priority. Perhaps we should though, because being happy has clear health benefits. Researchers have discovered that happy people have stronger immune systems than unhappy people; they don't pick up as many colds or get struck down as often by a flu virus. Their blood pressure is lower, and they have better protection against heart attacks and stroke. Happy people also deal better with pain, and bounce back faster after an operation. Their life expectancy is longer, too.

Studies also indicate that happy people take better care of their health. They have regular checkups and do more exercise than unhappy people, and don't forget to put on sunscreen.

But what if you're not naturally the life and soul of the party? Or you don't wake up in the morning grinning from ear to ear? Not to worry, the good news is that research shows we can all – no matter how gloomy – learn to be happy. The only trouble is, we're often not that good at predicting what will really make us happy. So take our quick quiz to find out the best way for you to achieve bliss – and be healthy.

Quiz

Which of these things would bring you the greatest joy? Choose three.

- Moving to the countryside
- Getting married
- Going to the gym
- Supporting a good cause
- A relaxing day fishing
- Being slim
- Taking an evening class in something you really want to learn
- Going on holiday with a group of your best friends
- Tidying up your room, flat or house
- Winning one million euros

---

4 Compare your answers to the short quiz above in small groups. Explain your choices.

5a Read the information on the quiz on page 164. With your group, discuss the comments. Would you like to change any of your original choices?

5b Now answer the following questions.

1 What do we learn about stress?
2 Name two things that will have an immediate effect on us.
3 How important does money appear to be for achieving happiness?
4 Which things does the article say are not much fun, but can increase happiness?

6 How would you describe the overall style of this article?

a) humorous   c) lively
b) serious   d) flippant

SPEAKING

7 Work in groups. Discuss the quotes below. What do they mean? Do you agree with these ideas? Why / Why not?

1 'I refuse to spend my life worrying about what I eat. There is no pleasure worth forgoing just for an extra three years in the geriatric ward.' John Mortimer, British dramatist, novelist and lawyer (1923–2009)

2 'A human can be healthy without killing animals for food. Therefore if he eats meat he participates in taking animal life merely for the sake of his appetite.' Leo Tolstoy, Russian novelist (1828–1910)

3 'To wish to be well is a part of becoming well.' Seneca, Roman philosopher and dramatist (4BC–65AD)

4 'True enjoyment comes from activity of the mind and exercise of the body.' Alexander von Humboldt Prussian/German scientist/naturalist and explorer (1769–1859)

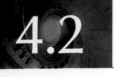

SPEAKING

1 Have you heard of the American film director, Michael Moore, and his films?

Student A: turn to page 158.

Student B: turn to page 160.

LISTENING

2a ▐1.22▌ Before listening to a review of *Sicko*, do you think these statements are true or false? Listen and check.

What seems to be the problem?

Waiting Room

MICHAEL MOORE
SiCKO

1 Michael Moore films are renowned for their objectivity.

2 Healthcare in the USA is financed through taxation.

3 US healthcare expenditure is the world's largest.

4 The US health system is in the top five of the world.

5 Healthcare is government funded in Cuba and the UK.

2b Listen again. Make notes on these points.

- The flaws in the US healthcare system.
- Moore's perspective on different healthcare systems.
- The reviewer's opinion of the film.

READING

3 Read the article and answer the following questions.

1 What does the article's title mean?

2 What is the aim of the journalist in writing this report?

3 What are the key features of the Cuban system?

4 In your opinion, does the journalist think Moore was fair to focus on Cuba as a contrast to the USA?

4 Read the article again and answer these questions.

1 How does the opening paragraph show 'a healthcare system that is extensive, accessible and ropey'?

2 How do life expectancy, infant mortality rates and health expenditure in Cuba and the USA compare?

3 What are the secrets of Cuba's healthcare success?

4 What do we learn about Cuban doctors' sense of vocation?

5 What are your thoughts on the contrast between the US and Cuban healthcare systems?

First world results on a third world budget

(1) According to Michael Moore's latest film *Sicko*, Cuba's medical care puts America's to shame. Rory Carroll investigates.

As a tropical sun rises over Havana, two dozen pensioners perform a series of stretches and gentle exercises in a small plaza, shaded by palms. Meanwhile, two blocks away, in a small shabby office, two doctors receive a steady stream of phone calls and patients. Although the doctors can deal with most cases, serious ones are referred to the antiquated Calixto García hospital.

(2) This snapshot of Havana shows a healthcare system that is extensive, accessible and, at times, ropey. What is unique is the blend of third world conditions with a progressive ethos and first world results.

(3) Michael Moore's documentary, *Sicko*, holds up Cuba as a model. Whether it is a consultation or open heart surgery, citizens are entitled to free treatment. As a result, this impoverished Caribbean island has better health indicators than its much wealthier neighbour 90 miles across the Florida straits.

(4) According to the World Health Organisation, a Cuban man can expect to live to 75 and a woman to 79. In addition, the probability of a child dying aged under five is five per 1,000 live births. That is better than the USA and on a par with the UK, yet these world-class results are delivered by an annual expenditure of $260 per person, less than a tenth of Britain's $3,065 and a fraction of America's $6,543.

Averting illness

(5) There is no mystery about Cuba's core strategy: prevention. From promoting exercise, hygiene and regular check-ups, the system is geared towards averting illnesses and treating them before they become advanced and costly. Other prevention strategies take the form of health advice adverts and tips on fighting mosquitoes.

(6) Simple, free access to GPs is a bedrock of healthcare. It is estimated that there is one doctor for every 175 people, compared to 485 in the UK. 'We are told to encourage them to contact us. And they do, all the time, day and night,' says one GP, somewhat ruefully. Cuban doctors have a reputation for dedication. With an average monthly salary of just $20 they cannot be accused of entering the profession for money. One neurosurgeon spoke of hitchhiking to work and operating on an empty stomach.

(7) Cuban healthcare is no utopia. At times, it is ragged and harsh. However, the virtues are no myth. People live as long as they do because the system, overall, works. To be poor and sick in Cuba is tough, but it is not to be forgotten.

5 Find words and phrases in the text which mean the following.

1 a continuous or regular flow

2 a smooth mixture

3 a philosophy or set of guiding principles

4 have the right to

5 financially poor

6 equal or similar to

7 designed for

8 a paradise, or place of perfection

GRAMMAR: cohesion 1 (linkers)

6a Put the highlighted words in the review into the correct categories below.

a) **additive linkers:** *Furthermore,*

b) **contrastive linkers:** *Whereas,*

c) **causal linkers:** *Since,*

d) **temporal linkers:** *After,*

6b Which of these conjunctions and linking devices link ideas:

a) across two separate sentences?

b) across two clauses in a single sentence?

➡ **Language reference and extra practice, pages 140–141**

7 Look at the linking phrases in the box below and answer the following questions.

| after   after that   as   as soon as   as well as this
| consequently   even so   even though
| for this reason   furthermore   in contrast
| moreover   nevertheless   nonetheless
| on the other hand   otherwise   similarly   since
| therefore   until   whereas   while   whilst |

1 Which group in Exercise 6a does each linking phrase belong to? Some may belong to two groups.

2 Do they link ideas across sentences or clauses?

GRAMMAR TIP

The linking devices which connect ideas across two sentences are usually conjunctive adverbs. When you connect ideas with these you can use a semi-colon, rather than a full stop.

Cuba is a relatively poor country; nevertheless, it has an exemplary healthcare system.

8 Rewrite the sentences below using one of the linking phrases in brackets.

1 Although the Americans spend the most on healthcare, they don't have the world's best system. (even so, whereas)

2 The Cubans emphasise prevention of illness. In contrast, the Americans emphasise treatment of illness. (as a result, whereas)

3 Cuba is a relatively poor country. Consequently, it makes sense for its government to focus on prevention as this is cheaper. (although, since)

4 While I was reading the article, I realised that while spending a lot of money on healthcare is probably a good idea, it doesn't necessarily lead to the best results. (furthermore, even though)

5 If the government doesn't improve healthcare, people will continue to die unnecessarily, and the current approach is also a waste of money. (furthermore, otherwise)

9 Complete these sentences with your own ideas. Compare your answers with a partner.

1 My government helps _____ . As well as this, it _____ .

2 In my country, _____ . As a result, _____ .

3 People in my country _____ , whereas in the USA they _____ .

4 One thing that is great about my home town is _____ . Furthermore, _____ .

5 I _____ , otherwise I _____ .

VOCABULARY: health care

10 Explain the differences in meaning between these words.

1 Doctor   Surgeon   General Practitioner (GP)   Paramedic   Pharmacist   Consultant

2 Doctor's surgery   Clinic   Hospital   Pharmacy   Hospice

3 to see the doctor   to have a check-up
to have an operation   to have a scan / an x-ray

4 a lack of funding   out-dated equipment
long waiting lists   post-operative infection

5 alternative medicine   palliative care
preventive medicine   conventional medicine

SPEAKING

11 In small groups, describe the healthcare system in your country. Use the points below to help you.

- organisation
- funding
- positives/negatives
- personal experience
- the future

WRITING

12 Write two paragraphs describing and evaluating the healthcare system in your country.

SPEAKING

1 Answer these questions.

1 What is your image of a typical nurse? Where does this image come from?

2 What qualities does a nurse need?

3 Do you think all nurses have a strong sense of vocation?

READING

2 Read the article quickly. What is/are the main problem(s) the writer mentions, and what solutions does he propose?

3 Read the article again and answer the following questions:

1 What is it that makes the doctor most unhappy during a normal working day?

2 What kind of nurse does the doctor like and respect?

3 What does the doctor think patients should be worried about?

4 Why do you think the doctor has written this article?

5 What do you think of the doctor's views?

VOCABULARY: the language of emotion

4a Find words in the article that describe events and their impact on people's feelings, e.g. *exciting, frightened*. Which of the words you found are synonyms or near-synonyms?

4b Complete the gaps in the sentences below with the best words from the box.

antagonised	disillusioned	disorientating
elated	exasperating	exhilarating	inspiring
invigorating	rejuvenated	relieved	

1 I was feeling rather stale before my holiday, but came back _____ .

2 Her leadership was _____ and made everyone want to do their best.

3 The sponsored climb of Mount Kilimanjaro was a/an _____ experience. It was absolutely brilliant!

4 We usually go for a/an _____ 5km run before we start work.

5 The new government hasn't lived up to expectations, so people are now _____ .

Microsoft Internet Explorer

File Edit View Favorites Tools Help

Back Forward Stop Refresh Home Search Favorites History

Address

Mail Online

| Home | News | Sport | TV&Showbiz | Femail | Health | Science |

You mag | Live mag | Books | Food | Gardening | Promos | Mailshop | Mail

Are nurses angels? I don't think so.

Many nurses, he admits, are magnificent. But equally, says this hospital doctor, many are lazy and uncaring. His bitterly outspoken attack is bound to provoke fury – but raises uncomfortable questions about the system he believes has ruined nursing as a vocation. For obvious reasons he wishes to remain anonymous.

As a young doctor, I witness many distressing scenes on a day-to-day basis. But there is nothing more upsetting than seeing patients suffer because of basic laziness – and incompetence. On each shift, I find myself constantly having to check and check again to ensure the nurses caring for my patients do their job properly.

Of course, I have worked with some admirable nurses who do more than their job description and will skip breaks and work late to ensure their patients are well cared for.

But nurses of this calibre are becoming less common and the problem stems from higher up in the system. When the standards in a department are institutionally poor, young, enthusiastic nurses are certain to have their confidence and ambition gradually eroded.

Part of the problem is that nursing has been dumbed down. Compared with the past, nursing is now looked down upon. But, paradoxically, nurses' training today is much more academic, conveying the idea that the hands-on stuff no longer matters as much.

Many nurses no longer have a sense of vocation; instead it's all about becoming a manager. It seems to me that many nurses enter the profession almost as an afterthought.

Done

LISTENING

5 [1.23] You are going to hear a speech by a VIP at a graduation ceremony for student nurses. Listen and answer the following questions:

1 What advice does she give?

2 What questions does she ask?

3 How would you answer her questions?

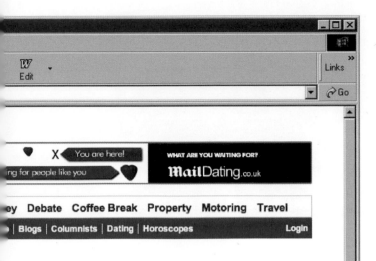

But if I was a patient, what would really worry me is the announcement that nurses are to be given the power to prescribe all medicines, as well as having full responsibility for diagnosis, treatment (including surgical operations) and discharge of patients, without supervision from a qualified doctor.

What we really need is for nurses to stay as nurses. We need nurses who really care for their patients and who recognise, as we all should, that the career of caring is one to be highly respected.

....

Are nurses really lazy and incompetent – or is it doctors who are the problem? Tell us in reader comments below.

This junior doctor is not to be considered representative and clearly has more to learn about multidisciplinary working. By whingeing about his nursing colleagues, he is likely to further damage the stressful working relationship he is in.
Hospital nurse

I've been nursing for 36 years, and the majority of nurses remain as committed and passionate about nursing as I do. Having just finished another long day caring for terminally ill patients ... I feel quite disheartened, and am on the verge of crying.
Sue

Nurses go into the profession knowing the money isn't brilliant, but we enjoy the satisfaction that the care we provide on a daily basis is as holistic and as professional as the system will allow.
Ian, a cardiac nurse for seven years

GRAMMAR: future forms with *to be*

6a Look at these sentences from the reader comments and then find other examples of future forms with *to be* in the reading and listening texts.

*He is **likely to** further damage the stressful working relationship …*

I'm on the verge of *crying.*

6b Choose the correct word to complete the explanation below.

We often use these forms to describe future events that will occur immediately or in the *near / distant* future. We mainly use them in more *informal / formal* situations.

6c Answer these questions about the forms in exercise 6a.

1 Which of them are used when we want to:

a) emphasise that something will happen soon?

b) say that something will definitely happen?

c) say that something is expected to happen at a particular time?

d) say that something will probably happen?

2 Which of these forms take:

a) the infinitive   b) -ing?

➡ **Language reference and extra practice, pages 140–141**

SPEAKING

7 In a group, discuss the following.

1 As a patient, would you be happy for nurses to carry out the duties mentioned in paragraph 7 of the text?

2 Why are men a minority of nurses? Do you think more men will be nurses in the future?

3 Would you be prepared to do a job that you loved for very little money?

WRITING

8 Look again at the three replies to the doctor's article, then write your own reply in one paragraph.

SITUATION

The government health department regularly runs health awareness publicity campaigns aimed at members of the general public. Proposals for future campaigns are currently being discussed, with the subject, aims and the publicity strategy all under consideration. One proposal will be selected as the next campaign.

1 Look at the posters and discuss the following questions.

1 What can you see in each poster?

2 What is the main message and approach of each campaign?

3 What can you remember about similar health campaigns in your country?

2a **1.24** Listen to Charlie make his proposal for a health awareness campaign and make notes under the following headings:

• Subject of the campaign   _____

• Reasons for selecting this subject 1 _____
                                    2 _____
                                    3 _____

• Main aim of the campaign   _____

• Campaign strategy   1 _____
                                    2 _____
                                    3 _____

• Publicity campaign: methods, style and slogan _____

2b Do you think this is an important campaign to run? What are its strengths and weaknesses?

KEY LANGUAGE: justifying your opinions

3 In the meeting, Charlie has to justify his choice of campaign and his approach. Complete extracts 1–8 from the discussion with language that is used to justify opinions. Listen again to check your answers.

1 Right, well, one _____ this campaign _____ almost half of the population eat more …

2 So, you can see that this affects a large number of people, _____?

3 By _____ within just four weeks … your blood pressure will be lower.

4 That's _____ the kind of thing that people want to see.

5 _____ we do these two things, people _____ less salt.

6 The _____ that the problem's so widespread _____ a TV advertising campaign's _____ justified.

7 While _____ that'd be expensive, it'd be the most direct way …

8 You may well _____ , and the _____ is that salt kills slugs.

4 Match the example sentences (1–8) in Exercise 3 to some of the techniques used when justifying opinions. Some examples may be used more than once.

a) using adverbs to give emphasis and focus

b) showing causal and similar direct connections

c) asking or answering a rhetorical question

d) introducing a key point

e) illustrating a key point

f) dealing with a possible criticism

5 Which of these phrases or techniques do/don't you regularly use in discussions? Why?

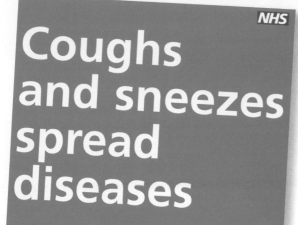

NHS

Coughs and sneezes spread diseases

always carry tissues | cover your coughs and sneezes | throw used tissues in a bin | always clean your hands

Stop germs spreading

© Crown copyright 2007 279593 1p 100k Feb07 (ESP)

MEMO

Health Awareness Publicity Campaign: points to consider
Which health or fitness issue should be addressed?
What is the target audience for the campaign?
What are the two or three key messages of the campaign?
What is the overall campaign slogan?
What campaign methods will we use?
How long should the campaign run for?
Can all this be done within budget?
What will the posters or other visual material look like?

Campaign Media Costs

€200,000	Producing a TV advert
€50,000	TV advertising for one month
€20,000	Producing a radio advert
€10,000	Radio advertising for one month
€20,000	Producing a newspaper advert or poster or leaflet
€40,000	Advertising in national newspapers for one month
€2,000	Distributing 10,000 posters/leaflets (to schools, medical centres, stations, etc.)
€40,000	Designing a website
€100,000	Organising 100 special events at schools/in workplaces

---

TASK: choosing and planning a publicity campaign

6 You work for the government health department and you have to decide which health issue to focus on, and then plan the different elements of the campaign. Read your information and decide why this is an important issue for the government to address with a publicity campaign.

Student A: Turn to page 159.

Student B: Turn to page 161.

Student C: Turn to page 162.

7 Have a meeting with the other members of your team. Follow these instructions.

1 Each person should present the information about their health issue and explain why it is important.

2 As a team, choose one of the issues and then plan the campaign. Consider the guidelines and points listed in the memo. You have a maximum budget of €400,000 (see table of campaign media costs, for your reference).

8 If there is time, produce a mock-up of a campaign poster or other visual communication document.

9 Present your campaign to the other groups in the class.

OTHER USEFUL PHRASES

Inviting someone to speak

So, what's your presentation about?

Let's hear what you have to say.

Tell us about the issue you've read about.

Responding to argument

That's quite convincing.

It's hard to disagree.

That doesn't sound so important to me.

Making a choice

So, which shall we choose?

Any preferences?

Which do you think we should go for?

STUDY SKILLS: analysing visual information

1 In small groups, discuss the following questions:

1 What do the letters WHO stand for? What do you know about this organisation?

2 Look at the WHO logo. What do you think it means?

3 Are some illnesses or diseases becoming more common in your country?

4 What do you understand by 'communicable' and 'non-communicable' diseases?

2 Look at the chart in Figure 1 on page 165 and answer the questions.

1 Where does the chart come from?

2 Is it a reliable source? Why?

3 Match these explanations with one of the terms (A–J) on the right of the chart.

1 very serious diseases caused by bacteria or a virus, and related to breathing or your lungs, e.g. pneumonia, avian influenza (bird flu), swine flu

2 brain diseases caused when the blood supply to the brain is disrupted in some way, e.g. stroke

3 deaths at or around the time of birth, e.g. stillbirth

4 diseases of the heart, e.g. heart attack, angina, chest pain

5 diseases in which waste from the bowels is watery, e.g. cholera

4 Look at the terms A–J on the right of the chart again. Which describe:

1 communicable diseases?

2 non-communicable diseases?

5 Discuss these questions with a partner.

1 Does the chart show every single cause of death?

2 How do we say these dates? 2004, 2009, 2012, 2020, 2030

3 Does the chart give information for every year between 2004 and 2030?

4 Choose one or two of the figures down the left-hand side of the chart. Write the exact number it represents.

6 Put the words below in the correct order to make a sentence describing what the chart shows.

death / between / chart / of / this / 2030 / shows / worldwide / and / 2004 / causes

7 What is the main trend we can see in the chart? Explain in your own words.

8 According to the information in the chart, are the sentences below true or false?

1 By 2030, malaria will have become the least significant cause of death.

2 The number of deaths from cancers will show a steady increase over the period 2014–2030.

3 In 2016, there will be about 6 million deaths from (ischaemic) heart disease.

4 The percentage of deaths from cerebrovascular diseases will remain almost stable between 2020 and 2024.

5 Deaths from tuberculosis will decrease sharply between 2020 and 2030.

6 Deaths from road-traffic accidents will overtake deaths from perinatal causes around 2016.

9 Are you surprised by anything in the chart? Why do you think these changes are expected to take place?

10 In your opinion, is the chart clear? Is there anything missing? Can you think of anything that would have helped you to understand the chart more easily?

WRITING SKILLS: describing visual information

11 Read the writing task shown below. Then put the stages (1–7) of the writing process in the correct order.

> The chart below shows the causes of death worldwide between 2004 and 2030.
>
> Summarise the information by choosing and describing the main features, and make comparisons where relevant. Write at least 150 words.

1 Check for mistakes, e.g. grammar, spelling, punctuation.
2 Look at any other written information on the chart.
3 Count how many words you have used to make sure it is right.
4 Read the title/heading of the chart.
5 Plan your answer. Decide what the main points are and make notes on them, including key data.
6 Look at the words/figures on the vertical and horizontal axes of the chart.
7 Write your answer (main points, plus supporting data). Use linking words.

12 Now read the description of the chart shown in Figure 1 and answer the questions.
1 What is the topic of each paragraph?
2 What is the difference between the first and last sentences?

13 Underline all the examples of approximation you can find in the description below, e.g. *about 14 million*.

14 Find examples of cohesion in the text. Underline all the reference words, e.g. *it, those* that refer to something mentioned earlier and say what they refer to.

15 When we describe a chart like Figure 1, are the statements below true or false?
1 You can just copy the title/heading of the chart and use it word-for-word in your answer.
2 You should try to give as much detail as possible.
3 As you write, it's a good idea to look back at what you've already written.
4 To avoid repetition, you should vary your vocabulary and sentence structures.
5 Try to include one or two complex sentences.
6 The overview must come at the end, as in the example above.
7 It's fine if your answer is a few words below the minimum length (say, 140 words).

16 Write at least 150 words about the chart in Figure 2 on page 165. Say what it shows and describe the main points/trends. Don't forget:
• to select information carefully
• to include a few key figures, where necessary
• to avoid excessive detail
• to use approximators where appropriate

> The chart shows the main causes of death worldwide between 2004 and 2030. Overall, the mortality rate is predicted to climb from just over 35 million in 2004 to approximately 39 million in 2030.
>
> In 2004, about 14 million deaths were attributed to communicable diseases. This represented close to 40 per cent of the total. By 2030, however, deaths due to these diseases can be expected to have fallen to around 7 million, representing less than 20 per cent of the total, with a particularly steep decline in deaths caused by diarrhoeal diseases and malaria.
>
> Conversely, deaths will rise for most non-communicable diseases, especially where cancer deaths are concerned. These will nearly double over the period. A further category is fatalities that are the result of road accidents. The latter will go up steadily from roughly 1 million in 2004 to somewhere in the region of 2.5 million in 2030.
>
> The main trend that emerges from the chart is that deaths from non-communicable diseases and accidents will increase, while deaths from communicable diseases will drop.

5 Fashions and consumerism

5.1 GLOBAL CONSUMERISM

Fashions fade, but style is eternal.
Yves Saint Laurent (1936–2008) French fashion designer

SPEAKING

1 In small groups, discuss the following statements with a partner. Are they true for you? Why / Why not?

1 I hate shopping.
2 Most of my favourite possessions are things that I've bought for myself.
3 I rarely buy things 'on impulse' simply because I like them.
4 It's really important to have a lot of branded goods.
5 I think people in my country are very materialistic.

READING

2 Read the information for a radio series. Name three aspects of global consumerism the programmes will explore.

3 In which of the four programmes might we hear about the following?

1 the effects of consumerism on demographic changes
2 the link between people's identities and their purchases
3 people who are fond of products from an earlier period of time
4 narrowing the gulf between the 'haves' and the 'have-nots'
5 consumerism that is not simply an urban phenomenon
6 consumerism as a recent phenomenon
7 consumer education

LISTENING

4a `1.25` Listen to this extract from the programme about Japan and answer the questions.

1 What evidence is given to support the idea that Japanese people 'love brands'?
2 Why do brands have such value in Japan?
3 What happened in Japan between the end of the Second World War and the mid-1990s?
4 Why have young women been the single most influential group of consumers in recent years, and why is this considered a problem?
5 Do Japanese people think there is a solution to this problem? And if so, what is it?

4b Discuss the following questions with a partner.

1 What do you think will happen to Japanese consumer society in the future?
2 What is the most interesting piece of information you have learned about consumerism in Japan?
3 Which of the other three programmes would you most like to listen to? Why?

VOCABULARY:
consumer collocations

5a Which of the words in the box form common collocations with *consumer*?

consumer choice

advice	boom	choice	confidence
demand	desire	goods	issues
pain	price index	products	society
spending	trends	watchdog	wish

5b Use the collocations from Exercise 5a to complete these sentences.

1 A _____ makes sure consumers are treated fairly and that products are safe.

2 The _____ was followed by a severe downturn.

3 With so many models on the market, good _____ is essential.

4 We've all heard of the _____ , but what does it mean? Well, it's one in which buying goods and services is considered to be very important.

SPEAKING

6 Work in two groups, A and B. Read the information below. Plan your argument, then have a debate.

Group A: You belong to a pressure group that wants people in your country to be less materialistic in the future. Think of some reasons why your country should be less of a consumer society in the coming years.

Group B: You know that there is a powerful pressure group that wants your country to be less materialistic. Think of some reasons why your society should be – or should continue to be – a consumer society in the future.

Global consumerism

This special four-part series investigates consumer trends around the world. What can they tell us about the mindsets of different countries? We visit Germany, Botswana, India and Japan and find that what people buy defines, to an ever greater extent, who they are or who they would like to be. But what's driving our passion to consume? And does it increase our fulfilment?

India In the first programme of this series looking at consumer issues around the globe, we focus on the gap between rich and poor, and how it could be bridged by the construction of new shopping malls, not only in cities, but also in the countryside. In addition, we explore the relationship between the country's new consumerism and its people's mental health.

Germany This programme examines consumerism as a political statement in the former German Democratic Republic (East Germany). Consumer products from the period before the fall of the Berlin Wall in 1989 – and subsequent reunification with West Germany – are viewed with nostalgic appreciation, a phenomenon known as 'ostalgie'. Because life in the east of the country is now changing very quickly, there is a great appetite for products that evoke a more stable era.

Botswana This is the story of an emerging consumer society. Thanks to the discovery of diamonds in 1966 and a number of years of sound government, Botswana's economy is relatively healthy, creating a new breed of consumer. Yet credit and personal debt are major issues here. So who has responsibility for promoting sensible spending habits? Is it the job of schools, of the banks, or of religious organisations?

Japan In the last programme of this globetrotting series, we look into the reasons why this advanced consumer nation is obsessed with brands. Why is this the only country in the world where people trust brands so much they will buy a car without taking it for a test drive? We also see the impact of consumerism on the shrinking birth rate and on the family.

HAUTE

WHAT IS HAUTE COUTURE?

Haute couture refers to high-quality clothes, hand-made exclusively for a particular customer. The French words roughly translate as 'high fashion'. Haute couture is a craft and the techniques used can be very time-consuming. The clothes are made with great attention to detail and finish so that they are a perfect fit, even taking into consideration the customer's body stance.

ORIGINS OF HAUTE COUTURE

Paris had established itself as a leader in European culture in the time of Louis XIV, when the art, music, architecture and fashions of the court at Versailles were copied around the continent. With the accession of Napoleon III in 1852, Paris again became a fashionable imperial capital.

Around this time, two things happened that were to revolutionise fashion and would give birth to modern haute couture. One was the invention of a fast and efficient sewing machine. The other was the arrival in Paris of an English dressmaker, Charles Frederick Worth, who was to become the father of haute couture. Worth transformed the role of the dressmaker into that of an artist, a fashion designer. Initially, only his wife was going to wear his creations but they quickly became popular with Parisians. In 1858, he entered into a business partnership that enabled him to open his own shop, effectively founding the first true house of haute couture. Rich, fashion-conscious women flocked there from around the world and Worth produced garments for royalty (the French Empress Eugénie and Britain's Queen Victoria were clients) and for the families of business magnates.

SPEAKING AND READING

1 **In pairs, discuss the following questions.**

1 What are your experiences or ideas of Paris?

2 What do you think of the clothes in the pictures?

2a **What do you understand by the term 'haute couture'? Read the first paragraph of the magazine article and check your answer.**

2b **Read the rest of the article. Are the statements below true or false?**

1 The importance of Paris in the world of fashion had nothing to do with the rulers of France.

2 The originator of haute couture was not French.

3 Haute couture is quite a wide-ranging term.

4 Companies do not expect to make money with haute couture.

5 More young people are buying haute couture.

3 **In small groups, discuss the following questions.**

1 Haute couture is variously referred to as an art, as a craft and as a business. Which of these three things do you think best describes haute couture?

2 What do you think the rules are that define whether something is haute couture? Check on page 166.

3 Why do you think the rich may be happy to show off their wealth these days?

4 Why do you think haute couture customers are getting younger?

5 Do you think Paris will maintain its position as a fashion capital? Do you think cities like Mumbai and Shanghai will be equally important in 20 years' time?

GRAMMAR: future in the past

4a **Look at the example from the text and complete the gaps in the rule.**

Two things happened that were to revolutionise fashion and would give birth to modern haute couture.

We usually use past tense forms or _____ when we are referring to a point in the _____ , but we want to describe an event that was still in the _____ at that time.

4b **Find and underline examples of the 'future in the past' in the article.**

4c **Which of the forms you have found describe:**

a) something that happened later?

b) something that did not happen later?

➡ **Language reference and extra practice, pages 142–143**

COUTURE

HAUTE COUTURE TODAY

The term haute couture now encompasses not only the clothes, but also the fashion designers and fashion houses. It is protected by French law and there are simple but strict rules about what is or is not haute couture.

This is an elite world with a customer base of only about 2,000–3,000 people. A simple dress can easily cost 50,000 euros yet, in spite of the high prices, haute couture is frequently unprofitable. Instead, it is used by the companies as a loss leader that enables them to build brand identity that will help them sell other products like perfume and lipstick to a mass market.

The demise of haute couture has often been predicted. 30 years ago, people thought that it was likely to disappear, as it was too expensive and too remote from most people's lives. Today, however, haute couture is thriving as the rich get richer, and there are more of them. 'If you've got it, flaunt it' seems to be their motto. Also, because of globalisation, extreme wealth is no longer confined to North America or Western Europe. Interestingly, the average age of customers is declining, too. All this means that it is not uncommon these days to find a 20-year-old Thai princess in the front row of a Paris couture show. Fans of haute couture argue that it is timeless, and that it will only die out when no one is interested in beauty or luxury.

5 Find suitable ways to complete the gaps in these sentences.

1 The famous supermodel was going to _____ , but fell ill just a few hours before the show.

2 She struggled to make a living when she first arrived in Paris, but she would later _____ .

3 No one realised it at the time, but it was to _____ advances of the modern era.

4 _____ Paris was certain to lose its position as the world's fashion capital.

6 Write some sentences about members of your family or about famous people, using the future in the past. Read your sentences to a partner.

My parents were going to emigrate to Argentina, but they changed their mind at the last minute. What happened was that …

VOCABULARY: compound adjectives formed with nouns

7a Put the four adjectives below into one of the categories 1–4.

time-consuming   high-quality

hand-made   fashion-conscious

1 noun + adjective
2 noun + present participle
3 noun + past participle
4 adjective + noun

7b Now put these adjectives into one of the categories 1–4 in Exercise 7a.

eye-catching   jet-black   big-name   world-renowned

7c Where could you use the words from Exercise 7b in the article? Find suitable places.

SPEAKING

8 In groups, discuss these questions.

1 How would you define luxury? What distinguishes luxury from ordinary?

2 Why is luxury important to people?

3 What kind of luxuries interest you most? Why?

WRITING

9 Write a brief description (about 100 words) of a luxury item you possess.

SPEAKING

1 **In pairs, discuss the following questions.**

1 What do the pictures on this spread show?

2 What do you know about the arguments related to these controversial practices?

READING

2a **Look at the newspaper headlines 1–6. What do you think each story is about?**

1 'Lawsuit accuses fashion house of running sweatshops'

(New York Times)

2 'Fashion for size zero* fuels rise in eating disorders among models'

(The Independent)

3 'Discrimination on the ramp**?'

(The Indian Times)

4 'Green is the new black'

(The Guardian)

5 'Fur flies on the catwalk'

(The New Zealand Herald)

6 'Buy it, wear it, chuck it: the price of fast fashion'

(The Independent)

* size zero – the smallest clothes size in America
** ramp – the catwalk at a fashion show

2b **Match the headlines (1–6) to the story extracts (a–f).**

a) Holding signs reading 'Burberry: Fur Shame' and chanting 'Fur is dead', three animal-rights [1]_____ took to the catwalk during the Burberry show at Milan Fashion Week.

b) As many fashion houses do, Donna Karan International asserts that it should not be held responsible for wage and hour [2]_____ committed by factories with which it contracts.

c) The recent rise in such [3]eco-_____ indicates that people want change … the market shifted to accommodate neo-environmentalists' growing interest in green products and their need for variety and [4]_____ .

d) The fashion industry's [5]_____ with size zero could be driving an even bigger increase in eating disorders among models than previously thought.

e) Growing demand for cheap clothes is putting an increasing social and environmental strain on the world, a report has said. It questions the [6]_____ of the 'fast fashion' that is growing in [7]_____.

f) After the [8]_____ 30 years back of black faces on catwalks, fashion in the first decade of the 21st century has turned relentlessly white.

VOCABULARY: suffixes (nouns 1)

3a **Make nouns by combining the suffixes in the box with the words below.**

| -ability   -ist   -ity   -ion (x2)   -ness   -ence (x2) |

active   conscious   convenient   emerge   obsess
popular   sustain   violate

3b **Complete the gaps in Exercise 2b with the nouns from Exercise 3a.**

3c **Think of more nouns with these endings.**

LISTENING

4a 1.26 **Listen to the opening of a radio programme about fashion and social responsibility and answer these questions.**

1 Which newspaper stories in Exercise 2b does the radio show refer to?

2 Who do you think will defend the fashion business, Sarah or Diana?

4b 1.27 **Who do you think will make these points? Listen and check.**

1 Monitoring conditions in suppliers' factories is not straightforward.

2 Fashion companies aim to increase profits.

3 Thin models have a negative influence on women's self-perception.

4 Designers are artists who want to show their work in the best way possible.

5a **Listen again and make notes on the arguments presented by Sarah and Diana.**

5b **Who do you think makes the strongest case overall? Who do you side with and why?**

GRAMMAR: emphatic structures

6a `1.28` **Inversion Complete these sentences from the radio programme. Listen and check.**

1 _____ sooner has _____ attached one than he picks up the next from the thousands in the bag.

2 _____ do the audience realise _____ two models, the Ramos sisters, are missing today …

3 At _____ time are _____ aware of the effect this fast fashion is having on the environment.

6b Answer these questions about sentences 1–3 from Exercise 6a.

1 What is unusual about the subject-verb word order after the opening phrases?

2 Why does sentence 2 above include the word *do*, while the others do not?

7 `1.29` **Fronting Complete these sentences from the radio programme. Listen and check.**

1 Even _____ dangerous _____ the effect this has on the models.

2 … damning _____ may have been, but _____ it certainly wasn't …

8a `1.30` **Cleft sentences Complete these sentences from the radio programme. Listen and check.**

1 _____ 's the enforcement of these rules _____ fashion chains have to focus on …

2 It's _____ that kind of shallow change _____ I'm talking about …

3 _____ the companies _____ is maximise their profits …

4 _____ you need to do _____ change the whole approach of the industry towards body size.

8b Answer these questions about the sentences in Exercise 8a.

1 How many clauses are there in each sentence?

2 Look at the first clauses. Which ones concern the object of the verb in the second clause, and which concern the verb itself in the second clause?

8c Rewrite the sentences in Exercise 8a.

a) The industry …   c) The companies …

b) I am …   d) You need …

➡ **Language reference and extra practice, pages 142–143**

9 Rewrite these sentences using emphatic structures.

1 The first designs were terribly dull. The second designs were much more vibrant.

The first designs were terribly dull. Much …

2 The models at the party were all well-known. Kate Moss was the most famous of them all.

The models at the party were all well-known. Most …

3 He has designed clothes for film stars and he has also opened stores all around the world.

Not …

4 We mustn't use child labour under any circumstances.

Under…

5 The press officer denied the accusation about the use of sweatshops.

It …

6 People are concerned about the cost of a product, not its environmental impact.

It …

7 The fashion industry encourages young girls to worry about their body size.

What …

8 The designer created new styles out of organic materials.

What …

SPEAKING

10 Work in small groups to debate these topics.

1 The fashion industry should be compelled to only use models that are of average body size.

2 The use of animal fur to make clothes should be banned.

3 Parents should not encourage children under 12 to choose their own clothes.

4 The customer is to blame for the increasingly throwaway consumer culture.

SPEAKING

1 In small groups, discuss the following questions.

1 Which fashion and clothing stores are successful in your country? Why?

2 Are there any stores that are not doing very well? Why?

3 As a consumer, what makes you choose one store over another?

2 Look at the various business strategies below. Can you think of any stores which employ any of these strategies?

1 Offering something for everyone.

2 Targeting a particular market, e.g. the fashion-conscious under 35s.

3 Having a low-price strategy:
   a) a no-frills approach to store design and logo
   b) a limited range compared to other stores
   c) not stocking well-known brands
   d) sourcing internationally from suppliers in developing economies

4 Having an up-market strategy:
   a) fashionable, branded clothing and quality products
   b) higher prices and renowned designers
   c) providing a high quality in-store environment

5 Cutting costs by closing under-performing outlets.

6 Maintaining a strong store brand identity through logos and shop design.

7 Advertising widely and staging publicity events.

8 Having a wide product range, not just clothing.

SITUATION

All Seasons is a well-established clothing retailer with 50 stores in its home country and five stores abroad. In recent years, sales have been declining and the company is in danger of making a loss. Ten of the domestic stores are losing money, and the five stores abroad are breaking even. The company sells clothes for the general mainstream market, catering for men, women and children. Most of the stores also sell household products such as kitchenware, bed linen and vases. All products are in the medium to high price range. A store that was once the family choice now struggles to attract people into the shops and to provide the fashion that is desired. The board of directors are planning a recovery strategy.

3 `1.31` **Listen to the CEO of All Seasons outlining the problems facing the company. Make notes on the main points from the consultant's report.**

Three main areas:

1 Shops and Facilities
 stores –
 changing rooms –
 tills –
 customer service –
 overall –

2 The Products
 positive points –
 look and design –
 cost –
 overall range –

3 The Market
 current target market –
 consultant's opinion –

Extra Points
 Accessories –
 Homeware –
 CEO's main interest –
 Finance –

KEY LANGUAGE: discussing hypothetical ideas

4a `1.32` **During the CEO's presentation, some of the directors discussed possible changes. Listen and complete the gaps in the extracts below.**

1 ¹_____ we did have a café, wouldn't that just reduce our sales space? And also, it'd mean that ²_____ to have food storage and preparation facilities. Most of our stores are in restricted high-street locations, I'm not sure how feasible ³_____ .

2 If we ⁴_____ new designs by major designers, rather than use our own in-house designers, ⁵_____ more up-to-date. Mind you, we'd need to produce the clothes quickly then, ⁶_____ we'd still be behind the times.

3 Just on that point, I was wondering if we ⁷_____ an element of specialisation, rather than make a wholesale change.

4 If we had a special range, say one for kids, but still ⁸_____ a wide general range for customers, ⁹_____ ourselves from other stores without losing our current customer base. ¹⁰_____ a chance to market the special range and use this as a way to get people into our stores.

5 I think a special range is an interesting idea, but surely ¹¹_____ be better to target one part of the market much more aggressively. Admittedly, ¹²_____ mean taking a big risk and possibly losing some of our traditional customers …

4b Now answer these questions.

1 Why do the speakers use this particular language in this kind of discussion?

2 Which words mean 'if' and 'if we didn't'?

| TASK: developing a recovery strategy |

5 Work in groups of four. You are on the Board of Directors for All Seasons. You are going to decide how to save the company. Before the meeting, prepare your ideas and review your notes from the consultant's report.

Student A: turn to page 159.

Student B: turn to page 160.

Student C: turn to page 162.

Student D: turn to page 163.

6 Hold the meeting and discuss the four different proposals. How can All Seasons become a destination store? Use the meeting guidelines above to help your discussion.

Meeting Guidelines

Target market?

Specialised ranges or complete change?

Store makeover: Appearance? Facilities?

Product range: Clothing – design, quality, price?

Homeware? New product lines?

Marketing: Advertising? Logo change?

Finance: Store closures? Redundancies?

OTHER USEFUL PHRASES

Making a proposal

I think the best way forward would be …

There are several reasons why I think this.

Firstly, … Secondly, …

I've told you about …, so let's move onto …

To conclude, …

Disagreeing

I think it'd be a mistake to concentrate on that.

I'm really not sure that'd the best way forward.

I'd have to disagree with you on that, I'm afraid.

STUDY SKILLS: reading complex texts effectively

1 Look at the title of the article and read the first paragraph. Answer the following questions.

1 What type of text is this?

2 What are the key words in the title?

3 What are the two things you learn about youth culture?

2a Building an overview Read the text quickly and follow the points below.

- Read to find the main topic **only** of each paragraph. (This will often be given in the first sentence of a paragraph.)

- Make a note of the main topic of the paragraph.

2b Look at your overview notes from Exercise 2a. Which paragraphs are closely connected?

3 Use your overview notes to identify in which paragraph you might find information about:

1 Hip-hop culture no longer being an urban phenomenon

2 People's earnings increasing in the late 1940s

3 Punk influencing the wider fashion industry

4 Reading for detail Pay attention to complex noun phrases and reference words. Identify the following noun phrases and references in the text.

1 The subject of 'is' (line 2)

2 The object of 'led' (line 7)

3 'with which' (line 12)

4 'them' (line 17)

5 'this' (line 30)

6 The subject of 'is' (line 46)

5 Read the whole article in detail and add notes about the key points to your overview notes. Identify the supporting points and argument that connect to the topic of each paragraph. Compare your notes with a partner's.

6 How would you describe the relationship between youth culture and mainstream fashion in your country? Are there any distinct youth sub-cultures?

COMMERCE, PUNK AND HIP-HOP: THE EMERGENCE OF YOUTH CULTURE AND ITS RELATIONSHIP TO THE MAINSTREAM

Whilst the existence of distinct styles of fashion and music that are associated with young people is undoubtedly an important feature of the Western world, it has not always been so. With regard to clothes, for example, for most of
5 history, young people could only choose from mainstream adult fashions as that was all that existed. (Rouse)

Significant economic developments after 1945 led directly to young people making their own decisions concerning taste and style. Principally, there was a huge demand for
10 labour which led to an elevation in salary levels, particularly for young people, who then had relatively large amounts of disposable income with which they could enjoy their lives in the period between school and marriage. (Abrams p.9)

This increase in disposable income meant that these
15 young people became an identifiable consumer market and many industries, such as television, fashion and music, produced goods and services that were directly aimed at them. In a sense, youth culture was defined by the products that were produced specifically for young people by
20 industry and commerce.

However, not all types of youth culture develop in this way. Whilst much of youth culture has been a result of commercial activity, there are undoubtedly smaller sub-cultures which are stylistically innovative and which are
25 created by the young people themselves. Punk and hip-hop cultures illustrate this, and also reveal further connections between mainstream society and youth culture.

The punk culture of 1970s England may be seen as a direct reaction by young people against the intense
30 commercialisation of youth fashion and music. This sub-culture was not the result of the commercial targeting of the young by industry, rather it was created independently by young people. However, punk culture went on to form a different connection with the mainstream culture when its
35 style was adopted by the fashion industry, such that models had green hair, clothes were ripped and cosmetics companies sold make-up in vivid colours. (Rouse).

This adoption of an innovative youth sub-culture by the mainstream culture is also present in the
40 historical journey of hip-hop culture. Rap music and an urban look of baggy jeans, sports shoes and baseball caps, emerged from a very specific social and geographical sphere, namely the young black culture of inner city North America. Yet, this specific
45 style has now spread amongst young people of all races across the world, from Boston to Beijing, and is as much suburban as it is urban. This has occurred because of the direct marketing of this specific sub-culture to the wider youth market by companies on
50 a global scale to substantially increase their profits. For example, in 1992, MTV launched a music show entitled 'Yo! MTV raps', and, by 1993, 80 percent of teenagers 'favoured the [Hip-hop] style'. (Speigler p.447)

Thus, it can be seen that youth culture is directly connected to mainstream consumer culture, although this relationship is not as simple as may first be assumed.

WRITING SKILLS: summarising

7a Identifying main points You are going to summarise the article on page 56 in 150–200 words. Complete the flow chart for the first half of the article with the words in the box.

adults	defined	feature
products	1945	spend

Youth culture/style a ¹_____ of Western societies ➝
not always the case ➝
young people wore same clothes as ²_____
this changed after ³_____ ➝
young people had more money to ⁴_____ as they wanted due to elevation of salaries ➝
businesses targeted young people's disposable income by making special ⁵_____ for them ➝
youth culture ⁶_____ by these products.

7b What information has been left out? Why?

8 Avoiding plagiarism As you make notes or a flow chart, it is important to use your own words in order to avoid plagiarism. Analyse the flow chart in Exercise 7a and identify language that has been changed from the original.

9 Rephrase the following ideas:
1 due to an elevation of salaries
2 disposable income
3 youth culture was defined by these products

10 Make a flow chart for the second half of the text. Compare your flow chart with a partner's. Have you left out similar pieces of information? How have you changed the language?

11a Compare the first sentence below with the first part of the flow chart in Exercise 7a, then with the original text. What are the differences? How many clauses does this sentence have?

While youth culture is a part of Western societies, this has not always been the case as, for a long time, young people only had adult clothes to choose from.

11b Change the rest of the flow chart for the first half of the text into two or three sentences. Use linking words such as *however, as, consequently.* Compare your sentences with a partner's.

11c Complete the full summary of the text, using the flow chart you made in Exercise 10.

Fashions and consumerism   UNIT 5   57

6 Technology and change

In this unit

Grammar
- the passive
- causatives

Vocabulary
- technology words
- dependent prepositions
- idioms and phrasal verbs with *get*

Scenario
- A radio debate

Study skills
- advanced dictionary skills

Writing skills
- a sales leaflet

6.1 ATTITUDES TO TECHNOLOGY

If I had asked people what they wanted, they would have said faster horses.
Henry Ford (1863-1947) Founder, Ford Motor Company

SPEAKING AND READING

1 In pairs, discuss the following questions.

1 What do you understand by the word 'technology'?

2 How have advances in technology affected your working/studying and social life?

3 What kinds of advances would you like to see in the next 20 years?

4 Is the latest technology always an improvement? Can you give any examples when it hasn't been?

2 Do the technology quiz on page 169 and then check your answers on page 166.

3 Do you think we rely on technology too much? Why / Why not? Discuss with a partner.

4 Which item of technology do you think is the most:

a) important?

b) useful?

c) controversial?

d) unpopular?

e) pointless?

VOCABULARY: technology words

5a Put the adjectives in the box below under the correct heading.

out-of-date   up-to-date

> behind the times   cutting-edge   ground-breaking
> innovative   new-fangled   obsolete   old-hat
> outdated   outmoded   pioneering   redundant
> retro   revolutionary   state-of-the-art

5b Which two adjectives from the box are more informal than the others? Use a dictionary to help you.

5c Complete each sentence using a suitable adjective from the box. There may be more than one possible answer.

1 I don't understand those _____ phones. I just want something simple that I can call people on.

2 That device was _____ before it even went on the market. Nobody uses them any more.

3 This really is a _____ development. It will change the way we communicate for ever.

4 It's not exactly _____ technology, but it's still a pretty useful piece of equipment.

READING

6a Read the message board opinions and answer the questions below.

1 Which of the people are for / against / undecided about the question?

2 Which points do you agree / disagree with? Which is closest to your own point of view?

6b Summarise each person's argument in one sentence.

7 What do you notice about the way the writers on the message board express their opinions? Is the style:

a) formal or informal?

b) subjective or objective?

c) well-structured or disorganised?

d) emotional or unemotional?

8a Find examples of the following in the message board texts.

a) rhetorical questions

b) colloquial language

8b What other stylistic features do you notice? Why do you think they are used?

9a Complete the following with the correct preposition. Look back to the message board to check your answers.

1 What does a fear of technology stem _____ in your opinion?

2 Which item of technology has had the biggest impact _____ your / your parents' life?

3 Has the rise _____ the popularity of social networking sites resulted _____ better understanding between men and women?

4 Does technology contribute _____ the happiness of mankind?

5 Is the expansion _____ robot technologies a good thing?

6 Do you think technological advances will lead _____ people living on other planets?

9b Discuss your answers with a partner.

WRITING

10a Write your opinion for a message board on the following question.

Have technological advances had a positive effect on people's lives in your country?

10b Exchange your writing with a partner and write a response.

Welcome [Web Search]

Views and Insight – message board – have your say- TODAY!

| Technology | News | Maps |

Browse

Have technological advances had a positive impact on peoples' lives?

All the really fundamental changes have been connected to advances in technology. Think about all the lives which have been saved due to breakthroughs in, for example, medicine. And what about the general extended life expectancy? What about transport and communication? Some people have always been anti-technology. There are always dramatic changes going on, especially now, in terms of communication. The Internet is amazing and has had an awesome effect on people's lives. Sven

It's true, technology has altered people's lives but I'm not sure it's been for the better. A lot of stress stems from the fact that technology speeds everything up in our already fast paced world. We're now reachable 24 hours a day and we expect instant answers, and this impacts on people's work/life balance. There are also the dehumanising effects of technology – we've become slaves to machines. What about the dangers of things like GM crops – or 'Frankenstein foods'? It's dangerous to mess about with nature. Advances in technology breed laziness and contribute to a sedentary lifestyle. Look at all those kids who would rather play a computer game than kick a ball around. Jose

Technology can fix all society's problems. Even during wars there's a great impetus for technological development. Cars which cause pollution resulting in global warming are now being superseded by hybrid and electric ones. They will reduce the carbon footprint. BTW, those of you who think technology is so bad: WHY ARE YOU USING THE INTERNET TO TELL US THIS?!! Andrea

Technology is a double-edged sword. There have been radical changes brought about by inventions like the telephone, car and the Internet. But, the important thing is that control of technology is power. It's the way it is used which is important. For example, some technological advances are not always used in a good way. What about the rise in cosmetic surgery, artificial intelligence, cloning, designer babies, people living forever? Where's technology taking us? This, together with a move towards an ever-greater reliance on technology is leading us to a nightmare vision of the future. Arwa

Technology has a lot to answer for. Never mind improving people's lives, it accounts for the increase in pollution and exploitation. Lots of people are killed in wars because of so-called technological advances. As for the expansion of access to the Internet, there are millions of people in the world who haven't even made a phone call yet!! There's a real digital divide. Technological advances because of their uneven distribution actually have a negative effect on people's opportunities. Major technological change is basically destroying the planet. I doubt we can save it in time. It's really all about greed. I guess this is more to do with human nature rather than technology itself, though. Jane

---

READING

1 In groups, rank the following in terms of how much they have changed the world:

the printing press, electricity, antibiotics, mobile phones, the Internet

2 Work in groups of three. Read one of the articles and explain what the technology is to your group.

3 Read the other two articles and answer the following questions.

1 What is 93 million miles away?

2 Will people pay more or less attention to their doctor?

3 How do you change the DNA in a cell?

4 Why do you think the writers use the underlined words?

4 What do the following words or phrases from the articles mean?

1 at peak oil
   a) at the highest level of oil production
   b) at the highest price for oil

2 arrays
   a) groups of buildings
   b) collections of solar panels

3 by trial and error
   a) by making lots of mistakes over time
   b) by testing different methods in order to find the most suitable one

5 Match the words 1–8 from the articles to their definitions a–h.

1 aspiration	5 trait
2 radiant	6 hunch
3 profound	7 synthetic
4 commensurate	8 chromosome

a) having a strong influence or effect

b) a strong desire to have or achieve something

c) heat or energy sent out in the form of waves

d) a particular quality in someone's character

e) matching something in size, quality or time

f) a feeling that something is true or will happen

g) a part of every living cell that contains our genes

h) produced by combining different artificial substances

6 Each author makes a strong claim. What is it, and do you agree?

7 In your groups, discuss which of the three ideas will change the world the most.

Ian McEwan

Author

By nearly all insider and expert accounts, we are or will be at peak oil somewhere between now and the next five years. Even if we did not have profound concerns about climate change, we would need to be looking for different ways to power our civilisation. How fortunate we are to have a <u>safe</u> nuclear facility a <u>mere</u> 93 million miles away and fortunate too that the dispensation of physical laws is such that when a photon strikes a semiconductor, an electron is released. My hope is that architects will be drawn to designing gorgeous arrays and solar towers in the desert – as expressive of our aspirations as medieval cathedrals once were. We will need new distribution systems too, smart grids – perfect Rooseveltian projects for our hard-pressed times. Could it be possible that in two or three decades we will look back and wonder why we ever thought we had a problem when we are bathed in such beneficent radiant energy?

GRAMMAR: the passive

8a Find and underline all the passive forms in the articles.

8b Now say which tense each passive is.

9 Read the uses of passive (a–g) and match them with the samples (1–7).

a) The agent is obvious.

b) The agent is unimportant or we don't know who the agent is.

c) If the subject of a sentence is long, we often make the verb passive so that the long phrase comes at the end.

d) We often make a verb passive so that new information comes at the end.

e) We want to avoid mentioning the agent (so as not to blame someone, or avoid responsibility).

f) We want to focus on issues rather than on the people involved, especially in scientific and academic English.

g) We are describing rules and procedures.

1 The technician was sacked yesterday.

2 The final chapter sums up all the issues that have been discussed throughout the book

3 The trainees were impressed by the brand new state-of-the-art laboratory on the ground floor.

4 Penicillin is one of the most widely used antibiotics. It was discovered by Alexander Fleming in 1928.

5 Mistakes were made.

6 The research will be carried out next year.

7 Safety glasses must be worn in the laboratory at all times.

➡ Language reference and extra practice, pages 144–145

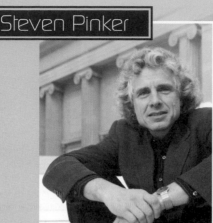

Steven Pinker

Psychologist and author

This past year saw the introduction of direct-to-consumer genomics. A number of new companies have been launched. You can get everything from a complete sequencing of your genome (for a <u>cool</u> $350,000), to a screen of more than a hundred disease genes, to a list of traits, disease risks, and ancestry data. Here are some possible outcomes: personalised medicine, in which drugs are prescribed according to the patient's molecular background rather than by trial and error; an end to many genetic diseases; cafeteria insurance (where you choose your own level of cover) will no longer be viable for insurers if the highest-risk consumers can load up on generous policies while the low-risk ones get by with the bare minimum; the ultimate empowerment of medical consumers, who will know their own disease risks and seek commensurate treatment, rather than relying on the hunches and folklore of a paternalistic family doctor.

Craig Venter

Scientist

We have now shown that DNA is absolutely the information-coded material of life by completely transforming one species into another simply by changing the DNA in the cell. By inserting a new chromosome into a cell and eliminating the existing chromosome all the characteristics of the original species were lost and replaced by what was coded for on the new chromosome. Very soon we will be able to do the same experiment with the synthetic chromosome. We can start with digitised genetic information and four bottles of chemicals (the four nucleotides of the genetic code) and write new software of life to direct organisms to do processes that are desperately needed, like create renewable biofuels and recycle carbon dioxide. As we learn from 3.5 billion years of evolution we will convert billions of years into decades and change not only conceptually how we view life but life itself.

10 In pairs, look at the text below and choose five places where the passive might be more appropriate.

Areha is a good example of a new town. In 1967, Eduardo Raffo designed it. The huge empty spaces and beautiful green landscapes delighted him. The Areha Development Corporation hired Raffo at the start of the project, but in 1969 they sacked him and appointed a young Italian designer instead. The authorities formally designated Areha a new town on 2 February 1972. Areha prospered for many years, but many changes have happened since the recent recession. The two main engineering companies closed down last year. However, the planners deliberately located Areha at a point equidistant from four large towns, and people expect it to recover quickly once the recession is over.

SPEAKING

11 In groups, discuss the following questions.
1 How has the world been spoilt by technology?
2 What has been lost due to technological change?
3 How has culture been affected?
4 Do you think technological innovation is/has been dominated by men?

WRITING

12 Write a short paragraph on the following question.

What technology will change the world the most in the next ten years?

Ten years in:

How Google raced ahead

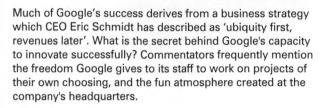

Much of Google's success derives from a business strategy which CEO Eric Schmidt has described as 'ubiquity first, revenues later'. What is the secret behind Google's capacity to innovate successfully? Commentators frequently mention the freedom Google gives to its staff to work on projects of their own choosing, and the fun atmosphere created at the company's headquarters.

'People in Google have up to 20 per cent of their time to 'play' with ideas and initiatives which might be of interest to the customers,' explains Phil Anderson, a client director at Ashridge Business School. 'There is also a wonderful physical environment – the Googleplex – where people are provided with free food, coffee and 'play areas'.' Google staff say that typically half of all new products and features result from 'personal project' time.

However, this is not the only way Google promotes innovation. Another key component is Google's technology platform. Tom Davenport, a professor of information technology and management at Babson College in Massachusetts, explains that this infrastructure 'allows Google to rapidly develop and roll out services of its own or its partners' devising'.

The emphasis, he adds, is 'not on identifying the perfect offering, but on creating multiple potentially useful offerings and letting the market decide. There is no need for Google to do market surveys to forecast trends: the information is in Google's database.'

Richard Hunter, a group vice-president at Gartner and Gartner Fellow, says that most companies ask, 'What information do we need to run the business?' But Google asks, 'How can we get our hands on every piece of information in the world – never mind if we do not know what to do with it all right now?'

Davenport thinks that 'while few organisations can match the magnitude of Google's infrastructure investments, many could create reusable software components, bake them into its infrastructure, and make them accessible to the enterprise – or to members of the extended enterprise who might be inspired to use them in building and delivering their own applications.'

Google has taken the 'suggestion box' a step further, by encouraging staff to submit ideas and allowing colleagues to comment on and rate them. Staff can also submit code for projects being run by other teams – such as a feature enhancement – without asking permission, and have the code incorporated into the testing process.

One of the reasons Google is able to put this much trust in its employees is that it recruits very carefully and continues to manage them in ways that encourage innovation.

READING

1 In groups, discuss what you know about Google.

2a Predict whether the following statements about Google are true or false.

1 Google staff spend half their time on their own ideas and initiatives.

2 Google is successful because it carries out extensive market surveys.

3 All Google staff have to assess ideas submitted to the 'suggestion box'.

4 Google takes great care when hiring new staff.

2b Read the article to check your answers.

3 How does Google encourage innovation?

4 Complete the gaps in the sentences with the words in the box.

> enhancement   infrastructure   initiative
> innovation   magnitude

1 There has been a lot of _____ in the teaching of Information Technology recently.

2 The earthquake has badly damaged the region's _____ . All the basic systems and services such as transport and power supplies have been affected.

3 These mistakes will not lead to the _____ of our company's reputation.

4 You need to have a lot of _____ to do this job. You have a lot of responsibility.

5 I don't think you understand the _____ of the problem. This is going to take months to sort out.

5 Find and underline nouns in the article which combine with the words below to make common collocations.

1 business   4 market

2 physical   5 software

3 information   6 suggestion

6 Discuss the following:

1 Would you like to work at Google? Why / Why not?

2 What sort of working environment encourages innovation?

LISTENING

7 **2.1** **Listen to somebody talking to a careers advisor. Answer the following questions.**

1 Why was he made redundant?

2 Why was he upset about the way he was made redundant?

3 What advice did the advisor give him?

VOCABULARY: idioms with *get*

8 **Complete the gaps in the sentences using the idioms (1–5) below. You will need to make some changes to the idioms first.**

1 get somebody down

2 get on somebody's nerves

3 get the hang of something

4 get on like a house on fire

5 get off to a flying start

a) Peter is really struggling with the new technology. He just hasn't _____ yet.

b) My boss has an annoying voice. It really _____ .

c) The computer support guy is really helpful and friendly. We _____ .

d) We went on a team building course and our team _____ . We completed the first task ahead of all the other teams.

e) I know this technology course is frustrating, but don't let it _____ .

GRAMMAR: causatives

9a **2.2** **Listen and complete the following extracts.**

1 I had an interview and then they _____ leave the building immediately.

2 I wasn't _____ clear my desk.

3 They didn't even _____ me say goodbye to my staff.

4 Apparently, they'd even ____ all the locks _____ …

9b **Now answer the questions.**

1 Which sentence means someone employs someone else to do something?

2 Which sentence means someone forces someone else to do something?

3 Which sentence means someone permits or doesn't permit someone else to do something?

4 Which verb do we use instead of *let* in the passive?

➥ **Language reference and extra practice, pages 144–145**

10a **Read the following pairs of examples and answer the questions.**

1 In which sentence is the emphasis on the fact that Ali was responsible for arranging the action, a or b?
   a) Ali's apartment was redecorated last week.
   b) Ali had his apartment redecorated last week.

2 In which sentence is the emphasis on having an experience rather than on arranging the action, c or d?
   c) Nadine had her car stolen at the weekend.
   d) Nadine had her car repaired at the weekend.

10b **Answer the following questions.**

1 Which sentences above (a–d) are causatives?

2 Which sentence is passive?

3 Which sentence is the non-causative use of '*have something done*?

GRAMMAR TIP

In informal / spoken British English *get* is used to express causatives.

I got my hair cut this morning.

11 **In pairs, ask and answer questions using the prompts below.**

car	hair	cut	change
lawn	tyres	mend	paint
house	clean	fix	

A *What have you done to your hair?*

B *I had it cut.*

SPEAKING

12 **In groups, answer the following questions:**

1 What positive and negative changes (moving house, moving to another country, changing school, losing / changing your job, etc.) have you had in your life?

2 What changes do you expect to have to make in the future?

I wasn't allowed to travel on my own until I was 18. When I was 18 my parents let me go to a summer school in Australia and that changed my life.

I was made to change school when I was 16 and I really found it difficult to make new friends.

SITUATION

A radio station has a weekly programme called 'Science and technology'. The station has organised a competition based on the theme of 'modern technologies'. Listeners were invited to write a short paragraph in response to the following debating topic:

The modern technology that has brought the most benefits to mankind and will continue to do so is ...

Listeners completed the statement with their chosen technology. Four of the listeners' responses have been selected by the programme organisers. The writers of the responses will now take part in a radio debate. They have been asked to present the case for their technology and to defend their arguments before a studio audience. At the end of the programme, there will be a vote and the winner will receive a cash prize.

> The four topics for the debate are:
>
> **Electric cars**
>
> **Genetic testing**
>
> **Robot technology**
>
> **Surveillance technology** *
>
> *(CCTV cameras, telephone tapping, speed cameras, etc.)

1 Read the situation. In groups, discuss what you know about each of the topics.

2 To help candidates prepare for the debate, the programme organisers have sent them an audio presentation about mobile phones. The presenter puts the case for mobile phones and answers questions from the audience. Work in small groups and discuss the following questions:

1 What arguments do you think the presenter will use to persuade her audience that mobile phones have brought the greatest benefits to mankind?

2 What criticisms of mobile phones do you think the audience will make?

3a **2.3** Listen to Part 1 of the presentation and
answer the following questions.

1   Why does the speaker mention the figure 4 billion?

2   What reasons does she give to persuade her
    audience that mobile phones are 'an extraordinarily
    versatile piece of equipment'?

3b Listen again and complete the gaps in the
sentences.

1   I think the facts speak for themselves, _____?

2   The total number of mobile phone subscriptions
    _____. Yes, 4.1 billion…

3   I'm sure _____ mobile phones are an _____
    piece of equipment.

4   It's _____ what this small electronic _____
    can do.

5   I'd like to give you just one other _____
    example of the use of mobile phones.

3c Which of these techniques are used in
sentences 1–5 above?

a) repeating a word or phrase

b) using an emotive adjective

c) using a rhetorical question

d) giving an impressive statistic

e) appealing to the audience

3d Read Track 2.3 on page 178 and find other
examples of the persuasive techniques above.

4a **2.4** Listen to Part 2 and answer the questions.

1   What counter-arguments does the speaker use to
    deal with the following criticisms?

a) Mobile phones often annoy people.

b) They cause problems when drivers use them.

c) People may have allergic reactions.

d) The radiation from mobile phones is harmful to
    users.

2   What other benefits of mobile phones can you
    think of in addition to the ones mentioned in the
    presentation?

4b Read Track 2.4 on page 178. Underline:

1   the expressions the speaker uses to concede
    arguments.

2   the expression she uses to introduce her most
    persuasive argument.

3   the rhetorical question she asks to persuade her
    listeners that mobile phones are indispensable.

5a Work in groups of four. Each group chooses one
of the modern technologies on page 167. Structure
your presentation using the following points.

* what the technology is
* what its uses are
* what criticisms have been made of the technology
* what the technology's benefits are
* conclusion

5b In your groups, take turns to present the case
for your chosen technology and answer questions
from the other members of the group.

5c As a group, decide which technology has been
most beneficial to mankind. You cannot vote for the
technology you presented in the debate.

OTHER USEFUL PHRASES

Persuading

There's no doubt that …

It's undeniable that …

Surely / Clearly / Obviously…

No one can dispute the argument that …

I'm sure you can all agree that …

Conceding points

I accept that …

There may be some truth in the argument …

It's true that…

However …

There is an argument that …

To some extent this is true, but …

STUDY SKILLS: advanced dictionary skills

1a Dictionaries can help you to find the meaning of a word, but they can also help you in many other ways. In groups, discuss the various ways in which a dictionary can help you.

1b What are the advantages of using a monolingual dictionary? Are there any disadvantages?

2a **2.5** Claudia and Mina are talking in the college canteen. Claudia has just bought a new dictionary. Listen to the conversation and tick the features of the dictionary mentioned.

Claudia says that in her dictionary, you can find out:

1 the part of speech of words
2 how words are spelled
3 the American term for a British word
4 how a word is pronounced
5 if a noun is countable or uncountable
6 the meaning of idioms and phrases
7 how important a word is
8 the grammar of a word
9 what words are often used with other words.

2b Listen again and answer the following questions:

1 Which section of Claudia's dictionary will help students to use it effectively?
2 Where can you find out if a noun is countable or uncountable?
3 How does the dictionary show that a word is used frequently?
4 Why does Claudia particularly like the dictionary?

3 Look at the extract from the Longman Dictionary of Contemporary English for the word 'plug'. Answer the questions.

1 In this extract, what part of speech is **plug?**
2 How common is the noun **plug** in spoken English?
3 Is the noun **plug** countable or uncountable?
4 How is **plug** pronounced?
5 Which meaning of the word **plug** is being used in this example?

My car won't start. I think the plugs are damp because of the heavy rain.

6 What expression means that someone won't give you more money for your project?
7 According to the extract, what must you do to continually improve your English?

8 Why would someone in Britain use a **plug** to put a framed painting on the wall?
9 What does it mean if someone says, 'He was **plugging** his new book in the TV interview'.
10 What is the American English word for **plug?**

4 Work in pairs. Ask each other more questions about the dictionary entries for 'plug'. The first person to get five correct answers is the winner!

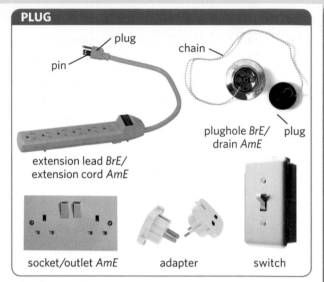

plug¹ **S3** /plʌg/ *n* [C]
1 ELECTRICITY **a)** a small object at the end of a wire that is used for connecting a piece of electrical equipment to the main supply of electricity: *The plug on my iron needs changing.* | *an electric plug* **b)** *especially BrE informal* a place on a wall where electrical equipment can be connected to the main electricity supply SYN **socket, outlet** *AmE*
2 BATH a round flat piece of rubber used for stopping the water flowing out of a bath or SINK: *the bath plug*
3 ADVERTISEMENT *informal* a way of advertising a book, film etc by mentioning it publicly, especially on television or radio: **put/get in a plug (for sth)** *During the show she managed to put in a plug for her new book.*
4 IN AN ENGINE *informal* the part of a petrol engine that makes a SPARK, which makes the petrol start burning SYN **spark plug**: *Change the plugs every 10,000 miles.*
5 pull the plug (on sth) *informal* to prevent a plan, business etc from being able to continue, especially by deciding not to give it any more money: *The Swiss entrepreneur has pulled the plug on any further investment in the firm.*
6 TO FILL A HOLE an object or substance that is used to fill or block a hole, tube etc: **[+of]** *You can fill any holes with plugs of matching wood.* → EARPLUG
7 FOR HOLDING SCREWS *BrE* a small plastic tube put in a hole to hold a screw tightly
8 A PIECE OF STH a piece of something pressed tightly together: *a plug of tobacco*

(Longman Dictionary of Contemporary English – Fifth Edition)

WRITING SKILLS: a sales leaflet

5a Read the sales leaflet below. Then look up the following words and phrases in your dictionary. Find out as much information as you can about each one, e.g. pronunciation, part of speech, meaning, how it is used.

workout   equipment   testimonial
on the ball   guarantee

5b In pairs, compare the information you have found in your dictionaries.

6 In small groups, discuss the following questions.

1   How does the writer get the attention of the reader?

2   What information in the first two paragraphs would be particularly interesting for readers and persuade them to read on?

3   How does the writer create desire in the minds of readers so that they feel they really need the equipment?

4   What evidence does the writer provide to back up claims that the equipment will make you fitter and healthier?

5   What methods does the writer use to persuade the reader to take action and buy the product?

7 Find and underline words/phrases in the leaflet which:

1   exploit the reader's desire

2   have a strong impact

3   are examples of collocations

4   are examples of persuasive language

8 Find four words/phrases in the leaflet which are formal and four which are informal.

9a `2.6` A company trainer is giving a talk to staff on writing a sales leaflet. Listen to Part 1 and answer the following questions.

1   What are the two main topics that the trainer covers in this part of the interview?

2   What does the acronym AIDA stand for?

9b `2.7` Now listen to Part 2. Note down the key points that the trainer makes in her summary. Then compare your points with a partner.

10 Write a sales leaflet for the surveillance product Eagle Night Vision Binoculars. The specifications are given on page 164.

Vibrant-Plate is an exercise plate which is designed to improve your fitness quickly, easily and more conveniently than a time-consuming workout at a gym or fitness centre.

Vibrant-Plate was developed in the United States by a famous trainer of Olympic athletes who worked together with scientists from Space Research to produce this revolutionary equipment for improving people's fitness.

The equipment's proven technology stimulates your muscles and tones up your body.

Your muscles generally contract once or twice a second, but when you stand on Vibrant-Plate, the vibrations cause your muscles to contract at a rate of 30 to 50 a second. So, you get a high-speed workout in a short time. It's the ideal solution for people who lead busy lives but want to keep fit.

Vibrant-Plate

Use Vibrant-Plate ten minutes each day and you will:

• **Lose weight quickly**

• **Improve your health**

• **Be fitter and more energetic**

• **Feel and look younger**

• **Save time and money**

**unhappy about your weight?
want to be fitter?
more healthy?
look better?**

Here is one of many testimonials that we have received:

"I've been using Vibrant-Plate for about six weeks now and I've already lost 8 pounds. I'm over the moon because I've tried so hard to lose weight in the past and failed. It's incredible! Now I look great and feel wonderful. I'm more self-confident, always on the ball at work and the life and soul of the party when I go to discos. I'm really enjoying my new slim self."
Marta Gonzales.

Vibrant-Plate

Price: 320 euros. 3-year guarantee. Money refunded if you're not satisfied.

(10% discount if you order before October 30) One of the cheapest vibrator plates on the market. Guaranteed to be as strong as more expensive brands.

Order today using the attached form, and we will contact you within 24 hours to arrange a free delivery. Or: log on to our website for an order form: www.Vibrant-plate.com

For further technical information, call: 0800 295 6600 or email: Vibrant-plate@hotmail.com.

GRAMMAR

1 Discuss the questions.

1 Is there an obesity problem in your country?

2 Many western countries have a problem with obesity. What are the factors in causing a population to become obese?

Are fad diets fuelling the obesity problem?

Leila Patterson reports from the Gastro 2009 conference in London

Fad diets are known to be a source of potential harm to the individual. [1]*As well as this / On the contrary*, they may be ultimately responsible for worsening the obesity issue, doctors warned today. If we are to avoid a hugely obese nation by 2050, the population needs to be made aware of the shortcomings of these fads. [2]*Whereas / Moreover*, doctors claim, pathological eating disorders such as anorexia and bulimia are fuelled by ruthless promotion of unhealthy diets and foods, along with the obsession for size zero models on the catwalk.

Never before has there been such a proliferation of different regimes available, from the raw food diet to the Hollywood grapefruit diet. One of the most popular is still the Atkins diet, [3]*although / even so* only 2 per cent of women believe that it is good for their health. The diet, which cuts out almost all carbohydrates, was first introduced by Robert Atkins in the 1970s but recently enjoyed a resurgence in popularity, selling millions of books worldwide. [4]*On the other hand / Despite* the fact that these food fads are often based on a scientific theory, the nutritional content of the diets has rarely been tested because they are so complex.

Some doctors feel fad diets may have a restricted use: [5]*while / because* they may be harmful in the long term, what they can do is provide a short-term 'fix', for example, quick weight loss for an imminent event, such as a wedding, arising from cutting out a whole food group from the diet. [6]*However / Furthermore*, according to medical experts, any diet that severely restricts the intake of a particular food group should be avoided, [7]*otherwise / as* the body needs a balance of all food groups to maintain optimum health. [8]*Furthermore / In contrast*, dieters must be aware that they are almost bound to regain any kilos lost once they revert to their former eating habits. [9]*Similarly / Consequently*, all fad diets that promise sustainable weight loss should be viewed with suspicion. The one thing that all experts agree on is that weight reduction can be maintained in the long term only by decreasing calorie intake and increasing physical exercise. [10]*Nonetheless / Therefore*, people wishing to lose weight should seek out diets adhering to this principle which have been tried and tested by thousands of people around the world.

2a Read the article quickly. Does it mention any of the factors you discussed in Exercise 1?

2b Read the article again, more carefully. Find evidence to justify these statements.

1 The British people have a problem with obesity.

2 There may be one or two valid reasons for following a fad diet.

3 There's only really one effective way to lose weight.

3a Choose the correct linking words in the article.

3b Find examples of the following in the article, and then compare with a partner.

1 a passive in a simple tense

2 a passive infinitive

3 a sentence with a long subject that has been made passive

4 a sentence in the passive where known information has been brought to the beginning

5 an example of *be* + adjective + infinitive to express the future

6 an example of *be to* to express the future

7 an example of inversion

8 an example of a cleft sentence

4 Writers try not to repeat the same words too often in texts, so they find alternative words or paraphrases. Find the way the writer refers to these things in the texts.

1 problem (one more way)

2 diet (two more ways)

3 weight loss (three more ways)

VOCABULARY

5a Complete the table with these words and phrases connected with medicine.

alternative medicine   check-up   flu virus
general practitioner (GP)   heart attack   operation
palliative care   paramedic   premature ageing
scan   surgeon   X-ray

health professionals	health problems	ways of diagnosing	types of treatment

5b Now write three or four sentences, each of which containing at least two of the words from the chart and make a link that will help you remember them.

After my last check-up, my GP sent me for a scan.

UNITS 4–6

6 Complete the sentences with a collocation or a compound adjective. Choose one word from Box A and one from Box B.

A

> consumer cutting fashion high immune
> life revolutionary

B

> changes conscious edge expectancy
> salt intake spending system

1 In most developed countries the average _____ is now around 80 or over.

2 One of the problems of being really stressed is that it can lower the efficiency of your _____ .

3 As the pound has fallen so much against the euro, the _____ by British people in Europe has really decreased.

4 There were _____ in the village once the water pump had been installed.

5 Younger people tend to be more _____ than older people, and want to update their wardrobe every year.

6 The new car manufacturer is at the _____ of automotive technology.

7 Doctors blame a _____ as a major cause of heart and circulation problems.

KEY LANGUAGE

7a [2.8] Listen to three business people discussing their shop. Match the people with the opinions. Which person is most committed to the business?

Ivan a) thinks there's little point in keeping the business going any longer.

Jaya b) believes they should target the local market more closely.

Patty c) thinks the shop needs to go more downmarket in what it sells.

7b Complete the sentences with phrases from the box. Who do you think said each sentence? Listen again and check your answers.

> Actually, I think   I was wondering
> One reason I favour this   Suppose
> The fact that   The facts speak
> While I accept   You can see

1 _____ we started to stock much cheaper clothes …?

2 _____ we're in a very affluent part of the country means we should focus on people with money.

3 _____ if we'd do better to go more upmarket.

4 _____ is that we know we can't compete on the fashion stuff …

5 _____ for themselves, don't they?

6 _____ what I mean, can't you?

7 _____ your arguments, I can't help feeling there are other solutions.

LANGUAGE CHECK

8 There is a missing word or a mistake in word order in each of these sentences. Find and correct the mistake, then look at the pages to check your answers.

1 Alex had a heart attack when he was only 50, though even he had looked after his health. (page 40)

2 This medication is to not be taken internally. (page 43)

3 I was going order you that book from Amazon, but I completely forgot. (page 50)

4 What the board plans to do boost production by introducing faster machines. (page 53)

5 We could hardly hear anything in the classroom yesterday as a drill being used in the room next door. (page 60)

6 This is the third time I've had stolen my bike from outside the office! (page 63)

7 The children who arrived at the school were made go home because of the weather conditions. (page 63)

LOOK BACK

9 Find the exercises in Units 4–6 where you …

• read about a successful health system (Unit 4)
• examine different ways of expressing the future (Unit 4)
• interpret information presented in a chart (Unit 4)
• listen to a programme about consumerism in Japan (Unit 5)
• look at ways of forming compound adjectives (Unit 5)
• learn how to manipulate word order for emphasis (Unit 5)
• do a quiz about your use of new technology (Unit 6)
• write a posting for a message board (Unit 6)
• simulate a radio debate (Unit 6)

People and ideas

7.1 CREATIVITY

The best way to have a good idea is to have lots of ideas.
Linus Pauling(1901–1994) Scientist and author

SPEAKING

1 **In pairs, answer the following questions.**

1 Do you think creative people are born or made?

2 What do you understand by these terms?

   a blue sky thinker, a lateral thinker, someone who thinks outside the box

3 How creative do you consider yourself to be?

2a **Try this test of lateral thinking.**

1 Where are all men equally attractive?

2 On which side of a cup is it best to have the handle?

3 How might someone be severely injured by being hit by some tomatoes?

4 Where do the biggest carrots grow?

5 What living thing has only one foot?

6 How many birthdays does a typical woman have?

7 A cowboy rode into town on Friday. He spent one night there and left on Friday. How do you explain this?

2b Discuss your answers with a partner, then turn to page 164.

LISTENING

3 **2.9** **You are going to hear a lecture about creativity. How do you think the speaker will answer these questions? Listen to Part 1 and check.**

1 How would you define creativity?

2 How can you recognise a creative person?

3 In which areas of work do you think it is a useful quality to have?

4 How is creativity different to innovation?

4a **2.10** **Listen to Part 2 of the lecture. Put the following stages of the model of the creative process in the correct order.**

a) illumination   d) intimation

b) preparation   e) incubation

c) verification

4b **Listen again and make notes on what stages a–e above mean.**

READING

5 **Look at the photos on the left and answer the questions.**

1 Who are the creative people in the photographs?

2 What do you know about them?

3 What do you think they have in common?

6 **Read the article and decide if the following statements are true, false or not given.**

1 Left-handed people are better at language learning than right-handed people.

2 Right-handed people have a more holistic approach to tackling problems.

3 Left-handed people are generally wealthier.

4 Right-handedness has associations with the law.

5 In the past, left-handedness was considered undesirable.

6 More US presidents have been left-handed than right-handed.

7 **What's your reaction to the text?**

VOCABULARY: idioms with *hand*

8 **Complete the following sentences (1–8) with the correct idiom from the box.**

> a safe pair of hands   give me a hand
> got my hands full   hand in hand
> hands are tied   on hand   time on my hands
> turn her hand to anything

1 I have so much work to do at the moment. I've really _____ .

2 It's amazing how multi-talented she is. She can _____ .

3 You can trust him with any task. He's _____

4 I'm bored. I've got nothing to do. I've got _____

5 I'm sorry, I'd love to help you but I'm afraid I'm not allowed to. My _____ .

6 If you need anything I'm just a phone call away. I'm always _____ to help.

7 I'm really finding this problem very difficult to solve. Do you think you could _____ ?

8 Mental illness can be a problem for very gifted people. Some people say that genius goes _____ with madness.

In another instalment in our series on 'gifted people', Jane Frank takes a look at a very special group.

On the other hand

If you want a quick insight into someone's abilities, throw a ball and see which hand they catch it with. Left-handedness is relatively uncommon, accounting for less than 10 per cent of the population. However, Chris McManus in his book *Right Hand, Left Hand* argues that left-handers as a group have up to now produced an above-average number of high achievers. Interestingly, five out of the last seven US presidents have been left-handed.

Research by Dr Alan Searleman of St Lawrence University has shown that left-handed people are more intellectually gifted, with more of them having IQs of over 140 compared to their right-handed counterparts. They are also more creative, successful and eloquent, with vocabularies up to a third wider. This is perhaps why there are more left-handers in creative professions such as music, art and writing. So-called 'lefties' are also often better at sport. Left-handed college graduates in the US have also been found to be 26 per cent richer. Perhaps surprisingly, left-handedness is three times more common in males than in females.

So, what differentiates them? Left-handers' brains are said to be structured differently. One theory is that they process information via 'visual simultaneous' methods, where several threads of thought can be processed at the same time, making it easier for them to multi-task and solve problems than for right-handers. The latter, according to the theory, process information using analysis, breaking problems down into pieces and analysing them one at a time. Left-handers use synthesis, which means they solve a problem by looking at it as a whole.

In spite of all their talents and skills, historically, left-handed people have often faced prejudice and discrimination. The origins of the word 'left' have negative connotations in many languages. For example, 'gauche', 'sinister' and 'awkward' are among translations from French, Latin and German. In English, the word 'sinister' became identified with evil or bad luck. Schools in many societies forced children to use their right hands, which seriously affected their development. In contrast, 'right' is a synonym for 'correct' or 'proper', and can stand for authority and justice in English and in many European languages.

In the final analysis, however, it may be that left is in fact better than right!

SPEAKING

9 **In small groups, discuss the following questions.**

1 What do you understand by the phrase an 'artistic temperament'?

2 Which of the following adjectives do you associate with creative people?

arrogant, romantic, emotional, insular, sensitive, unrealistic, selfish, difficult

3 Which creative person (living or dead) would you like to meet? Why?

SPEAKING AND LISTENING

1 Answer the following questions.

1 Why do people become famous?

2 Who do you know that was more famous posthumously (after their death)?

3 Which people used to be famous in your country, but aren't now?

4 Who is famous in your country, but won't be famous ten years from now?

5 Why does fame fade away?

6 Do you know any people who were forgotten and then rediscovered?

2 What do you know about Keynes, Aristotle and Ibn Battuta?

3 2.11 In groups of three, choose one of the three people above, listen to a radio programme about them and make notes about the person you chose. Then share your points with the group.

READING

4 Read the article and say if the statements below are true, false, or not given.

1 Ibn Battuta was the only medieval traveller who is known to have visited all the Arab lands.

2 He made the Hajj to Mecca more than once.

3 He dictated a record of his travels to a court scribe.

4 His accounts of his travels were found in North Africa.

In the year 1349, a dusty Arab horseman rode slowly toward the city of Tangier on the North African coast. For Ibn Battuta, it was the end of a long journey. When he left his home in Tangier 24 years earlier, he had not planned to travel distant roads for all of the long years from young man to middle-age. From his mount, Ibn Battuta surveyed the white spires and homes of Tangier spreading in a crescent along the Atlantic Ocean. He tried to remember how the city had looked when he left it behind almost a quarter-century ago.

In 1325, Ibn Battuta had been a young man of 21, reluctantly leaving his parents to make his first Hajj, or pilgrimage, to Mecca some 3,000 miles due east. He had covered those 3,000 miles and then had gone on to travel another 72,000 miles! Many Muslims made the pilgrimage to the Holy City but then returned home, for it was not an age when people were accustomed to straying from home for long periods. When Ibn Battuta began his travels, it was, in fact, more than 125 years before such renowned voyagers as Columbus, de Gama and Magellan set sail. It was no wonder, then, that Ibn Battuta returned to his native city, where his parents had died in his absence, to find himself a famous wayfarer. A contemporary described him as 'the traveller of the age,' adding, 'He who should call him the traveller of the whole body of Islam would not exceed the truth.'

Ibn Battuta was indeed the traveller of his age. His wanderings took him to Spain, Russia, Turkey, Persia, India, China and all the Arab lands. His description of the religious, political and social conditions of the lands he visited – in some cases the only record – give insight into medieval Eastern civilisation. Authorities, who estimate Ibn Battuta's journeys at more than 75,000 miles, say that the distance was not exceeded by anyone until the age of steam.

Travellers have many reasons for visiting foreign lands. Marco Polo was a merchant and Columbus an adventurer. Ibn Battuta, however, was a theologian, poet and scholar, and a humanitarian in an age when life was cheap. He left Tangier to visit the holy places of his faith and found himself curious about the wide world and eager to learn more about it.

Strangely enough, Ibn Battuta's exploits were lost to the Western world for 300 years. Not until the 19th century, when his *Rihla (Travels)* was discovered in Algeria, did his extraordinary roamings come to light. In contrast, Marco Polo dictated an account of his journeys to a contemporary while they shared a prison cell in 1296, and copies had circulated all over Europe by the 15th century. Had Ibn Battuta's work received the same attention, his name would rank alongside Marco Polo's as a synonym for world travel.

Ibn Battuta, Traveler from Tangier

5 **Match the words in the box to their definitions.**

| contemporary crescent humanitarian |
| pilgrimage reluctantly renowned |

1 someone who lives or works at the same time as someone else

2 a curved shape that is wider in the middle and pointed at the ends

3 unwillingly

4 a person concerned with improving peoples' living conditions

5 a trip to a holy place for a religious reason

6 famous and admired

6 **Complete the gaps in the sentences with the words in the box above.**

1 He was not ambitious and took the post _____ .

2 The moon appeared as a dazzling yellow _____ .

3 They hoped they would get the chance to go on _____ to Mecca.

4 Ali was my _____ at university. We studied together at Oxford.

5 She's _____ as a brilliant speaker.

6 He was a _____ who was dedicated to preventing unfair treatment.

GRAMMAR: quantifiers

7 **Look at the quantifiers in bold in Track 2.11 on page 180 and the three highlighted in the text and put them in the table. Then add as many quantifiers as you can.**

+ singular noun	+ plural noun	+uncountable noun
	many	

➡ Language reference and extra practice, pages 146–147

8 **Circle the correct answers. There may be more than one correct answer.**

1 _____ Muslims are instructed to go on a pilgrimage to Mecca.
   a) All   b) Every   c) Much

2 Ibn Battuta had _____ adventures on his way to Mecca.
   a) a few   b) many   c) much

3 _____ of the exploits of Ibn Battuta were recorded until 1354.
   a) none   b) no   c) a little

4 Ibn Battuta is one of the most remarkable travellers of _____ time.
   a) every   b) all   c) little

5 Ibn Battuta had not planned to spend _____ time in the Maldives.
   a) many   b) much   c) a lot of

9 **Answer the following questions.**

1 How does the inclusion of *of the* before a plural or uncountable noun change the meaning?

I need some information.
I need some of the information.

2 What is the difference between:
   a) every   all   each ?
   b) little   a little   few   a few ?

3 What do we put after:
   a) either?
   b) neither?

4 What is the difference between?

I like all classical music.
I don't like some classical music.
I don't like any classical music.

10 **Complete the text below with appropriate quantifiers:**

Nearly [1]_____ of the problems of philosophy were defined by Socrates, Plato and Aristotle. However, Aristotle is known for being one of the [2]_____ figures in history who studied almost [3]_____ subject possible at the time. He wrote [4]_____ texts on the sciences and the arts. He also wrote [5]_____ texts on ethics , the major one being *Nichomachean Ethics*. His most famous work was [6]_____ *Nichomachean Ethics* or *Politics*. In *Politics* Aristotle says:

'Democracy is when those who do not own [7]_____ property, but are poor, have authority in the system of government. [8]_____ men are rich, but [9]_____ are free. Democracy is when [10]_____ free citizen has authority. It is democracy when [11]_____ the citizens can deliberate about everything.'

Very [12]_____ information is known about what Aristotle looked like, but he was known to be a kind-hearted man devoted to his family and his friends. He liked to spend a [13]_____ of time walking with his students discussing philosophical problems.

SPEAKING

11 **In groups, talk about people who are famous in your country but who are not well-known in the rest of the world. What are the reasons for this, do you think?**

SPEAKING

1 In small groups, discuss the following ideas. Which do you think are good and which do you think are bad? Why?

1 Making all countries drive on the right rather than the left.
2 Painting all roofs in cities white to save energy.
3 Arranging all products in supermarkets alphabetically.
4 Making all young people join the army for a year.
5 Making chewing gum illegal.
6 Wearing facemasks when you have a cold.

READING

2 Scan ideas A–C from a *sharing good ideas* website to find the following information:

1 the most common type of book on the book-swapping website
2 what satellite navigation was first used for
3 the inventor of the light bulb

3 Read the ideas (A – C) and answer the questions.

1 Which text mentions something that:
   a) was not immediately clear to the writer?
   b) has improved since its first appearance?
   c) is fundamentally the same as when it first appeared?
   d) has outlived its usefulness?
2 Which idea appeals to you the most?
3 What other great ideas can you think of?

Sharing good ideas

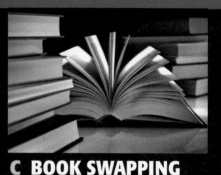

A LED BULBS

B SATELLITE NAVIGATION

C BOOK SWAPPING

People choose electronic LEDs (light emitting diodes) because they last for ages, never break and reduce your energy bill. Traditional light bulbs haven't changed much since Thomas Edison invented them in the late 1870s. You flip a switch and the bulbs give you light. They are simple but they are fragile and don't last very long. LEDs light up almost immediately and can take a knock, given their solid construction. They are used in flashlights and miner-style head torches. They are being used more and more in homes due to their falling prices. Originally, there was a problem with their blue-white colour, which was a side effect of a chemical used in their manufacture. Now they give off a warm, yellow light. Conversion to LED lighting would reduce our energy consumption by approximately one third, cut our energy bills and reduce carbon emissions.

Although it is difficult to come up with a rigorous set of criteria to evaluate how good an idea is, many drivers would agree that satellite navigation systems (sat navs) are indispensable. I'd have bought one years ago if I'd realised how brilliant they were. It has transformed my driving and taken all the stress away. You just type in the correct post code and the sat nav guides you to your destination. The instructions spoken aloud prevent you from getting lost. It's a great concept. Satellite navigation was originally used for military applications such as the delivery of weapons and the tracking of troops. These days, the technology is used by pilots, sailors, explorers and taxi drivers. And, from my point of view, the best thing is that my wife isn't going to say to me, 'If you'd brought a map, we wouldn't be lost now!'

If I had a euro for every book I had read once and then dumped on a shelf, I would be a rich woman. Many of us own hundreds of books that will never be read again. Up till now the only book sharing I have done has been with friends and my book club.

You could try www.readitswapit.com. This is a website that lets you exchange the books you won't read again for books that you do want to read. All users of this ingenious website provide a list of their unwanted books. If you find a book you like, you email its owner. The owner then looks at your list. Hopefully they will see a book they like. Then you both send each other your books. Simple. Currently, there are a lot of thrillers and mysteries such as *The Da Vinci Code*, but if you look hard enough, you'll find something you like.

4a Find words in the texts which mean the following:

1 the amount of electricity, gas, oil or energy that is used (Text A)

2 substances that are sent out into the air (Text A)

3 careful, thorough, and exact (Text B)

4 so important or useful that it is impossible to manage without it (Text B)

5 an idea or thought (Text B)

6 works well and is the result of clever thinking and new ideas (Text C)

4b Write your own sentences using the words above.

VOCABULARY: irregular plurals

5a Complete the gaps below.

	SINGULAR	PLURAL
1	criterion	_____
2	phenomenon	_____
3	hypothesis	_____
4	_____	analyses
5	_____	theses

5b Correct the incorrect sentences below.

1 He wrote an excellent doctoral theses.

2 There is a strange phenomena that occurs every year in this part of the world.

3 You still haven't proved this hypothesis.

4 What are the criteria for selecting the best idea?

5 We are carrying out a detailed analyses of the test results.

GRAMMAR: conditionals

6a Look at these examples from the text. Which type of conditionals are they? Check your answers on page 146, Language reference, G2.

1 I'd have bought one years ago if I'd realised how brilliant they were.

2 If I had a euro for every book I had read once and then dumped on a shelf, I would be a rich woman.

3 If you find a book you like, you email its owner.

4 If you look hard enough, you'll find something you like.

5 If you'd brought a map, we wouldn't be lost now.

6b Which pattern does the mixed conditional follow?

7 Which conditional do we use to talk about:

1 likely conditions? (things which are very likely to happen)

2 unlikely conditions? (things which might happen, but probably not)

3 impossible conditions? (things which are unreal and did not happen)

4 general conditions? (things which can occur at any time and often occur more than once and their results)

8a Match the conditional clauses (1–8) with a pair of clauses (a–h) to form sentences.

1 If they'd brought a map,

2 If you solve the problem,

3 If I were you,

4 If I had my own car,

5 If I'd worked harder,

6 If you don't leave right now,

7 I'll phone the hospital

8 If the ball touches the line,

a) I'll phone the police. / you'll regret it.

b) it's in, not out. / don't blow your whistle.

c) I could have gone to college. / I'd have passed the exam.

d) I'll buy everyone dinner. / you'll feel a lot better.

e) I'd listen to her very carefully. / I wouldn't tell her.

f) I'd go away every weekend. / you wouldn't have to take me to work.

g) if you don't have time. / if you want.

h) they wouldn't be lost now. / they would have arrived on time.

8b Match the examples above to their functions below.

1	advice	5	criticism
2	offer	6	regretting
3	promise	7	threats
4	instructions/rules	8	imagining, wishing

WRITING

9 Write a short entry for the *sharing good ideas* website.

SITUATION

Camomila is a city in South America. It is situated on flat land and surrounded by mountains. Several rivers and streams run through the city. At times, there is heavy rainfall and the summers tend to be very hot and humid. The population has grown steadily over the years to 1.5 million because of immigration and its appeal as a popular destination for ecotourism (it is not far from the Amazon rainforest). There is now a thriving industrial area, with many multinational companies, a growing number of electronics enterprises, and large commerce and service sectors. This has brought many problems.

The new mayor of the city, Eduardo Alves is determined that Camomila will become a model city in South America. To solve the problems, he has enlisted the help of a firm of consultants, JB Urban Planning (JBUP). This is an international group of young, dynamic architects and city planners. They have been told that any solutions they offer must be 'practical, inexpensive and involve the participation of the local community, as much as possible'.

1 Read the situation and discuss the following question.

What problems do you think have arisen because of:

a) the climate?

b) the rapid increase in population?

2 [2.12] The mayor, Eduardo Alves, accompanied by the councillor responsible for environmental affairs, Manuela Lopes, is meeting the Director of JBUP. Listen to Part 1 of their conversation. Make notes on the problems which have arisen concerning:

1 green spaces

2 the downtown shopping district

3 buses

4 trains and stations

5 flooding

6 children

KEY LANGUAGE: approving ideas, expressing doubt/objections

3a 2.13 Now listen to Part 2, as Fabio and Christina from JBUP join the group.

1 What does the mayor propose to make the city 'greener'?

2 What advantages of his proposal does he mention?

3b Match the functions (a–c) to the extracts (1–12) from Part 2.
  a) approving ideas
  b) expressing doubts/objections
  c) offering counter arguments

1 Sounds like a great idea.

2 I'm not too keen on this one.

3 I think there'll be some real problems.

4 It would be a very expensive option.

5 But, looking after the trees might not be such a big problem …

6 I think it's a really good suggestion.

7 Some of the projects must be for the long term.

8 Will it really work?

9 I just don't think it's feasible.

10 You have to trust local people and give them responsibility.

11 It's a good project in my opinion.

12 It may not cost as much money as you think.

3c In pairs, practise saying the expressions in Exercise 3b.

TASK: a new plan for Camomila

4 Work in groups. Choose six problems from those identified in JBUP's report. Brainstorm ideas for solving the problems and note down your solutions.

5a You are members of JBUP. Working in a group, discuss your ideas for solving the city's problems. Try to agree on a plan for the future development of Camomila.

5b Decide which solutions should be given priority and which could be delayed until a later date.

OTHER USEFUL PHRASES

Prioritising

Solving the problem of … is a priority …

We need to give this matter priority …

We need to find a solution urgently …

The most urgent problem is …

Delaying action

It could be put off / put back …

It could be put on the backburner …

We could look at this later …

We needn't take any immediate action …

Making alternative suggestions

Another possibility might be …

It might also be worth … (+ verb in –ing form)

An alternative solution could be to …

Another approach could be …

JBUP – Report

The federal government has given the city a large grant to finance its urban plan. However, the mayor and city council will welcome solutions which represent value for money, are relatively inexpensive and involve the local community.

PROBLEMS

• Traffic jams in the downtown shopping district.
• Frequent flooding in the city.
• Lack of green spaces in the city.
• Too many small buses; an unreliable train service.
• Not enough places for young and old to meet.
• No reliable system of dealing with rubbish; usually left outside houses and buildings.
• Insufficient hotels for tourists; poor quality and service.
• A lack of courtesy towards tourists. Many complain of a lack of respect from young people at night. Overcrowded housing; shabby, run-down houses and apartments, especially in the highly populated, new town area.
• Too many 'street children'.
• Crime on the buses and trains.
• Architects don't create green spaces when they build schools, office blocks, apartment buildings, etc.
• Lack of facilities in the city: not enough hospitals, theatres, cinemas, art galleries, museums.

STUDY SKILLS: critical thinking

1 In groups, discuss the statements below and decide which one most closely reflects your opinion.

The main purpose of education is to:

a) pass on knowledge to a child.

b) help a child to fulfil his or her potential.

c) encourage a child to express themselves freely.

d) prepare a child for their adult life.

2 Read the essay question below. Then look at the essay on the topic on page 79. Answer the following questions.

> How relevant are the ideas of Jean Jacques Rousseau to today's educators? Discuss the question and state your opinion on the topic.

1 What is the writer's opinion concerning the topic?

2 In what part(s) of the essay can the reader find the writer's opinion?

3 What area of education does the essay focus on?

3 In pairs, discuss the questions.

1 Which two of Rousseau's ideas does the writer present in the essay?

2 What evidence does the writer give in each case to show that Rousseau's ideas are still relevant to today's educators?

3 What do you think are the strongest pieces of evidence he offers? Give reasons for your answers.

4 Has the writer presented his arguments in a logical, coherent form? Give reasons for your answer.

4 Find words/phrases in the text which mean the following.

1 effect or influence (paragraph 1)

2 to give/communicate (para. 2)

3 behaviour that is the same as most other people's (para. 2)

4 emphasised (para. 4)

5 presented a point of view (para. 5)

6 the basis of (para. 6)

7 cannot be challenged or debated (para. 7)

8 having a strong effect on something or someone (para. 7)

9 better than (para. 7)

5 Read the last paragraph of the essay again. Summarise in one sentence the difference between the child-centred and teacher-centred approaches to education.

6 Read the essay again. In groups, make a list of questions you have about the essay and discuss them.

7 Work in pairs and try to persuade each other that your approach to teaching children gets the best results.

Student A: prepare an argument in favour of the child-centred approach to educating children.

Student B: prepare an argument for the teacher-centred approach to educating children.

8a Tick the ideas below you think Rousseau would have agreed with. Read and check.

1 educating children to develop their character and moral sense

2 using education to teach children self-control and to be good human beings

3 including physical training in the curriculum

4 giving children a lot of books to read

5 ensuring that the child does not learn anything that he or she is not ready to understand

6 educating children's emotions before their reasoning

7 getting students to memorise facts

8 recommending teachers to do more talking in the classroom than their students

9 paying careful attention to the environment in which children study

10 encouraging children to draw conclusions from their experience

11 teaching young adults a manual skill, such as carpentry, as a means of making a living

12 seeing the role of the teacher as facilitating opportunities for learning

8b Which of the above do you think should be the aims of educators?

9 [2.14] Listen to a teacher talking about 'critical thinking'. In pairs, make notes about his key points. Then compare the accuracy of your notes with other pairs.

WRITING SKILLS: an opinion-led essay

10 Fill in the gaps in the text below with the words in the box.

> evidence ideas overall persuade
> reasons summarised

An opinion-led essay gives an opinion and supports it with **1**_____. The aim of the writer is to **2**_____ the reader to agree with the opinion, and to show **3**_____ for a particular opinion. The introduction gives an **4**_____ view of the essay. In the main body of the essay, evidence is presented that supports the thesis. The most important **5**_____ usually come first. In the conclusion, no new evidence is given. The main idea is **6**_____ and the argument is restated.

11 Do you agree or disagree? In the opening paragraph of an opinion-led essay, you should …

1 introduce the subject of the essay.

2 refer to the main point(s) in the question.

3 copy several phrases from the question.

4 try to paraphrase the question.

5 state clearly your opinion on the topic.

6 indicate the scope of the essay.

12a Look again at the essay on Rousseau. Analyse the structure that the writer has used to present his or her ideas in the essay.

12b Discuss your analysis of the structure with a partner.

13a **Essay planning** Work in groups. Think of some arguments for and against the opinion expressed in the essay. For each argument, try to support it with reasons and evidence.

13b Use the structure below to plan the stages of the essay.

- Introduction (general statement, introduce the subject)
- Body (arguments + evidence, most important ideas come first)
- Conclusion (summary, restatement of your opinion)

14 **Essay writing** Write an essay. Choose one of the following tasks.

1 Write an opinion-led essay strongly agreeing or disagreeing with the writer of the essay below.

2 Choose an influential thinker and write an opinion-led essay on whether you agree or disagree with his/her ideas.

---

1 *Jean Jacques Rousseau* was a French philosopher and educationalist writing in the 18th century. He set out his ideas on education in a novel entitled *Emile*, published in 1762. This describes the ideal education of the book's main character, Emile. Rousseau's ideas on education, presented in the book, have influenced generations of educational thinkers and still have a strong impact on modern educational practice, particularly in the area of primary education.

2 According to Rousseau, the main purpose of education was not to impart information but to bring out what was in each person. Children should be allowed to express themselves and to develop their own views of the world, rather than submit to repression and conformity. Education, therefore, should consist of allowing the child as much freedom as possible.

3 There is no doubt that Rousseau's idea, which was taken up by later educationalists, has greatly influenced a modern approach to education called 'child-centred learning'. This focuses on the needs of children rather than on those of teachers and administrators. The child-centred teacher tries to create an environment which will

encourage children to discover new skills and knowledge. Teachers using this approach do not focus on imparting information but on helping children to discover information. Such teachers create activity centres in the classroom, encourage peer tutoring, and get children to work together on group projects.

4 The importance of Rousseau's ideas was highlighted in John Darling's 1994 book, *Child-Centred Education and its Critics* (1994:17). The author argues that the history of modern educational theory is a series of footnotes to Rousseau.

5 Another of Rousseau's important ideas

was that things rather than people should be used to train a child. He argued that a teacher or parent should never lecture or preach to a child and that experience and interaction with things was a more effective teacher. For example, when Emile breaks a window, he finds that he gets cold because the window is not repaired. This is an example of discovery learning.

6 Rousseau's ideas of using things to train a child is at the heart of the world famous Montessori method of teaching children. In Montessori schools, which can be found all over the world, the classrooms are filled with games and equipment which children can use to learn skills and gain knowledge. The essence of Montessori teaching is that children learn by experience rather than being told things by a teacher.

7 It is undeniable that Rousseau has been very influential in promoting a child-centred approach to learning rather than a teacher-centred approach. In a child-centred approach, the child is an active, responsible participant in his or her own learning. This approach is surely preferable to the teacher-centred approach, which has the teacher in an active role and the students in a passive, receptive role.

8 Journalism and media

In this unit

Grammar
- verb patterns
- prepositional verbs

Vocabulary
- the media
- people in the media
- idioms with *keep*

Scenario
- Sailing close to the wind

Study skills
- research skills

Writing skills
- a features article for a magazine or newspaper

8.1 BREAKING NEWS

In journalism there has always been a tension between getting it first and getting it right.
Ellen Goodman (b. 1941) American Pulitzer Prize-winning journalist

SPEAKING

1 In small groups, discuss the following questions.

1 'Newspapers will soon be a thing of the past.' Do you agree with this statement? Why / Why not?

2 Where do you get the news from, e.g. TV, newspapers, radio, the Internet? Why?

2a Complete the gaps in the statements with the words in the box.

> bias   deadline   privacy   record
> scoop   sources   speculation

A good news journalist …

1 never misses a _____ .

2 respects the _____ of public figures.

3 deals in facts rather than _____ .

4 will do almost anything for a _____ or to break a story.

5 always identifies their _____ .

6 allows people to speak off the _____ to protect themselves.

7 reports honestly, objectively and without _____ .

2b Which statements in Exercise 2a do you agree with? Which are the most important? Discuss your reasons with a partner.

3a What are the following people's roles in the media? Discuss your ideas with a partner.

a) editor   e) reporter

b) anchor   f) correspondent

c) publisher   g) paparazzo

d) producer   h) columnist

3b In your opinion, is working in the news media an attractive profession? Why / Why not?

LISTENING

4 `2.15` Listen to six people working in the media talking about their jobs. Which part of the news media do you think they work in? Why?

a) print media

b) broadcast media (TV / radio)

5a Listen again. What do you think their jobs are? Choose one of the job titles (a–h) from Exercise 3.

5b What difficulties with their job does each speaker mention?

6 Which job would you most like to do? Why?

VOCABULARY: the media

7a Look at some of the expressions used by the speakers. What do you think they mean?

a sound bite   broadsheets   chequebook journalism
circulation figures   libel laws   media coverage
ratings war   spin   the tabloids   viewing figures

7b Match the meanings with the expressions in Exercise 7a.

a) the number of newspapers sold

b) the number of people who watch a broadcast

c) popularity battles with rival channels / networks / programmes

d) official rules governing what you may say about people in print

e) present a positive view of something to influence people

f) paying people for information

g) amount of time / space given to a subject

h) very short part of speech or statement

i) the 'popular press'

j) quality newspapers / the 'quality press'

READING

8a Read the newspaper headlines. What do you think the stories are about?

8b Which headlines refer to:

1 losing a job?

2 a rescue?

3 new rules / laws?

4 an investigation?

5 a planned reduction in something?

6 death?

7 a romance?

8 an argument / fighting?

9 Answer the following questions.

1 Which tenses / verb forms are used?

2 Which time do they refer to?

3 What do you notice about the language used in the headlines?

10 Rewrite the headlines as full sentences.

A The government is going to take strong action against crime on the Internet.

SPEAKING

11 Work in groups. You are producers of a 30-minute news programme with an audience demographic of 18–35-year-olds. The headlines below are the possible stories for today's edition of the programme. Follow the steps below.

1 Discuss the possible content of each story and decide how interesting they would be for your viewers.

2 Choose five for your programme. You may also include one extra item of 'breaking news' (your own idea).

3 Decide a running order for the stories.

4 Decide how much time will be spent on each story. Will it contain an interview? If so, who will you interview?

5 Present your ideas to another group.

A GOVT TO CRACK DOWN ON NET CRIME

B FLOODS TOLL RISES

C MINISTER QUITS OVER COVER-UP

D tv stars split to wed

E MOVE TO CURB JUNK FOOD SALES

F NATIONAL SPEED LIMITS SET TO CHANGE

G PM PLEDGES TAX CUT

H CAT SAVES OWNER FROM BLAZE

I Olympic chief in vote rigging row

J MURDER PROBE: POLICE QUIZ MODEL

K FOOTBALL BOSS AXED

L UN urged to act over new clashes

READING

1 What qualifications and training do you think are needed for a career in journalism?

2a Read the article and choose the best sub-heading.

According to Simon Jenkins, the best journalists are great writers with an extensive knowledge of the English language and a solid training in how to write.

Are journalists born or made? According to Simon Jenkins, while the basics can be taught, first there has to be an intense curiosity about the world and a love of the written word.

2b Read the article again and answer the following questions.

1 What does the writer find upsetting in written English these days?

2 What does the writer compare learning the technique of writing clear English to?

3 Which parts of speech did the writer's sub-editor like and which did he not like?

4 Where did the writer learn how to write clear English?

5 What do the best journalists do when they meet an exciting person or visit a beautiful place?

6 What are the most important qualities for journalism?

7 What is more important: a story or journalism?

3 Which of the sub-editor's rules does the following paragraph break?

It is interesting to see that the three key problems were punctuality, truancy and bad behaviour. Unfortunately, the police had to be called to the run-down state school on several occasions.

Simon Jenkins, The Guardian

A Journalists are creatures of nature not nurture. The profession develops from instinct, from a peculiar way of seeing and describing the world. It may be objective in practice but it is subjective in motivation.

B Journalism is expressed in the written or spoken word, but I have never regarded that as its essence. The technical skill is that of creating clear and succinct sentences, which any profession should inculcate. This can be taught and should be part of any core curriculum. Its absence from so much of written English nowadays, from users' manuals to student exam questions to government white papers, is deplorable. I sometimes think a well-produced newspaper is that last redoubt of clear English. There is no talent for such technique. While some people pick it up quickly, it must be acquired, as must a skill at playing the piano. Like many ingénue journalists, I acquired it first in the trial and error of a student newsroom and then went on to a more formal training, in my case with the Times Newspapers.

C The latter's Educational Supplement, then integrated with the main paper, possessed two invaluable bits of equipment. One was a source of stories, the politics of education, to which little harm could be done by my reporting. The other was a ferocious Irish sub-editor. He would score through superfluous words, underline bad grammar and mercilessly spike articles, leaning back in his chair, removing his glasses and asking the classic question of any journalism teacher: 'Now, what is it you are really trying to tell me?'

D I absorbed his maxims like mother's milk. Never begin a paragraph with 'it'. Make every paragraph a single idea. Nouns and verbs are the workhorses of a sentence, never qualifiers. Delete every adjective and adverb from your story and reinsert only those that appear essential. Never use sloppy words such as *supply*, *problem*, *accommodate* and *interesting* and try to use concrete not abstract nouns. The best punctuation is a full stop.

E That training was a privilege greater than anything I acquired at school or university. It was the toolkit for a career, always to be kept oiled and polished. I watched colleagues floundering as they sought to fashion stories in ignorance of its framework.

F I used to ask aspiring journalists whether they kept a diary. What was their instinctive response to meeting an exciting person or visiting a beautiful place, to any highly charged emotion? Did they crave to communicate their experience through the written word? It is the best indicator I know of a natural reporter.

G The qualities essential to journalism thus extend far beyond an ability to write. They are those of curiosity, an uninhibited mind, native cunning and an eagerness to communicate, summed up in the gift to narrate. Such is the raw material on which the story depends and without which there is nothing to say. There can be a story without journalism, but no journalism without a story.

4 Find and underline adjectives in the text which mean the following:

1 based on opinions and feelings rather than on facts (paragraph A)

2 clearly expressed with no wasted words (para. B)

3 very bad (para. B)

4 extremely useful (para. C)

5 unnecessary (para. C)

6 carelessly expressed (para. D)

7 hoping to be successful at something (para. F)

8 not restrained in any way (para. G)

5 Paraphrase the following sentences from the article in simple English.

1 I absorbed his maxims like mother's milk.

2 I watched colleagues floundering as they sought to fashion stories …

LISTENING

6a **2.16** **Listen to an experienced journalist talking to a group of students and answer the questions.**

1 What advice is given to those who want to go into journalism by:
a) Joseph Pulitzer?
b) the speaker?

2 What current topic in journalism is the speaker going to look at towards the end of the talk?

6b Listen again and complete the gaps in the extracts.

1 I'd like to congratulate you on receiving the 'Best _____ .

2 First of all, I'm not going to apologise for being a journalist, even though we are not _____ .

3 I can't stand listening to complaints about _____ .

4 'Put it before them briefly __ _____ , clearly so they will _____ , picturesquely so _____ and above all, accurately so they will _____ ,'

5 Always treat the reader with _____ and don't …

6c Check your answers in Track 2.16 on page 182.

GRAMMAR: verb patterns

7 Look at the following list of common verb patterns. Look at Track 2.16 on page 182 and underline the different verb patterns.

1 Verb + infinitive with *to*

2 Verb (+ object) + infinitive

3 Verb + infinitive without *to*

4 Verb + *-ing*

5 Verb + preposition + *-ing*

6 Verb + object + preposition + *-ing*

8 What is the difference in meaning between the two sentences?

1 *You don't want them to stop reading.*

2 *You don't want them to stop to read.*

9a Which of the verb patterns in Exercise 7 above do the following groups of verbs belong to?

a) likes or dislikes

b) recommendations

c) intentions

d) thought

9b Can you think of any other verbs which belong to the four groups in Exercise 9a?

➡ Language reference and extra practice, pages 148–149

10 Use the correct verb pattern to complete sentences 1–9 in your own words. Then compare your sentences with those of a partner.

1 I don't mind _____ .

2 My parents persuaded _____ .

3 I promised _____ .

4 Next year I really want _____ .

5 My parents always encouraged _____ .

6 I can't stand _____

7 Once I blamed my friend _____ .

8 I remember _____ when I was a child.

9 When you go out, you must remember _____ .

SPEAKING

11 In groups, discuss the following statements:

1 'People in the public eye should not expect to have private lives.'

2 'Journalism is not a respectable profession.'

READING AND SPEAKING

1 What do you know about Twitter, Flickr and other forms of new social media?

2 Read the article quickly and say which 'mainstream media' and which 'social media' are mentioned.

3 Read the article again and answer the following questions.

1 How were the following social media used in Mumbai?
   a) Twitter   d) Google
   b) Metroblog   e) Flickr
   c) Wikipedia

2 Which words does the writer use to make the text exciting?

3 Why does the 'mainstream media' use 'social media'?

4a Match words 1–5 with words a–e to make collocations from the article.

1	eyewitness	a)	information
2	background	b)	accounts
3	media	c)	media
4	mainstream	d)	footage
5	video	e)	analyst

4b Make sentences using the collocations above.

5a Work in groups. Which of the social media formats mentioned in the article have you used?

5b How do you feel about the use of social media for news gathering? Do you think they will replace the mainstream media in the future? Discuss your ideas.

---

http://www.newsroundup.org

Mumbai attacks: Twitter and Flickr used to break news

home | articles | about us | courses | blog | site map | contact us

Anyone who doubts the power of the social web need only take a **look at** the activity on Twitter when terrorists attacked a hotel in Mumbai.

Mere moments after the first shots were fired, Twitter users in India, and especially in Mumbai, were providing instant eyewitness accounts of the unfolding drama.

Messages, known as 'tweets', were being posted to the site at a rate of around 70 tweets every five seconds when the news of the tragedy first broke, according to some estimates.

A group of bloggers based in Mumbai used their Metroblog, which **dealt mostly with** the everyday minutiae of life in this bustling city, as a news wire service, bringing its readers, and the wider world, news of the incident as it unfolded.

On Wikipedia, a new page about the terror attacks was set up within minutes of the news breaking, with a team of citizen editors adding a staggering amount of detail, often in real time, to provide background information about the attacks.

Someone even created a Google Map showing the location of buildings and landmarks at the centre of the incident, with links to news stories and eyewitness accounts. But perhaps the most amazing and harrowing first-hand account of the Mumbai attacks came from Vinukumar Ranganathan who grabbed his camera and headed out onto the streets of the city, taking a series of photos. He has uploaded more than 112 photos to Flickr.

New media analyst Cherian George said events such as the Mumbai attacks have highlighted the emergence of citizen journalism and user-generated content.

'If the event is highly dispersed and affects very large numbers of people, it would be physically impossible for a very large news organisation to keep track of every development,' Mr George told Reuters.

VOCABULARY: idioms with *keep*

6a Match idioms 1–6 with their meanings (a–f).

1 keep a close eye on
2 keep a low profile
3 keep an open mind
4 keep your wits about you
5 keep your fingers crossed
6 keep in with

a) get all the facts before making a judgment
b) stay alert
c) stay friendly with
d) monitor very carefully
e) avoid attracting attention to yourself
f) hope for a positive outcome

6b Complete the gaps in the sentences with the idioms from Exercise 6a.

1 Try to _____ the editor. He could help your career.

2 When you're reporting from a war zone, you've got to _____ .

3 We need to _____ this story. Things are changing fast.

4 Just _____ that we are the first ones to get this story.

5 Its not clear yet if he's guilty. We need to _____ .

6 It will be hard to interview her. She tends to _____ .

'Those kind of events show the great potential for all these user accounts to be valuable to the mainstream media.'

Indeed, many mainstream media outlets, including CNN, used video footage and photos sent in from people on the ground in Mumbai to illustrate their reports, and many television stations, radio stations and newspapers were also keeping a close eye on Twitter and the blogosphere in the hope of finding out more information.

Despite the obvious value and immediacy of these eyewitness accounts, there are signs that the blogosphere is struggling to know what to do for the best when these sort of incidents occur.

While Twitter and other social media are not yet in a position to replace the mainstream media, there can be no doubt that they provide a powerful communication platform.

GRAMMAR: prepositional verbs

7a Look at the highlighted prepositional verbs in the article and complete the rule.

Prepositional verbs are the combination of a _____ and a _____ .

7b Does the verb *look* have the same meaning in these sentences? If not, what changes the meaning?

a) I haven't had time to look at the news on the Internet.

b) Police are looking into the disappearance of two children.

c) His dad left him here to look after the business while he's away.

7c Replace the words in bold with the correct form of prepositional verbs in the box.

> come across   come up   get on   get over
> look at   look into   look like   look round

1 Anyone who doubts the power of the social web only needs to **observe** the activity on Twitter.

2 How are you **progressing** at work?

3 A free microblogging service that started a few years ago, Twitter **resembles** an onscreen bulletin.

4 An opportunity has **arisen** for a Twitter correspondent at Sky News.board.

5 I am resisting an urge to **investigate** Twitter in case it is as addictive as Facebook.

6 If Twitter ever suffers a catastrophic failure it cannot **recover from**, you will still be protected from any data loss.

7 We **inspected** the new office to see if the building was suitable.

8 I've seen a really interesting anecdote on Twitter. I **found** it by chance.

GRAMMAR TIP

We can put adverbs of degree and manner between the verb and preposition, but not between the preposition and object.

It dealt mostly with the everyday minutiae … ✓
It dealt with mostly the everyday minutiae … ✗

➡ Language reference and extra practice, pages 148–149

8 Put the words in italics in the correct order.

1 The *article looked like exactly on Tweet the blog* a

2 I *thought never much about Twitter* until my son showed me how it worked.

3 *The media fast-moving had dealing events the problems with.*

4 Would *mind story you into looking this?*

5 People *accuse falsely of a lot of things the media.*

9 Complete the text with prepositional verbs.

Journalists need to be familiar with technical developments in the media. They shouldn't just ¹_____ social networking sites, they need to use them because familiarity with the tools is important. They need to ²_____ their sources from Facebook, MySpace and Twitter and any other type of social media source as carefully as they would verify traditional sources. They need to restrict access to private profile information that they don't want the general public to ³_____ by chance. They need to manage their time efficiently and manage their friends on social networks so they can ⁴_____ tweets, status updates and endless emails. Although blogging and tweets may ⁵_____ conversation, journalists must be mindful that they represent more than just themselves.

WRITING

10 Write a short paragraph on the following question.

Is it more important to get news fast or accurately?

SITUATION

The *Daily Chronicle* is a daily newspaper in Chicago. Its features articles focus on scandals in government departments or on misconduct by prominent personalities. The newspaper often sails close to the wind to get its stories and its journalists have been accused of invading people's privacy and showing bias in their reporting. When chasing stories, the newspaper's editor and reporters inevitably face ethical dilemmas.

1 Read the situation above. What do you think the phrase 'often sails close to the wind' means?

2a Read about the following dilemma that the newspaper must resolve.

> The editor of the sports section of the *Daily Chronicle* has been offered copies of confidential emails sent by the head coach of a top baseball team to the owner of a rival team. The source of the emails wishes to be paid $100,000 for the copies. The emails reveal that the head coach is considering leaving his present job to coach the rival team. This would be a bombshell in the sporting world and a report in the newspaper about the coach's plans would greatly increase its circulation.

2b In pairs or small groups, discuss the following.

1 What are the advantages and disadvantages of running a story about the head coach based on information in the emails?

2 Should the Sports Editor publish a story about the head coach based on what he has learned?

KEY LANGUAGE: being cautious

3a 2.17 Listen to the Sports Editor, Dan, discussing the dilemma with the Chief Editor of the *Daily Chronicle*, Margaret Lawson. Answer the questions.

1 What reason does the Sports Editor give for wanting to buy the emails?

2 What are the Chief Editor's reasons for *not* wanting to buy the emails?

3 What is the Sports Editor going to do now?

3b **Being cautious** Listen again and complete what the Chief Editor says.

1 We need to _____ this one _____ , Dan … If you don't get your facts right, he could _____ and get substantial _____ .

2 Dan, there's a problem with this material. We have no idea how our source got the information. Maybe he did something _____ , and if that's the case, we could be in very _____ .

3 I don't think our readers will thank us for running the story. It's a very _____ issue. If we get our facts wrong, it'll have a _____ on our reputation. We wouldn't be able to say where we got our information from, so it would look like pure _____ on our part.

4 No, sorry, we need to _____ on this one. I've got a bad feeling about it. It could land us in _____ if the emails are not genuine.

TASK: resolving ethical dilemmas

4a In pairs, read the descriptions of the ethical dilemmas below. Choose ONE of the situations and decide which role each of you will play.

4b Prepare for your role play. Make notes on what you'll say. Then, role play the situation and decide what decision should be taken, with your reasons.

5 Join another pair and tell them what decision you made, with your reasons. Ask them if they agree with your decision.

6 As a group, discuss what guidelines you could give journalists faced with the kinds of dilemmas described.

An undercover operation
Chief Editor or Investigative Reporter

Two journalists want to do an investigative report on a group of nursing homes. There are rumours that the homes are badly run. The rooms are said to be dirty and unhygienic, and the staff uncaring and insensitive. Relatives of residents claim that the residents are neglected and not fed on time. The two journalists wish to carry out an undercover operation to investigate the claims. They want to get a job at the nursing homes and film secret evidence of bad practice. The question is: should the undercover operation be carried out?

The newspaper proprietor
Chief Editor or Journalist

Journalists from the Business Section of the *Daily Chronicle* are currently investigating the activities of a powerful international businessman. They have discovered that he is guilty of tax evasion and has also been running his company in an improper way. They wish to expose the businessman's illegal activities. The Chief Editor, who has only been in the job six months, mentioned this to the owner of the newspaper. The owner said 'Mr X is a good friend of mine and helped me earlier in my career to make several important deals. I don't want him to receive any unfavourable publicity.' The question is: should the Chief Editor authorise the journalists to write the features story?

The fashion show
Chief Editor or Journalist

A group of *Daily Chronicle* journalists attended a press lunch hosted by the fashion designer, Emilio Conti, to commemorate his 40 years in the fashion business. After the lunch, all the journalists were given a bag that contained a press kit and a box that the journalists did not open until they left the restaurant. The box contained a Rolex watch worth about $5,000, with a certificate of authenticity.

Some of the journalists from other newspapers gave the watches back. The *Daily Chronicle* journalists have a good relationship with Emilio Conti and don't want to offend him. The question is: what should they do about the gifts they've received?

A confidential document
Chief Editor or Political Correspondent

A politician has given some information to the *Daily Chronicle's* Political correspondent about the content of a report on the state of the army's equipment. The document is classified information and the findings of the report have not been made public. Its findings are very controversial and critical of the condition of the army's equipment. The politician told the correspondent, 'Use the information, but don't quote me.' The question is: should the journalist write an article based on such confidential information?

OTHER USEFUL PHRASES
Considering implications

It could be too risky.

It might damage our reputation.

It may be illegal.

They could take us to court.

They might take legal action.

They might sue us.

Proposing solutions

The best thing to do is …

The answer to this is to …

The way to deal with it is to …

The best way forward is to …

STUDY SKILLS: research skills

1 Think about a writing task or project you have done which required research. In pairs, discuss the methods you used to gather your information.

2 Discuss which of the following sources you have used and for what purposes. Which source have you found the most useful? Why?

1 libraries
2 academic journals
3 newspapers
4 trade magazines
5 company/institutional literature
6 public relations departments
7 directories
8 government records
9 statistics from international organisations
10 interviews (face-to-face, by telephone)
11 questionnaires
12 agents

3 In groups, discuss what kinds of research you would use for the following writing tasks. Give your reasons.

1 A paper on US population trends to be read in a university seminar.
2 An article for a newspaper on a historic monument in your town.
3 An essay on a 20th-century philosopher required for a Masters course in Philosophy.
4 A report on the latest electrically-driven cars for a motor magazine.
5 A chapter on a modern crime for an *Anthology of Famous Crimes*.
6 A biography of a famous living pop singer or musician.

4a **2.18** Listen to a lecturer talking to university students about using the Internet and web documents for research purposes. Make notes under the following headings:

- Currency
- Authority
- Objectivity
- Coverage
- Style and functionality

4b Check your notes with a partner.

5 Look at these websites for the American film star, Leonardo DiCaprio. You are asked to write a profile of him for a film magazine. Which of the following websites do you think would be:

a) the most trustworthy?
b) the best sources of information for your article?
c) probably not worth looking at?

Microsoft Internet Explorer

File Edit View Favorites Tools Help

Back | Forward | Stop | Refresh | Home | Search | Favorites | History | Mail

Address

Web Images Videos Maps News Shoping Mail more

[Search]

Web Show options

L E O N A R D O D I C A P R I O - Official Website
http://www.leonardodicaprio.com/ Official website of the actor with biographical information, news, photos, filmography, awards, information about his environmental causes, art gallery.

Leonardo DiCaprio http://www.imdb.com/name/nm0000138/ View legal, agent and manager contact information for Leonardo DiCaprio on IMDbPro. ... View 20 in-development credits for Leonardo DiCaprio on IMDbPro.

THE DiCAPRIO ZONE: The #1 place to find everything about Leo http://www.geocities.com/Hollywood/Set/4040/ 24 Aug 2007 ... An extensive site about Leonardo Dicaprio. Features include a popular chatroom and message board, hot pictures, movie reviews.

Leonardo DiCaprio at The Insider http://www.theinsider.com/celebrities/Leonardo_DiCaprio
The Insider has Leonardo DiCaprio celebrity information, news, pictures and more. Get the latest Leonardo DiCaprio news and share your interest with other ...

Leonardo DiCaprio
http://j.webring.com/hub?ring=dicapring;id=3;prvw
The DiCapring contains fan sites dedicated to Leonardo DiCaprio, one of the greatest actors of his generation. On these sites you will find a great deal of
The interview:

Leonardo DiCaprio | Film | The Observer http://www.guardian.co.uk/film/2007/jan/28/awardsandprizes 28 Jan 2007 ... A child-star first Oscar-nominated at 19, Leonardo DiCaprio has 'come of age' with every movie since then. On eco-ethics, Martin Scorsese ...

Done

6 What other research would you do before writing the article?

WRITING SKILLS: a features article for a magazine or newspaper

7 Read the description of features articles and answer the questions.

Features articles appear regularly in newspapers and magazines. They are not front page, time-sensitive news stories. They provide information about an event, person or idea and they are usually human interest stories.

1 What features articles have you read recently?

2 Were they interesting? Enjoyable? Instructive? Why / Why not?

8 After choosing a catchy title for a features article, the writer must decide how to grab the reader's attention and indicate the central idea, sometimes called the 'angle', of the article. Look at the four types of leads (opening sentences) below and match them to the extracts (A–D) from a features article about Rupert Murdoch.

1 Quote – use of a quote that suggests the angle the writer will take.

2 Anecdote – a lead that tells a story.

3 Summary – tells who, what, when, where, why, how.

4 Surprising statement – stimulates the reader's interest with an unusual beginning.

9 **2.19** Listen to a journalist giving some tips to a group of students on how to write a features article and make brief notes. Compare your notes with a partner.

10 Write a features article for a serious newspaper. Choose one of the following tasks:

1 Write about Rupert Murdoch, the Australian newspaper proprietor, for a serious newspaper. Use the notes on page 168. If you have time, do some more research on Rupert Murdoch before you write the article.

2 Do some research on a well-known personality. Write an article on the personality for a newspaper or magazine which reports on current affairs.

A Billionaire Australian, American publishing tycoon, owner of some of Britain's most popular media and newspapers. He is the boss of News Corporation, one of the largest media organisations in the world. His name is Rupert Murdoch.

B Rupert Murdoch once said, 'Can we change the world? No, but hell, we can all try.' This is the attitude which has helped him to create one of the largest and most influential media groups in the world.

C He works at the age of 77, that's all Rupert Murdoch really does. He works. That's what brings meaning to his life. That's what gives him pleasure.

D I met him in his office in New York. He was wearing a smart jacket and tie, and greeted me with great warmth. He spoke fluently and with great authority when he talked about the future of newspapers and his plans for developing his Internet business. I began by asking where his publishing career started.

Law and society

9.1 HIDDEN RULES

Please remember that law and sense are not always the same.
Jawaharlal Nehru (1899–1964) Indian statesman

SPEAKING

1 Complete the gaps in the statements with the words in the box. In groups, discuss your opinion of each statement.

class	culture	economic
laws	policy	public

1 _____ development causes great social and cultural change.
2 People's friends and relationships are determined by their social _____ .
3 Government _____ directly reflects social attitudes.
4 _____ protest is futile as it never achieves its aims.
5 Youth _____ has little impact on mainstream society.
6 Relatively few _____ affect the public's general social behaviour.

READING

2 Read the book introduction and choose the book (1–3) from which it comes.

1 *Rules and why we need them* by a socialist politician.
2 *The Historical Development of English Society* by a social historian.
3 *Watching the English* by a social anthropologist.

3 Read the introduction again. Discuss the questions.

1 What are the main claims made in paragraphs 1 and 2? Do you agree with them?
2 In paragraphs 3 and 4, which three phrases describe the types of rules under investigation?
3 Which definitions of the word *rule* do these examples match?
   a) I generally go swimming early in the morning.
   b) You must not eat or drink in the classroom.

(1) The human species is addicted to rule making. Every human activity, without exception, is hedged about with complex sets of rules and regulations, dictating precisely when, where, with whom and in what manner the activity may be performed. Animals just do these things; human beings make an almighty song and dance about it. This is known as 'civilisation'.

(2) If you think about it, we all use difference in rules as a principal means of distinguishing one culture from another. The first thing we notice when we go on holiday or business abroad is that other cultures have 'different ways of doing things', by which we usually mean that they have rules about, say, food, mealtimes, dress, greetings, hygiene, trade hospitality, joking, status-differentiation, etc., which are different from our own rules about these practices.

(3) The object (of my observational research) was to identify the commonalities in rules governing English behaviour – the unofficial codes of conduct that cut across class, age, sex, region, sub-cultures and other social boundaries.

(4) Most people obey the unwritten rules of their society instinctively, without being conscious of doing so. For example, you automatically get dressed in the morning without consciously reminding yourself there is an unspoken rule of etiquette that prohibits going to work in

LISTENING

4a [2.20] **Listen to five extracts from a radio serialisation of the book. Answer the following questions.**

1 Which social context is discussed?

2 What is the underlying principle or rule that she draws out of each example?

4b Listen again and answer these questions.

1 What are the specific examples in each case?

2 What is the author's view of the role privacy plays in social rules?

3 What is the author's opinion of the reputation that drivers have?

4 Why does she describe the publican or restaurateur as 'poor'?

5 What is the author's claim about humour in other cultures?

6 Which fact do some foreigners think the English are relatively unaware of?

Kate Fox

one's pyjamas. But if you had an anthropologist staying with you, she would be asking: 'Why are you changing your clothes?'

(5) I am using a rather broad interpretation of a rule, based on four of the definitions allowed by the *Oxford English Dictionary*, namely:

- a principle, regulation or maxim governing individual conduct;
- a standard of discrimination or estimation; a criterion, a test, a measure;
- an exemplary person or thing, a guiding example;
- a fact, or the statement of a fact, which holds generally good; the normal or usual state of things

(6) Thus, my quest to identify the rules of Englishness is not confined to a search for specific codes of conduct, but will include rules in their wider sense of standards, norms, ideals, guiding principles and 'facts' about 'normal or usual' English behaviour.

VOCABULARY: idiomatic verb phrases

5a Match 1–9 with a–i to make complete verb phrases.

1	~~to make a song~~	a)	something for granted
2	to mind	b)	attention to yourself
3	to make	c)	something is amiss
4	to draw	d)	your own business
5	to wash	e)	something to a halt
6	to take	f)	~~and dance about something~~
7	to bring	g)	your dirty linen in public
8	to know	h)	your responsibilities
9	to shirk	i)	a scene

5b In pairs, find phrases from Exercise 5a in Track 2.20 on page 183 and discuss their meanings.

5c Choose the best verb phrases for the situations below.

1 She keeps asking me where I got the money from. I wish she would just _____ .

2 If you decide to become team captain, you can't be lazy and _____ .

3 I know you're angry, but please don't _____ , not here in the library.

4 You have to work at a relationship; you can't just _____ love _____ .

5 I _____ , but I'm not sure exactly what. Let's ask Sarah if she knows about any problems.

SPEAKING

6 Think about your society, and look at the following questions:

1 a) Discuss any 'unwritten rules' that apply to the contexts below.

- work / business
- public transport / cars
- restaurants / food
- homes / domestic life
- social / leisure time
- shopping / street life

b) What happens when people break the rules?

2 Are there any written, or explicitly spoken, rules concerning social behaviour? e.g. train companies ask passengers to let people off a train before boarding.

3 Are there any rules that should be written to improve social behaviour?

SPEAKING

1 With a partner, discuss the following questions:

1 Which of these examples of criminal, or anti-social behaviour are commonly associated with teenagers in your country?

- vandalism
- knife-crime
- car theft
- financial fraud
- shoplifting
- playing loud music in public places
- bank robbery
- graffitti
- street robbery

2 Do you think your country has a problem with juvenile crime?

2 Most countries have a minimum age of criminal responsibility. Guess where these countries go in the table below: The United States (in most states), Iran (girls only), China, The UK, Poland, Argentina. Check your ideas on page 164.

Age of criminal responsibility (Below this age, children cannot be dealt with as criminals.)	
7	Pakistan, Thailand, 1_____
9	Philippines 2_____
10	Ukraine, 3_____
11	Turkey
12	France, 4_____
14	Germany, Japan, Italy, Russia, 5_____
15	Iran (boys only)
16	6_____

3 How does your country compare to others? Do we need such an age? What is a suitable minimum age? How does it compare to other legal ages, e.g. age of marriage, driving?

VOCABULARY: justice systems

4a Complete the abstract for a paper on youth crime with the words in the box. Use a dictionary to help you.

care community service courts
custodial delinquency deter
deterrent offenders punishment
rehabilitation

Youth crime and punishment: a global perspective

Abstract: Despite frequent statistical evidence, and perhaps due to political and media claims, the public perceive juvenile 1____ to be increasing. This paper describes global approaches to juvenile justice, with a focus on the balance between rehabilitation and 2____ when dealing with convicted young 3____. Most countries have dedicated youth 4____ and juvenile detention centres. A few countries, such as Japan, deal with young offenders solely within the 5____ system rather than the justice system. Within justice systems there are two types of sentence – non-custodial and 6____. The former includes curfew and control orders, fines and 7____. In contrast to adult justice systems, there is often a stronger emphasis on 8____ than on simple punishment, although there is a recent trend in some countries, such as the USA, towards harsher punishment, which is justified as being a stronger 9____ to potential young criminals. Critics of this trend claim that imprisonment does not 10___ as it does not take into account the difficult backgrounds of many criminal adolescents.

4b Now answer the following questions about the abstract:

1 What do you know about the juvenile justice system in your society?

2 Is there a current trend in your country that is similar to that in the USA?

3 Where do you stand on the rehabilitation, punishment and deterrence debate?

READING

5 Read the brochures and compare two approaches to the treatment of juvenile delinquents in the USA. In what ways do they act as punishment, rehabilitation and deterrence?

LISTENING

6a 2.21 Listen to Part 1 of a talk on teenagers by forensic psychologist, Diana Kott. What is her argument and what is your opinion of it?

6b 2.22 Listen to Part 2 of her talk. Make notes on the following psychological traits.

- fairness
- respect
- encouragement not punishment
- reject imposed structure
- need guidance
- feel competent and successful
- need to belong
- family

7 In pairs, evaluate the two juvenile punishment programmes with regard to the key teenage psychological traits. Which programme is more appropriate for teenagers?

8 **2.23** Listen to Dr Kott's evaluation of the two programs. How similar are her points to yours? Make notes and compare with your partner.

GRAMMAR: adverbs of degree

9a Complete the gaps in the extract below with the correct adverb. Listen again and check.

1 …boot camps _____ address juveniles' psychological problems.

2 …the teenagers _____ lack the chance to determine the structure …

3 …they are _____ certain to see things as unfair.

4 The _____ complex range of tasks …

9b Answer these questions.

1 What types of words do these adverbs modify?

2 Which of the adverbs amplify or intensify the meaning of the word they modify?

3 Which of the adverbs decrease or soften the meaning of the word they modify?

9c Find more examples in Track 2.23 on page 184, and answer the questions.

1 What is the effect of those adverbs?

2 Can you think of any more similar adverbs?

3 You can say something is 'absolutely excellent', but not 'absolutely good'? Why? Which of the other adverbs are similar?

➡ Language reference and extra practice, pages 150–151

SPEAKING

10 In groups, discuss the following questions.

1 Look at the different types of punishments below. What are their advantages and disadvantages when dealing with juvenile crime? Is the seriousness of the crime relevant?
   a) imprisonment in a youth detention centre
   b) corporal punishment
   c) community service, e.g. cleaning streets
   d) psychological therapy
   e) electronic tagging, curfews and movement restriction
   f) fines

2 Is there a difference between the reality of juvenile crime and the public perception of juvenile crime in your country?

3 What is your general view of your country's legal and justice system?

BOSTON BOOT CAMP –
DISCIPLINE, STRUCTURE, REFORM

Based on the principles of military training and discipline, Boston Boot Camp gives juvenile delinquents a short, sharp shock that instils respect for authority, rigorous self-discipline and a sense of honor. We change their lives for the better and turn them into respectable members of society.

Teens stay at the camp for 30 to 60 days, removing them from the negative influences of their local community, peers and regular lifestyle. There is no TV, radio and Internet. They wear uniforms, live in dormitories and follow an intensive program of physical military training, work, drill exercises and educational experiences.

We operate on a 'Yes, sir! No, sir!' principle. If they obey and follow the rules, they are rewarded. If they break rules or show disobedience, they are punished with further physical exercises. This gives the teens meaningful consequences of their actions.

Our camps are a vital part of the juvenile justice system. We reform disrespectful youth, and our methods also act as a deterrent for would-be criminals and recidivists.

Aspen Forest
Wilderness Therapy Camp

Our camp offers a character-development program for troubled teens that promotes personal growth through living and surviving in the wilderness. The remote setting removes urban distractions, and our program's nurturing approach helps students address personal issues, achieve success, and develop their leadership potential.

The two-month program consists of two integrated dimensions. One involves learning camp-craft, hiking trips, nature education and physical activity. In order to overcome the challenges that nature presents, communication, teamwork, self-discipline and self-reliance are keys to success and students gain an understanding of actions and consequences.

The other dimension involves counselling, group therapy and reflective writing. The spiritual dimension of life in the wilderness, as a teen watches the sun set over the mountains, can encourage greater insight and personal change than a psychologist's office.

During the final stage, each student takes on leadership responsibilities and assists in teaching new participants. Family involvement is important: parents are in regular contact with their child's counsellor and engage in letter writing to their child.

SPEAKING

1 In groups, complete the quiz below.

> ### How much do you know about
> ### international migration?
>
> **1** Which TWO of these countries are NOT countries of strong emigration? Colombia, Morocco, Libya, Senegal, Angola, Portugal, Turkey, Kazakhstan, India, the Philippines.
>
> **2** Look at this list of the top ten countries accommodating international migrants. Which do you think are the top three? Canada, France, Germany, India, Russia, Saudi Arabia, Spain, Ukraine, the UK, the USA.
>
> **3** Which two countries do you think have produced the most refugees in recent years?
>
> **4** How many international migrants are women?
>   a) about 1/4   c) about 1/3
>   b) about 1/2   d) about 2/3
>
> **5** What percentage of international migrants are young people aged 15–29?
>   a) over 80%   b) over 50%   c) over 40%
>
> **6** What do we mean by the term 'brain drain'?

LISTENING

2a 🔲 **2.24** Listen to Pilar Martinez speaking about immigration at a meeting of European Union officials and tick the points she mentions.

1 The growth of the Spanish population.

2 The countries of origin of new immigrants to Spain.

3 The reasons for introducing the Law of Historic Memory.

4 The likely effects of the Law of Historic Memory.

5 The role of immigrants in local politics.

6 The relationship between economics and migration.

2b Listen again, makes notes on the points mentioned and compare your details with a partner.

READING

3 Many postgraduate students in the UK are required to keep a research diary as part of their studies. Read Belén's research diary quickly and answer the questions.

1 What is her dissertation going to be about?

2 Why has she decided to do this topic?

3 Which method of research is mentioned in the diary?

4 Read the diary again and give the date associated with:

1 people's creative ability

2 a promising discovery

3 a change in attitude

4 the reasons for a failure

5 a language problem

6 some non-professional guidance

7 a statement of principle

---

28 Feb
Struggling to find a topic for my dissertation. Talked about it with Amy, my best friend. Her advice was: 'Do something personal, that really means something to you.'

4 March
Think I've finally got a topic - international migration – but not sure about the precise take on it. Have got a strong affinity with the subject, as my parents came to the UK when I was two. Might investigate the Spanish community in London. Found one or two interesting books: 'Aventuras en la Nostalgia' (Adventures in Nostalgia) edited by Lala Isla looks a good bet – collection of life stories (mainly) of exiles from Spanish Civil War who grew up in London. Want ordinary people's voices to be heard in my own work – migrants too often presented as a problem or statistic.

6 March
Think I've got a better idea: immigration to Spain - perhaps focussing on Latin-Americans - since the millennium. Seems more international and contemporary. Read an interesting EU report about a Spanish government initiative to pay jobless non-EU immigrants – most of them Latin-Americans - to go home. They get about 10,400 euros in two lump-sums. Apparently, though, the plan's proving a flop so far. The immigrants' concern that life would be harsher in their own countries means that most of them want to stay put.

GRAMMAR: reporting using nouns

5a Look at these examples and find other verbs and nouns used for reporting in the diary.

He asked me to write up a proposal.

His comment that it was good to use my language skills and contacts abroad pleased me.

5b Choose three of the examples using nouns. What did the speaker actually say?

GRAMMAR TIP

Notice that quotes can be direct or indirect.

Her advice was: 'Do something personal'.

Her advice was to do something personal.

6 Look at the sentences in the diary using reporting nouns. Match them to structure 1 or 2 below.

1 His claim was that they'd lied. (This was false.)

2 His claim that they'd lied was false.

➡ Language reference and extra practice, pages 150–151

---

9 March

Met my supervisor, Gavin Travis, for the first time today. My excuse that I'd cancelled last Wednesday's meeting because I suddenly developed toothache didn't go down too well, so the atmosphere was a bit frosty to start with. Eventually, he warmed to me a bit. He was pretty enthusiastic about my topic and his comment that it was good to use my language skills and contacts abroad pleased me. He asked me to write up a proposal for next week. In the end, it was quite a productive meeting.

16 March

Gavin said my proposal was generally fine. His only complaint (well, suggestion, really) was that I should try to write in a more formal style.

24 March

Very interesting postgraduate seminar today at Princes College. The speaker (Caroline Morton) was from a think tank close to the government. Her main argument was that immigration has important economic benefits for a country as immigrants bring entrepreneurial spirit and inventive flair. Her point that the number of inventions patented in a particular area increases in proportion with the number of migrants was quite memorable. Afterwards, got talking to a guy who worked for the Spanish Embassy and claimed he used to date the actress Mónica Cruz.

2 April

Had a brainwave! Next time I visit my relatives in Madrid, I'll do some interviews with the carers from the Dominican Republic who look after my ageing great-aunt.

---

7 Complete the gaps in the sentences using a reporting noun from the verbs in the box.

accuse	answer	claim
declare	observe	remark

1 'I told you before: I've got dual nationality.'

'But we've discovered you haven't.'

His _____ that he had dual nationality turned out to be false.

2 'We want to stay in this country.'

'I'm afraid you can't.'

They asked for asylum, but the _____ was no.

3 'They're really backward.'

Her _____ about the immigrants' customs was offensive.

4 'A lot of them have got really good skills.'

The _____ that many of the migrants were highly skilled was made by several politicians.

5 'It's nonsense to say that border security is lax.'

The government issued a _____ that border security was not lax.

6 'You entered the country illegally.'

The_____ was levelled against him that he had entered the country illegally.

VOCABULARY: noun conversion

8a Which of the verbs and adjectives in the box can be used as nouns, without adding an affix?

best	catch	complain	do	find	hopeful
international	investigate	walk	white		

8b Use the nouns in the box to complete the sentences below.

1 We're having a little _____ to celebrate his 30th birthday.

2 The Anglo-Saxon rings were an astonishing archaeological _____ .

3 The teachers bring out the _____ in their students.

4 He's a talented young footballer and stands every chance of becoming a/an _____ next season.

WRITING

9 Has your country experienced immigration recently or in the past? Write a paragraph on what people in your country think about immigration.

SITUATION

In Australia, following a recent election, there is a new political party in government which intends to unify many of the currently separate state laws. The policy department is currently drafting new laws to fulfil the party's manifesto pledges. The initial proposals have had a poor reception as they were perceived as being too strong and as failing to take into account important exceptions. The policy department has to redraft the laws, maintaining their efficacy whilst eliminating their drawbacks.

1 Read the situation and the extracts from the manifesto and discuss the following questions.

1 What laws could be made to meet these manifesto commitments?

2 In your country, which laws relate to these particular issues?

2 Read the original law proposals below. Which manifesto commitments have not been addressed?

1 There will be a complete ban on the sale of chocolate and salty snacks to children aged under 16, and children will not be allowed to consume more than one sugary fizzy drink per day. Shopkeepers and parents will be liable to fines.

2 There will be a complete ban on the use of plastic shopping bags, enforceable with fines up to AU$10,000.

3 There will be a complete ban on the carrying of knives in public places.

4 All drivers entering city centres must pay a charge per visit of AU$75.

5 Parents of children who are absent from school without permission will be punished with fines or imprisonment.

A safer society

We can only have a safe society if we have strong laws that address the current problems. We will introduce new laws to deal with the recent rises in knife crime, aggressive anti-social behaviour and racial intolerance.

A greener society

The time to act is now, and we are the party that will take that action. We will reduce the use of cars, the use of plastic shopping bags and encourage the use of alternative energy sources.

A healthier society

At times, the government has to bring in laws that will promote a healthier society for the good of everyone. We will introduce legislation concerning smoking and unhealthy food.

An educated society

In this information age, we need to ensure that the education of our youth is at the forefront of government policy. We will introduce new laws to reduce truancy and also raise the minimum school leaving age to 17 across the nation.

3a `2.25` Listen to the discussion concerning the re-drafting of one of the laws in Exercise 2, and make notes on the following points:

• aim of the law

• strengths

• weaknesses

3b In pairs, discuss how you would choose to amend this law.

3c `2.26` Listen to the final decisions and answer the questions.

1 How do the decisions compare to your ideas?

2 What is your opinion of the amended law?

3 Is there anything similar in your country?

KEY LANGUAGE: balancing an argument

4a `2.27` Listen to extracts from the discussion in Exercise 3a and complete the gaps in the sentences below.

1 …lowest achievers. _____ , this law is not solely about children.

2 Now, _____ we're here to amend this law, I think that …

3 That's _____ , but it's _____ too inflexible…

4 Well, _____ it's important that the law sends out a strong message, _____ think there must be some …

5 Well, _____ that as a fair principle, we mustn't make it…

6 …about fines? _____ , imprisonment would be deterrence, but, overall, I'm not sure…

7 I see _____ , _____ one thing that I like about the current proposal is that…

4b The phrases in Exercise 4a are used to balance an argument, in particular to show that we accept the validity of one point, and also accept a contrasting, or conflicting, point. Answer the following questions.

1 Can you remember the arguments that surrounded the phrases in Exercise 4a? Check in Track 2.25 on page 184.

2 In each case, can you say which argument the speaker favours?

TASK: amending and modifying the law

5 You work in the policy department and have to modify the four remaining laws from Exercise 2. Group A students are responsible for laws 1 and 2, Group B students are responsible for laws 3 and 4. Discuss the assigned laws and identify their strengths and weaknesses. As you criticise the laws, propose amendments. As a group, decide which amendments to make and, finally, rephrase the law.

6 Form pairs with a student from the opposite group. Present your amended laws and the thinking behind the amendments. Evaluate the other student's amended laws. Should further changes be made to any of the laws?

OTHER USEFUL PHRASES

Focussing the discussion

So, let's look at the law concerning …

Can I just point out that …?

Let's concentrate on …

Accepting an argument

I can go along with that.

That seems sensible.

I don't have any objections to that.

Attending to detail

How shall we word the law, exactly?

Is that clear enough?

Does that cover everything?

Is there anything we've forgotten?

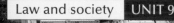

STUDY SKILLS: synthesising information

1 In groups, discuss the following questions and make notes on your ideas. Report the main points of your discussion to another group.

1 Have you, or anyone you know, ever been unemployed? Are you unemployed now? Describe your experience.

2 What are the causes and effects of unemployment – and the solutions?

3 To what extent should governments help unemployed people?

4 Martti Ahtisaari, the Finnish winner of the 2008 Nobel Peace Prize, said that youth unemployment is perhaps the greatest challenge in the world. Do you agree?

LABOUR ISN'T WORKING.

UNEMPLOYMENT OFFICE

BRITAIN'S BETTER OFF WITH THE CONSERVATIVES.

2 Read definitions 1–3 below. Choose the correct definition for the word *synthesis*.

1 A short statement that gives the main information about something, without giving all the details.

2 Something that has been made by combining different things, or the process of combining things.

3 A statement that expresses in a different (or clearer) way what someone has said or written.

3 It is sometimes argued that there are two main types of synthesis: 1) background synthesis, and 2) thesis-driven synthesis. Match each type with a description (a or b) and an example (c or d).

a) Information is brought together from a variety of sources and organised by topic. Aim: to inform.

b) Information from different sources is used to develop and strengthen an argument. Aim: to persuade

c) a lawyer in a court presenting a case for the prosecution or defence

d) a website listing flights available with different airlines

4 Think of one or two activities you often do as a student, and how they involve synthesis.

5 Put steps 1–6 for writing a synthesis in the correct order.

1 Write your synthesis using your own words and citing relevant authors.

2 Read material from different sources that will help you do the task.

3 Check the synthesis against the original texts to make sure it is accurate.

4 Find relationships between the points in your notes. Look for patterns and categories of information, common ideas, similarities, differences, contrasts, contradictions. Mark or highlight links between points using colours, letters or numbers.

5 Make notes of key, relevant points for each text in your own words.

6 Decide on the best order for the points you will use for your synthesis and write them all on one piece of paper.

WRITING SKILLS: a literature review

6 [2.28] Hassan is going to write a dissertation on the effects of unemployment on young people. He watches a podcast on writing a literature review. Listen and take notes to answer these questions.

1 What is a literature review?

2 What purposes does it serve?

7 Look at Hassan's notes for part of his literature review. What kinds of categories, similarities, etc. can you see? How would you organise the information with the aim of writing a synthesis?

Singh, V. (2004) *Youth unemployment*
- negative psychological effects (p 76)
- early experiences of unemployment > further periods out of work later on (young miss out on experience + training while unemployed) (p142)
- delays age young people leave home/become indep./have family - Australia (p167)
- detachment from labour market, reduces desire to work. Slacker phenomenon. (p215)

Ashcroft, T. (2007) *Unemployment amongst the young in the early 21st century*
- rejects claim made by Rossi (1998) that it encourages young people to do further training + 'increase their economic value' (p45)
- increases crime > increases costs of health services, policing (p121)
- unemployment early in life > lower earnings, under-employment + unemployment later. Scarring effect. 'Widespread youth unemployment could create a lost generation' (p189)

O'Donnell, M. (2009) *Wasted: the damaging effects of youth unemployment*
- low self-esteem, depression > harder to enter job market (p37)
- increases govt. spending on pub. services. (p65)
- nation's economic growth impeded by waste of young talent + energy (p174)

8 Now read Hassan's synthesis. How is the information organised?

A number of recent investigations into youth unemployment find the effects to be overwhelmingly negative.

Singh (2004) and O'Donnell (2009) study the damaging psychological effects. O'Donnell's argument is that unemployment causes low self-esteem and depression in young people, and makes it more difficult for them to find work later.

Singh and Ashcroft (2007) point out that unemployment early in life is often a predictor of unemployment later on. Singh's explanation is that young people fail to gain experience or be sent on training courses while out of work, reducing their subsequent chances of securing a job.

A further effect noted by Ashcroft and O'Donnell is the increase in government expenditure on public services such as health and policing – the latter the result of a rise in crimes committed by unemployed youths.

The only glimmer of hope is that mentioned by Rossi (1998, in Ashcroft), with the observation that unemployment sometimes encourages young people to do additional training and 'increase their economic value', although this is disputed by Ashcroft.

9a Read the synthesis again and find words that are used to report information.

point out

9b Which of the words you found in Exercise 9a could be replaced by the following?

1 observed
2 According to X,
3 In X's view,
4 touched on
5 examine

9c Does Hassan use a direct quote anywhere? If so, where?

10a Look at the photo. What do you know about the Great Depression?

10b Write part of a literature review on 'The Great Depression: Consequences'. Look at the notes on page 169 and synthesise the information. Write between 150 and 180 words.

A public kind of privacy
by our media columnist

Giles Smith

'Celebrity in privacy battle' – how often does one come [1]_____ like this in the news today? But what exactly is meant by privacy? This is a [2]_____ complex issue that varies from culture to culture. Many sociologists have made the observation that the concept of personal privacy is primarily a western construct, almost [3]_____ absent from societies such as the Australian Aborigines, whose lives are conducted very publicly.

In most respects today the individual is protected from invasion of privacy by laws such as the Data Protection Act, which prevents personal information [4]_____ or circulated without permission. The most common accusations of invasion of privacy seem to involve revelations of inappropriate conduct by public figures such as politicians, or the deplorable intrusions of paparazzi into celebrities' lives. However

much governments may urge [5]_____ its own affairs, most weeks bring new 'invasions of privacy'. News editors defend their revelations by stating that the information is 'in the public interest', which may be true when politicians are exposed [6]_____ irregular expense claims, but it is hardly so in the case of minor celebrities – that is surely just satisfying the public appetite for salacious gossip.

It is, of course, most regrettable and unacceptable when ordinary people become, however briefly, celebrities and therefore a target for journalists. Take the case of Kate and Gerry McCann, whose daughter Madeline mysteriously disappeared on holiday in May 2007. Although the couple initially welcomed the press into their lives, the pressure to provide more news soon became intolerable, and the situation got out of hand, as is shown by Mr McCann's recent contention that the reporters [7]_____ unfounded stories if there were nothing to report on a particular day. Surely it is vulnerable people such as the McCanns who should be protected from invasion of privacy, maybe even by law?

from jackideedee, posted two hours ago
I read this article with interest. Yes, we should sympathise with innocent members of the public who become reluctantly entwined with the press, but in the case of the McCanns, if they hadn't invited so much media coverage for their own purposes, they [8]_____ so many problems with them at the time, nor [9]_____ hounded by them even now.

from delray x-box, posted one hour, five minutes ago
I think jackideedee's comment that the McCanns brought the situation on themselves is [10]_____ unfair, but in the case of celebrities, it's their own fault. They want the press around when they're starting to become famous, but then they get fed up. Sorry, guys, but if you [11]_____ the heat, get out of the kitchen. If you want to be in the public eye some of the time, then learn to [12]_____ all of the time!

GRAMMAR

1 Read the article and responses quickly, ignoring the gaps, and answer the questions.

1 Does Giles Smith think that we need tighter privacy laws? If so, for what kind of cases?

2 Do the two postings agree with Giles Smith?

3 What does the writer of the second posting think of celebrities, do you think?

2a Now read the texts again and complete the gaps with the words below.

1 a) it across   b) a headline across   c) across a headline

2 a) highly   b) absolutely   c) completely

3 a) very   b) entirely   c) fully

4 a) from be revealed   b) from being revealed
c) from to be revealed

5 a) the media regulating   b) to regulate the media
c) the media to regulate

6 a) for filing   b) for file   c) for to file

7 a) would have simply repeated
b) will simply repeat   c) would simply repeat

8 a) wouldn't have had   b) wouldn't have
c) would have had

9 a) would they being   b) would they be
c) would they have been

10 a) slightly   b) little   c) bit

11 a) don't like   b) didn't like   c) hadn't liked

12 a) put up it with   b) put up with it
c) put it up with

2b Find and underline statements in the texts that report the following quotes. Which nouns are used to introduce the reported statement?

1 'The concept of privacy is a western construct.'

2 'The reporters would simply repeat unfounded stories if there were nothing to report.'

3 'The McCanns brought the situation on themselves.'

3 Discuss with a partner. How would you react in the following situations?

1 … if a stranger started taking photos of you in public.

2 … if you found someone looking through your bins.

3 … if you won a competition and your address and phone number was printed in the local newspaper.

VOCABULARY

4 2.29 Listen to seven short conversations and match each one with an idiom below.

a) She thinks he takes her for granted.

b) She offers to give her a hand.

c) He doesn't want to wash his dirty linen in public.

d) She doesn't want to make a scene.

e) She's keeping her fingers crossed.

f) His hands are tied.

g) He's got time on his hands.

5 Choose a word/phrase from Box A and one from Box B to complete each short summary.

A

create   policy   posing   restrict   youth

B

care system   custodial sentences
juvenile delinquency   rehabilitation
tabloid newspaper

1 After two boys of 11 were charged with attempted murder today, the government has promised to _____ tougher laws against _____ .

2 Judge Collins was insistent on _____ the question about press responsibility to the editor of the _____ that had exposed the so-called fraud.

3 Our reporters have unearthed a cover-up of extreme negligence in the juvenile _____ , which may be one reason behind the recent increase in _____ crime.

4 Judges have today urged the Home Secretary to _____ the use of _____ for young offenders; this just exacerbates the problem, they say.

5 We urgently need a coherent government _____ that tackles the ongoing debate about whether _____ or punishment is more effective for young offenders.

KEY LANGUAGE

6a **2.30** Listen to a discussion in a newspaper office. Which of the following opinions do you hear?

1 Running a sensitive story isn't entirely a business decision.

2 The story is very important for the newspaper's profitability.

3 The story isn't a particularly sensitive one.

4 The newspaper owner is happy with the idea of chequebook journalism.

5 It isn't a problem that the politician is asking for payment.

6 The politician might have an ulterior motive for revealing the cover-up.

6b Complete these phrases from the discussion, then listen again to check.

1 _____ said that, it isn't _____ about business.

2 That _____ _____ a great idea, Jim.

3 I have to point out that we _____ to think _____ _____ _____ very carefully.

4 If you don't get _____ _____ _____ , we _____ be taken to court.

5 I just don't _____ it's _____ because people will question the politician's motives ...

6 I see _____ _____ _____ , Fiona, but the point is that she's very likely to lose her job ...

7 You know, to be honest, I'm not too _____ on _____ _____ , either.

8 It's a very _____ _____ .

9 ... while _____ all these views, we _____ take a decision without having all the facts here.

10 If we get our _____ wrong, it'll have a _____ _____ on our reputation.

LANGUAGE CHECK

7 There is a mistake in each of these sentences. Find and correct the mistake, then look at the pages to check your answer.

1 Finally, I'd like to say all of journalists that have attended this conference today have been extremely brave. (page 73)

2 If I'd learnt to write with my left hand, I might not have had so many problems now I've broken my right wrist! (page 74)

3 We wouldn't have chosen to live here if we don't appreciate the mountains. (page 74)

4 The judge made the jury to leave the court while he spoke to the lawyers. (page 83)

5 The reporter was really pushy; she insisted asking me some very personal questions. (page 83)

6 I hadn't seen my car keys for weeks when I came them across yesterday in the dog's basket! (page 85)

7 We need to look into urgently the question of fossil fuel consumption. (page 93)

8 We enjoyed particularly the documentary about travelling round Australia. (page 93)

9 The defendant's assertion that he is at work at the time of the robbery simply wasn't true. (page 95)

LOOK BACK

8 Find the exercise in Units 7–9 where you ...

- read about left-handed people (Unit 7)
- find out about a forgotten 14th-century explorer (Unit 7)
- revise conditional sentences (Unit 7)
- study newspaper vocabulary and headline language (Unit 8)
- write about the importance of getting news (Unit 8)
- discuss an ethical dilemma (Unit 8)
- listen to parts of a book about the English (Unit 9)
- study how to form nouns (Unit 9)
- look at how to synthesise information (Unit 9)

10 Arts and entertainment

In this unit

Grammar
■ non-finite clauses
■ spoken English

Vocabulary
■ performance reviews
■ compound adjectives
■ academic verbs

Scenario
■ Reality island

Study skills
■ seminar/discussion skills

Writing skills
■ creative writing (a screenplay)

10.1 PERFORMANCE

There's no business like show business.
Irving Berlin (1888–1989) American Composer

SPEAKING

1 Look at the information about arts and entertainment in Scotland. Where do the missing percentages go in each table?

Table 1: 55, 50, 32, 8 **Table 2:** 61, 29, 14

Table 1	
Attendance by adults at arts and cultural events in the previous 12 months (2008). Figures as percentages.	
Arts festivals	9
Art galleries / exhibitions / events	45
Ballet / dance	2
Carnival / circus	25
Classical / traditional music	
Cinema	
Poetry / literary events	3
Rock / pop / jazz music	
Theatre / musicals	

Table 2	
Participation of adults in arts and entertainment in the previous 12 months (2008). Figures as percentages.	
Acting and performance	2
Crafts / drawing / painting	
Dance	6
Film / video / photography	9
Music (instrument and singing)	
Reading books	

2 In small groups, discuss the following questions.

1 What do the tables reveal?

2 How do you think your country would compare?

3 What arts events do you attend or participate in?

4 What events have you been to recently? Did you choose those events for the reasons below?

recommendations from friends / reviews in the media / previously enjoyed similar events or performers / the chance to see something new and different

READING

3 Read the mini-reviews from the listings magazine *Time Out, London*. Match the types of events (1-6) with the reviews (A–H). There may be more than one correct answer.

1	Theatre	4	Comedy
2	Music	5	Dance
3	Film	6	Art

4 Read the reviews again and answer the questions. Compare with a partner.

1 Which event(s)…
  a) have/has received an explicitly positive review?
  b) is/are in a non-central location?
  c) is the performer's first performance in Britain?
  d) is visually interesting?
  e) include an unusual use of everyday objects?
  f) features music of African-American origin?
  g) has/have a gender theme?

2 Which events would/wouldn't you like to go to?

VOCABULARY: performance reviews

5 Find words or phrases in the reviews which mean the following:

1 when a story from one medium is produced in another
2 a large group of singers
3 the list of performers appearing during a night at a single place
4 the place where a performance occurs
5 an incredibly talented person, a genius
6 a group of three people
7 a creator of dances
8 a group of actors or performers who work together on different projects

6a Complete the compound adjectives a–i with the words in the box. Check your answers with the text. What do they mean?

> award   awe   bass   British   female
> laughter   out of   Rambert   star

a)	-inspiring	f)	featuring
b)	-winning	g)	-heavy
c)	-packed	h)	-born
d)	the way	i)	-trained
e)	-studded		

6b Which two of these adjectives do you think the writer might have created specifically for these reviews?

Critic's choice

A On the Waterfront
Steven Berkoff returns to the stage in a new adaptation of the Academy Award-winning film about a boxer who takes on the mob.

B The Phantom of the Opera
Critics of this stage musical call it tired, but its lavish and bold set design is still awe-inspiring and it's a touching story of love and desire.

C Lost and Found Orchestra
Featuring dance, music, comedy and aerial performance, the orchestra comprises an incredible array of invented instruments (including vacuum cleaners and traffic cones), played by the 32 multi-talented performers, plus a choir.

D Amused Moose
Great night out at this award-winning comedy club with a laughter-packed bill.

E Kenny Wheeler
This out of the way venue keeps the quality sky high with another star-studded show featuring legendary UK trumpeter Wheeler and guitar virtuoso Parricelli. Catch this if you can, it should be a corker.

F An Experiment On A Bird In The Air Pump + Das Wanderlust
Evening of female-featuring bands, from the gothy, bass-heavy post-punk tuneage of female trio AEOABITAP to the reckless garage pop of toy instrument-abusing Das Wanderlust.

G The Weather Committee + Karl Wilson + Emy And The Band
Live acoustic hip hop, R&B and soul showcase.

H Thomas Noone
UK debut of British-born, Rambert-trained choreographer Thomas Noone and his company performing two pieces based on the complexities of personal relationships.

LISTENING

7a [3.1] Listen to interviews done after the events in Exercise 3. Which event did each person attend?

7b What did they think of the event? Listen again to complete the extracts below (use one to three words).

1 … well, the music is rather _____ .
2 _____ the cost of the ticket.
3 Goth music isn't really my _____ …
4 Well, it lived up _____ …
5 … that's _____ to say it's _____ worth seeing, just that it's _____ the best.

SPEAKING AND WRITING

8 With a partner, describe and review a few performance-based events that you have been to.

9 Write short reviews for your events from Exercise 8 in the style of *Time Out*.

VOCABULARY AND SPEAKING

1a Add to the list of types of music below.

pop, rock, jazz, world music

1b How would you define the types of music in the list? Discuss with a partner and check your ideas in a dictionary.

2a In small groups, discuss the following questions.

1 What kind(s) of music do you like/dislike?

2 Do you think classical music is the most international kind of music? Why/why not?

3 Is classical music only for certain kinds of people?

READING

3 Read the press release quickly. What is its aim?

4a Scan the press release and find the following information in one minute.

1 When the orchestra was set up.

2 The total number of young people who participate in the system.

3 The maximum age of the performers in the orchestra.

4 When the orchestra last performed in London.

5 How often the young people in Venezuela go to music lessons.

6 How far you should travel to listen to this orchestra.

7 How many performers there are in the orchestra.

4b Why do you think there is so much numerical information in this text?

5 How many people are quoted in the text? Are the quotes similar in any way?

6 Underline all the positive words and phrases in the text. Why are there so many?

7 In pairs, discuss the following questions.

1 What do you think about the Venezuelan system mentioned in the press release?

2 Have you got anything similar in your country?

3 Does/would it work in your country?

PRESS RELEASE

NEWS RELEASE

SIMÓN BOLÍVAR YOUTH ORCHESTRA OF VENEZUELA – RESIDENCY AT CARDIFF BAY CULTURAL CENTRE

To mark the tenth anniversary of the opening of Cardiff Bay Cultural Centre, we are pleased to announce that the exceptional Simón Bolívar Youth Orchestra of Venezuela and its charismatic conductor Gustavo Dudamel will be in Cardiff 17–21 September next year for a special residency. To focus the residency at the Bay Centre, the Orchestra will give two showcase concerts.

First seen in London in 2005, the Orchestra returned in 2007, to produce electrifying performances bringing wide-spread critical acclaim. Dean Jones, Head of Music at the Bay Centre, said: 'This special residency offers an amazing opportunity for Welsh audiences to watch and listen to one of the most dynamic groups of musicians in the world. This orchestra has tremendous energy, passion and a sense of fun, but also great technical skills. They're very accomplished musicians. And, of course, Gustavo Dudamel is a phenomenon.'

At the end of a concert by this orchestra, you won't hear polite clapping. Instead, the audiences are on their feet, stomping and roaring, doing the Mexican wave, demanding encore after encore. The atmosphere is closer to a carnival than a traditional classical music event. The *Daily Telegraph* wrote: 'Music-making this joyous is in a class of its own. If you hear of the Orchestra coming within 500 miles of you, book straight away'.

Founded in 1975 by the musician and economist, José Antonio Abreu, the Simón Bolívar Youth Orchestra has, since its inception, striven to offer new opportunities for musical excellence in Venezuela, touring with its Music Director Gustavo Dudamel and working with other world-famous conductors. Heading a national system, the State Foundation for the Venezuelan System of Youth and Child Orchestras, known simply as El Sistema, the Orchestra comprises over 200 young musicians aged from 16 to 20.

These gifted young performers are all products of a system that is of equal social, musical and educational importance. Six afternoons a week, hundreds of thousands of youngsters from some of the toughest neighbourhoods in Venezuela have free music lessons, and are provided with free instruments, taking them off the streets of the shanty towns where they live and away from drugs, guns, gangs and crime. They are literally given a new life, and their classes become a new family where they learn not only music, but also respect, discipline and teamwork.

Around 250,000 musicians from across Venezuela are involved with El Sistema, playing in pre-school orchestras, over 90 children's orchestras, over 130 youth orchestras and over 30 professional adult symphony orchestras. Simon Rattle, Director of the Berlin Philharmonic, has said of the Venezuelan system: 'This is nothing less than a miracle. From here, I see the future for music for the whole world.'

GRAMMAR: non-finite clauses

8 Read the sentences from the text. Look at the example and underline the non-finite clauses in sentences 1 and 2.

Founded in 1975, the Orchestra has striven to offer new opportunities.

1 Heading a national system, this orchestra comprises over 200 young musicians.

2 To focus the residency, the Orchestra will give two showcase concerts.

9 There are three main types of non-finite clause. Match them with the sentences in Exercise 8.

a) infinitive clauses

b) past participle clauses

c) -ing clauses

10a Read the explanation of a non-finite clause. Then answer the questions.

A non-finite clause has a lexical verb, but this verb does not indicate tense. We have to understand its reference to time (and person and number) from the context or surrounding clauses. Non-finite clauses are typically subordinate, and are usually combined with finite clauses in sentences.

1 In the sentences in Exercise 8, what are the lexical verbs that do not indicate tense?

2 What is the time reference of the non-finite clauses?

10b Find other examples of the different types of non-finite clause in the press release.

➡ Language reference and extra practice, pages 152–153

11 Complete sentences 1–6 below, using the non-finite clauses a–f. Choose the appropriate form of the verb in brackets and use appropriate punctuation.

a) (blamed / blaming) for an increase in street violence

b) (to reduce / reducing) the need for painkilling drugs by 50 per cent

c) (to escape / escaped) the monotony of suburban life

d) (producing / produced) more milk

e) (to watch / watched) by over 400 million people around the world

f) (to stimulate / stimulated) greater spending by customers

1 Certain kinds of music are played in shops
_____ .

2 The 1985 Live Aid concerts for famine relief in Ethiopia took place in London, Philadelphia and other cities _____ .

3 _____ the rapper was vilified by the media.

4 Tailor-made music programmes have a remarkable effect on some medical patients _____ .

5 Cows appreciate calming music _____ .

6 _____ they formed a band.

WRITING

12 Write a short press release (about 100 words) for a music event in your town or city.

SPEAKING

13 Discuss these questions.

1 Which instrument has the nicest sound, in your opinion?

2 Is music important to you? If so, why?

3 Have your musical tastes changed over the years? If so, how?

4 Is there any music / song you associate with particular events or people in your life?

5 Are any singers / musicians from your country popular abroad?

SPEAKING

1 In small groups, discuss the following questions.

1 a) Over the years, how has the Internet and digital technology changed entertainment?

   b) How do you use the Internet for entertainment?

2 What developments might occur in the future regarding digital entertainment?

READING

2 Read extracts A–D quickly and answer the questions.

1 Which extracts are about …
   a) producing material to show/share online?
   b) consuming online entertainment?

2 Match the extracts to their sources below.
   a) The abstract of an academic research paper
   b) A press release about a business research report
   c) A journalist's blog
   d) A newspaper article

3 In which extract are the following ideas mentioned?

1 Much entertainment will remain within small groups of people.

2 Internet entertainment and communities may be harmful for a nation.

3 Many people spend a lot of time online.

4 Many online sites or phenomena do not last long.

5 Being familiar with the Internet enhances personal credibility.

4 With your partner, read each extract carefully and then answer the questions.

1 Are such situations positive, negative or neither?

2 How does it compare to your country and your life?

VOCABULARY: academic verbs

5a Find verbs in the extracts with mean the following:

1 provide the means for something to occur (Text A)

2 supply something or spread something over an area (Text A)

3 change in form or quality (Text B)

4 show that something exists or is true (Text C)

5 support or make stronger (Text C)

6 weaken or reduce in importance (Text C)

7 use or purchase (Text D)

8 discover and name (Text D)

A This time last year I went down to Los Angeles to do a live debate about the merits of user-generated-content with a kid called Justin Kan. It was a surreal experience. Kan, a freshly graduated Yale philosophy student, had affixed an always-on video camera on his head. Everything in his life – absolutely everything – is streamed in grainy video onto his website. Back then, Kan was just starting a business called Justin.tv – a user-generated-content portal that enabled other self-broadcasting kids like himself to distribute their unedited lives on the Internet. Just another ephemeral web 2.0 thing, I concluded. After all, how many kids would be shameless enough to broadcast their entire lives to a voyeuristic world? I was totally wrong. The venture capital-backed Justin.tv is now a significant commercial success.

B Mohammed Lutf, the owner of an Internet café in Sana'a, Yemen, noted, 'Sometimes students use the Internet for their researches, but this happens rarely.' According to Lutf, the use of Internet varies during the day. In the afternoon, young kids between 7 and 16 visit the cafés to play games and listen to music. But evenings are when the majority of users will be seen, when young adults and people of all ages use the Internet for chatting, playing games and visiting various entertainment websites, sometimes until the early hours of the morning.

5b Now, use the verbs to complete the gaps in the sentences below.

1 Surveys _____ that the broadcast industry undervalued the public interest in user-generated content.

2 An attempt has been made to _____ global copyright laws in order to protect commercial content.

3 It is important to _____ the factors which lead to children deceiving parents about their levels of Internet use.

4 Video and music sharing sites tend to _____ consumers' respect for the rights of media producers.

5 Social networking sites enable users to rapidly _____ information to their peers.

6 The pattern of Internet use for entertainment _____ considerably according to age.

7 The data _____ us to draw clear conclusions concerning the future of entertainment.

8 Greatly increased Internet use will _____ both bandwidth and energy resources.

C The main results of this study about young Shanghainese indicate that the main motivation behind the Internet café use was entertainment and that the Internet use in the cafes was ritualistic, habitual and pleasure-seeking. For the urban youth culture, the Internet cafés provided a space where the youngsters could reinforce their identities as trendy, technology-savvy urbanites. The government and the public concerns were reflected in the phenomenon as the Internet cafés have been accused of eroding public morality.

D Up to a quarter of the entertainment consumed by people in five years time will have been created, edited and shared within their peer circle rather than coming out of traditional media groups. This phenomenon, dubbed 'Circular Entertainment', has been identified by Nokia as a result of a global study into the future of entertainment. 'The trends we are seeing show us that people will have a genuine desire not only to create and share their own content, but also to remix it, mash it up and pass it on within their peer groups – a form of collaborative social media,' said Mark Selby, Vice President, Multimedia, Nokia.

LISTENING

6 **3.2** Listen to a Canadian student webcast and put the following points in the order they are first made.

1 The Internet is of benefit to the world due to its search capacity.

2 Some parents do not let their children use the Internet.

3 Parents who restrict Internet use often don't understand the Internet.

4 Using the Internet leads to an inability to retain information.

5 The Internet does not encourage you to explore one topic deeply.

6 Television has many benefits.

7 Some parents do not allow their children to watch television.

GRAMMAR: spoken English

7a **3.3** Listen to pairs of extracts from the conversation in Exercise 6. Which feature of spoken English below does each short extract exemplify?

1 a Speakers interrupt, or talk over, each other. *(First extract)*
  b Listeners make short supportive comments, without fully interrupting. *(Second extract)*

2 a Speakers hesitate and use fillers such as 'er' and 'I mean'.
  b Speakers repeat words, especially when restarting a sentence.

3 a Frequent use of phrases such as 'I mean, you know, like, so' to organise speech.
  b Simple clause structure – a chain of ideas, linked simply with 'and, but, so, then, because'.

4 a Ellipsis – omitting grammatical words such as pronouns.
  b Sentences are incomplete because the speaker rephrases their idea.

7b Listen to and read Track 3.2 on page 186. Find more examples of the features of spoken English.

➡ Language reference and extra practice, pages 152–153

8 Replace the missing words in these examples of spoken English.

1 Must be loads of things to do in London at New Year. Check in *Time Out*.

2 Do anything last night?

3 **A:** Where shall I put this?
  B: Top drawer of the cabinet.

4 **A:** Proved you wrong there, didn't I?
  B: Can't believe I was wrong. Never happened before!

5 **A:** Shall I leave a note for Simon?
  B: Not worth it. On holiday for a month!

6 Come on! Everyone outside. Time for the family photo.

SPEAKING

9 Work in groups of five. Three students discuss one of the statements below. Two students listen for features of spoken English and make notes.

1 There's nothing wrong in parents banning their children from watching TV and / or using the Internet.

2 Using the Internet for entertainment will remain the preserve of young people.

3 Soon, people will spend more time viewing user-generated entertainment than commercially-produced material.

4 Young people are ignorant of the dangers of revealing their private lives online.

5 Downloading movies and music for free, without permission, is a criminal act and people should be prosecuted.

INTERNATIONAL ISLAND

SPEAKING

1 **In groups, discuss the following questions.**

1 What formats of reality show are there in your country? Are you a fan of any?

2 Why do you think people appear on these shows?

3 What do you think the producers will be looking for in contestants for 'International Island?' Consider the following:

- personality traits
- physical appearance
- hobbies and interests
- singing / acting skills
- practical skills
- age and health

2 **Read the producer's selection guidelines. Are they similar to your ideas?**

SITUATION

A production company is making a new TV and Internet reality show called *International Island*. The show will feature 12 contestants from all over the world who will live on a small, deserted, tropical island for three months. They will work together to build a community and survive without any modern conveniences, performing tasks to win food and points. The global public will vote each week to give points to different contestants. The contestant with the most points at the end will win a round-the-world trip. The production company is about to hold the auditions for the potential contestants.

3 **3.4** Read the situation and listen to two auditions. Which attributes do the candidates claim? Who would / wouldn't you choose to be in the show? Why / Why not?

Selection Guidelines

Although a good mix of people is required, the ideal candidates should …

- be interesting, have opinions and something to say. Be quick-witted and have a bright personality.

- have useful practical skills – they will fend for themselves, build their homes, cook and improve life on the island.

- be fit and healthy. We must avoid any major health problems during the show, and they will be living in basic conditions and not eating well.

- be entertaining, or ready to contribute to the fun. Remember, television is entertainment, and some challenges will not be of the survival type, e.g. there will be Tropical Karaoke.

- have an open mind with regard to this new experience and believe it will be a learning experience.

Also, good TV often means conflict. Selecting assertive personalities that might clash with other strong personalities would be good, but we don't want complete idiots who can't change. The audience wants to see the journey that these characters make, to see how they learn to live together.

KEY LANGUAGE: an informal talk

4a **Listen again to the auditions and complete the extracts below.**

1 _____ , all my life I've come first in everything.

2 _____ surviving on the island, well, I …

3 _____ , that doesn't mean that I'm perfect.

4 _____ , I'm single at the moment …

5 _____ , trying to win International Island will be a challenge …

6 I'm a builder, which I _____ is one of the reasons…

7 I like a good bit of banter, _____ , if there's a chance for a joke, I'll make it.

8 I guess I should say that, _____ , I'm pretty laid back …

9 I get along with most, _____ …

10 So, _____ , I reckon I'd be a great choice …

4b **Choose the formal expressions which match the meanings of the phrases in Exercise 4a.**

1 Generally speaking / By this I mean that

2 Consequently / As far as … is concerned

3 However / Additionally

4 I would just like to add that / With regard to the fact that

5 As one example of many / Moving on

6 believe / understand

7 As I explained earlier / To put it another way

8 Generally speaking / Significantly

9 As one example of many / To be precise

10 To begin with / Taking everything into consideration

5 **Find and underline more examples of language that would be useful in an informal talk in Track 3.4 on page 187.**

6 3.5 **Listen to the producers discussing the two candidates. Who do they select and why?**

TASK: auditioning

7 You are going to audition for *International Island*. First, prepare for your audition by creating a new character for yourself. Use these questions to help prepare.

1 What is your nationality? (choose an English-speaking country)

2 How old are you? (over 18)

3 What is your family, education and employment background?

4 What interests do you have?

5 How would you describe your personality? (think about strengths and weaknesses)

6 What special skills, abilities and qualities do you have?

7 Why should the producers choose you for the show?

8 What do you want to get from the experience?

9 What will you say in your audition?

7b Form large groups (6–8 students) and divide each group in half (As and Bs). First, the As are the producers, and the Bs take it in turns to audition for the show. The producers take notes about each candidate, and may ask interview questions.

7c Swap roles. The Bs are the producers, and the As now audition.

8 Following the auditions, each small group (the As and the Bs) meet as producers and decide which two candidates will be selected for *International Island*. Use your notes and explain your final choices to the other group.

OTHER USEFUL PHRASES

Recalling what someone said

Can you remember what he said about …?

She said …, didn't she?

What did he say about …?

What was it she said about …?

Explaining choices

The main reason I'd choose her is that …

What I really liked about him was that …

The thing that made me choose her was that …

I'd go for him because …

Making a decision

So, do we all agree that …?

Who is it going to be then?

We've got to choose someone; let's go for…

STUDY SKILLS: seminar/ discussion skills

1 You are going to hear part of a seminar on: 'The difference between real conversation and conversation in plays, radio and TV drama and films'. In pairs, discuss these questions.

1 Which plays, films and TV dramas have you seen recently?

2 What kind of skills do you think a dramatist / screenwriter needs?

2 Discuss the following questions.

1 What are the differences between
a) a lecture   b) a seminar   c) a tutorial?

2 What are the advantages of seminars for students? Are there any disadvantages?

3 Tick the skills below that you think seminars may be particularly good at developing.

1 listening actively

2 working with a wide range of different people

3 solving problems

4 communicating effectively by speaking

5 managing differences of opinion and conflict

6 training other people

7 leading a team

4 What can students do to prepare for a seminar? Make a list. Check your answers on page 166.

5a **3.6** Listen to Part 1 of the seminar and put these points in the order you hear them.

1 the way men and women speak is different

2 conversation is cooperative

3 shared background information helps participants understand each other

4 conversation has a lot of pauses, hesitations, etc.

5 utterances are repetitive and short

5b Tell a partner what you can remember about the points from Exercise 5a.

5c **3.7** Listen to Part 2 of the seminar and make notes on the main points. Compare your notes with your partner.

5d What kinds of personalities do the different students have?

6 Look at the bold phrases in the first paragraph of Track 3.6 on page 187. Decide which of the following functions they perform.

1 checking everyone has understood

2 stating the topic of the seminar

3 identifying your role in the seminar

4 making sure the scope of the topic is understood

7 In pairs, choose ten of the bold phrases in Track 3.6 on page 187 and decide what their function is.

8a Which of the phrases below would probably be said by the chair / seminar leader?

1 I see what you're getting at, but …

2 Sorry, I didn't catch that.

3 On balance, we thought that …

4 Lia, we haven't heard from you yet.

5 Miles put it well when he said that …

6 We're running out of time, so …

8b What is the function of the seminar phrases above?

9 As a group, choose ONE of the seminar topics below – or think of your own topic. Prepare for the seminar and practise what you want to say with your partner.

1 Why aren't more young people interested in theatre?

2 Soap operas – a powerful educational tool.

3 The predictable nature of TV drama.

4 Remakes of films – what's the point?

WRITING SKILLS: creative writing (a screenplay)

10 Have you seen or heard of the film *Slumdog Millionaire*? Read this synopsis of the film. Would you like to see it? Why / Why not?

Slumdog Millionaire is a colourful story set in modern India. Jamal Malik is an 18-year-old orphan from the slums of Mumbai, whose life changes when he becomes a contestant on India's *Who Wants To Be A Millionaire*? Just one question away from winning a fortune, he is arrested on suspicion of cheating. To prove his innocence, Jamal tells the dramatic story of his life on the streets, where he has learned the answers to the quiz show's questions.

11 Read an extract from the screenplay / shooting script of the film and answer the following questions:

1 What information do we get at the very beginning of this scene?

2 What do you notice about the balance of dialogue and description in this scene?

3 What do we learn about the personalities of Prem and Jamal from the scene?

4 What features of spoken language can we find here?

5 What are the main characteristics of the descriptive language?

12 Choose one of the following tasks.

1 Write a short extract of a screenplay of a film based on an incident in your life.

2 Continue the screenplay below.

Note: Think carefully about dialogue and don't forget to include some description of the characters, action and atmosphere.

EXT. COUNTRYSIDE. DAY.
The countryside is covered in a thick layer of snow. A young man, DAN, walks heavily across a field towards a tree. He is wearing summer clothes and is barefoot. There is another man, STEVE, standing under the tree. He is wearing thick winter clothes.

```
INT. STUDIO. NIGHT.

                    PREM
        So, what's it to be? Walk away and this cheque
        for sixteen thousand rupees is yours. Look, it's
        even got your name on it.

He produces a cheque and waves it at Jamal.

                    JAMAL
        I don't have a bank account.

Laughter from the audience. Prem is momentarily wrong-
footed.

                    JAMAL (CONT'D)
        But I'll take the cash.

More laughter, this time with Jamal, rather than at him.
Prem gets up and starts rummaging theatrically through his
jacket pockets and trousers.

                    PREM
        Nope. Looks like the Producer's stolen my wallet
        again-

                    JAMAL
        - I'll play.
Nobody was expecting this. Least of all Prem who has to
rearrange his features into one of surprised delight. He
sits down.

                    PREM
        You'll play?

                    JAMAL
        Why not?

                    PREM
        Well, well, well. We've got a wild one, here.

Prem tears up the cheque with theatrical slowness.

                    PREM (CONT'D)
        For sixty-four thousand rupees, Ladies and
        Gentlemen, the question once again.....
```

11.1 UPS AND DOWNS

Business? It's quite simple. It's other people's money.
Alexandre Dumas (1802–1870) French author

SPEAKING

1a List three successful businesses. Why do you think the businesses are successful? Compare your ideas with a partner.

1b Tick the practices below that you think apply to the businesses you mentioned.

A successful business:

1 constantly innovates, diversifies and takes risks.

2 pays fixed salaries without bonuses or other fringe benefits.

3 makes redundancies to cut costs.

4 keeps overheads down by manufacturing/ outsourcing abroad.

5 makes as much money for shareholders as possible.

6 invests heavily in PR and advertising to create brand awareness.

7 eliminates the competition to gain market share.

8 uses creative accounting to pay less tax.

9 gets customers to pay in advance but pays suppliers as late as possible.

1c Which of the practices do you think are common in business?

1d Which are the least acceptable to you? Why?

VOCABULARY: business and economic terms

2a Choose a word from each column below which when joined with *and* and *to* make common business and economic terms.

imports and exports

A	B
supply	loss
boom	exports
imports	liabilities
profit	mergers
takeovers	loans
income	debtors
mortgages	expenditure
creditors	demand
assets	slump

2b Match the words from Exercise 2a to the definitions below.

1 the relationship between the goods and services available and what consumers want to buy

2 periods when an economy or business is doing well or badly

3 things owned by a business and things owed by a business

4 the money earned and spent by a government or business

5 changes in the ownership and running of businesses

6 financial products on which interest is charged

7 people or organisations owed money by others or owing money to others

READING

3 What sort of information do you expect to find in the business pages of a newspaper / news website?

4a Read the stories on this page. Which are 'Business Bites' and which are 'Economic Bites'?

A _____

Paradise Place, the struggling luxury travel group is seeking a substantial cash injection to avoid almost certain bankruptcy, after recording further plunging profits this year. Any potential investor would be taking on $56 million of debt. According to a spokesperson, the company could go into administration within weeks unless a buyer is found.

B _____

Trade in counterfeit goods in the UK has escalated. New figures show that the trade in pirate DVDs, fake designer goods and other aspects of the underground economy, may have cost the government up to £1.5 billion in lost tax revenue in the past year. With tax revenues falling due to the economic slump, there is a real threat to future public spending, a spokesperson announced.

C _____

'Rabbit', the mobile phone giant, continues to go from strength to strength in a fiercely competitive market. Turnover and profits are well up on this time last year. It has just announced a further expansion of its workforce with the creation of 2000 new jobs and the opening of 350 new retail outlets across Europe over the next two years.

D _____

The Japanese stock market remains volatile. Yesterday was another day of heavy trading with share prices falling again. Although there was a slight recovery towards the end of the day, the forecast is bleak as market confidence remains low due to the effects of the global recession.

E _____

Business is booming for leading engineering company Phoenix Industries and its subsidiaries in Australia and South East Asia. Pre-tax profits rose by 23% according to interim results released this week and sustained growth is forecast for the rest of the year, which will please shareholders. The reported acquisition of the ailing Medusa Group could be completed by the end of next month.

F _____

There has been another surge in German unemployment figures announced today. Predictions are that they will reach a peak in the next three months. There are further gloomy forecasts that industry will be hit hard by the economic slump. Manufacturing output will drop sharply, while capital investment by firms will plummet. Meanwhile the inflation rate continues to climb, edging towards 4%.

G _____

In the US, falls in the exchange rate have led to a much more positive balance of trade. The trade deficit has been reduced significantly and the government hopes that this will stimulate growth and lead to a small surplus by early next year. There has been further speculation about the introduction of import tariffs and quotas to help the badly hit car industry.

4b Match the following headings to the correct story.

1 Black market boom
2 Investment fears
3 Paradise Lost?
4 Optimistic trade outlook
5 Takeover follows growth
6 Economy suffers downturn
7 Telecoms firm expands

4c Now, read the stories again and answer these questions.

1 Which companies are doing well/badly?
2 Which economies are doing well/badly?

5 Find words or phrases in the stories which mean the following:

1 shops
2 money earned from sales during a particular period of time
3 not genuine/original products
4 the general rise in prices
5 companies owned or controlled by a larger company
6 the failure of a business
7 difference between the value of a country's imports and exports
8 a negative balance of trade
9 a period of negative growth

6a Find words and phrases in the texts which refer to trends. Are they ↑↓ or something else?

falling ↓

6b What other phrases referring to trends can you add to the list?

SPEAKING

7a You are responsible for the distribution of the public spending budget for your country (i.e. the income from taxes, loans, etc.). Think about the different areas of spending in the table on page 160 and follow steps 1–3.

1 Fill in the budget for this year to show what you imagine the current situation is.
2 Decide on your priorities for next year.
3 Fill in the budget for next year.

7b Work in groups to present your ideas.

WRITING

8 Write a short summary of the main points of your budget.

SPEAKING

1 In groups, answer the following questions.

1 How much do you worry about:
   a) the money you have now?
   b) getting a job / keeping your job?
   c) having enough money when you retire?

2 Do you look carefully at what you spend?

3 How do you try to save money?

4 How do you think an economic recession affects:
   a) young people?
   b) elderly people?

READING

2 Read the article below, written in 2009 during the global financial crisis. Write an appropriate headline for it.

3 Read the article again and answer the following questions.

1 Who does the author say was to blame for the financial crisis?

2 What examples does the author give to show that we are not good at learning from past mistakes?

3 What evidence is there that mistakes are being forgotten?

4 Do you think the author is optimistic or pessimistic about the future? Give reasons for your answer.

4a A metaphor is a word or expression used in a non-literal way to represent something else. Find three metaphors in the text that involve parts of the body. What do they mean?

4b What other metaphors involving parts of the body can you think of?

Helen Tate asks whether we are capable of learning anything from the fallout of the financial crisis.

Even before the dust had settled on the wreckage of our financial institutions, the accusations were flying. Who was really to blame? Was it the arrogant and greedy investment bankers who were only too happy to take huge risks with loans and credit as long as they were taking home enormous bonuses? Was it the mortgage lenders, who were prepared to lend money to people far in excess of their creditworthiness? Were the politicians and regulators at fault for allowing debt to build up unchecked? Or were the homebuyers culpable for taking out loans they could never expect to repay? And let's not forget the savers, who were content to take the returns on offer without asking why the rates were so high.

Of course, the truth is that all of the above contributed to the collapse and, unless we stop pointing the finger at each other and focus on the serious business of recognising our collective responsibility for our predicament, we will find ourselves repeating the same mistakes.

Let's face it, we are not good at learning lessons from past errors. The Great Depression of the 1930s was, like the current crisis, preceded by a housing boom, a long period of cheap credit and a stock market crash. There are also disturbing parallels between recent developments and the events in Japan in the 1990s.

But already there are worrying signs of our amnesia. Investment banks are falling back into old habits, hiring high-fliers on mind-boggling salaries and bonus incentives to the mantra of 'We need good people'. Meanwhile, governments are wavering in their commitment to impose the tough financial regulations that they were banging their fists about only months ago. It is as though we can only look backwards for so long. Then we shrug our shoulders and head unwittingly in the direction of the next crisis.

The solution is not to vent our anger at each other. Instead, we all need to pause – bankers, borrowers, lenders, savers, legislators and regulators – and acknowledge our collective failure. Then we must have the courage to take the necessary steps, whether political, corporate or personal, to prevent yet another cycle of boom and bust.

VOCABULARY: confusing words

5a **Choose one of the words in brackets to complete each sentence below.**

1 We took out a personal _____ to pay for our holiday. (debt, loan)

2 Can you _____ me ten dollars until tomorrow? (lend, borrow)

3 The _____ reason for the company's failure was the recession. (principle, principal)

4 Our _____ are trying to get their money back. (creditors, debtors)

5 The _____ of the new legislation will be to increase the tax bill for small companies. (affect, effect)

6 This is sensitive information, so I must ask you to be _____ . (discrete, discreet)

7 Please keep the management informed of any changes as they _____ . (arise, rise)

5b **Write sentences with the words NOT used in Exercise 5a. Use a dictionary to help you.**

GRAMMAR: alternatives to *if*

6 **Read the article again and find other alternatives to *if* and add them to the list below:**

Necessary	*provided that, on (the) condition that, assuming, but for, not … until,*[1]_____
Imaginary	*in case, what if, suppose/supposing*
Unexpected	*even if*
Alternative	*whether (or not)*
Negative	[2]_____

7 **What is the difference in meaning (if any) between the sentences in each pair?**

1 a) If we do not learn lessons from the past, people will lose their jobs.
   b) Unless we learn lessons from the past, people will lose their jobs.

2 a) They were happy only if they were taking home enormous bonuses.
   b) They were happy as long as they were taking home enormous bonuses.

3 a) I'll attend the conference in case the Chairman is going.
   b) I'll attend the conference if the Chairman is going.

4 a) You can get a mortgage if you are self-employed.
   b) You can get a mortgage even if you are self-employed.

   ➡ Language reference and extra practice, pages 154–155

8 **Rewrite the sentences using the words in bold.**

1 If you hadn't been so generous, the charity would have closed down. **but for**

2 We will succeed if we all work together as a team. **as long as**

3 What would you do if you won the lottery? **supposing**

4 I will agree to those conditions if you increase my commission. **provided that**

5 If we don't win this contract, we'll all lose our jobs. **unless**

6 He will only sign the contract if we give him a pay rise. **unless**

7 If I don't see you again before you go, have a great holiday. **in case**

8 The search can tell us about his outstanding debts, if he has any. **whether or not**

9 They agreed to lend her the money if it was repaid by 1st December. **on condition that**

10 How are you going to finance your studies If you get a place at university? **assuming**

LISTENING

9a **3.8** **Listen to a banker talking about how he was made redundant during the financial crisis and answer the following questions.**

1 How did he find out he was going to lose his job?

2 What problems does he mention about people losing their jobs?

3 Why was he lucky?

4 Does he change his mind about anything while he's talking?

5 How do you think he feels now about the whole experience?

9b **Identify the features of natural spoken speech in Track 3.8 on page 189.**

SPEAKING AND WRITING

10a **Work in groups. Do you agree with the viewpoint of the article that everyone was equally to blame for the financial crisis? If not, who do you think was most to blame and why? Discuss your ideas.**

10b **Write a paragraph giving your opinion.**

SPEAKING AND READING

1a Work in groups to give some examples of times when you have had to negotiate in your life, e.g. with noisy neighbours.

1b Discuss the following questions:

1 Are you afraid of negotiating? Why / Why not?

2 When you negotiate, do you usually concede more than you should?

3 Do you get caught up in arguments when negotiating?

4 Do you think of negotiating in terms of winners and losers?

2a You are going to read some advice on negotiating. Think of five pieces of advice that might appear in the text.

2b Read the advice sheet and check which of your predictions were mentioned.

3 Read the advice sheet again. Which do you think are the five most useful pieces of advice? Why?

VOCABULARY: suffixes (nouns 2)

4 Make nouns from the verbs in the box by using the suffixes *-tion* and *-sion*. Check the spelling and meaning of any words you do not know in a good dictionary.

abstain admit clarify collide confuse decide discriminate eliminate extend indicate instigate negotiate permit

5 Complete the sentences with the correct noun from Exercise 4.

1 Rising house prices are a(n) _____ of confidence in the economy.

2 She felt a sense of _____ that she was not being promoted as quickly as her male colleagues.

3 The CEO's _____ that she had lied shocked the shareholders.

4 The unions will try to force further _____ from the management.

5 Alicia's been given a(n) _____ to finish her report.

6 Some further _____ of your position is needed.

7 No final _____ has been taken, but a merger between the two companies seems likely.

8 The inquiry was set up at the _____ of the Chairman.

NEGOTIATING TIPS

Are you a nervous negotiator? Or are you the aggressive type, who tries to win at all costs?
The advice below can help you to improve your negotiating skills.

■ First of all, find out everything you can about the other party. Preparation is vital. Clarify your priorities and be ready to concede less important points. Keep your negotiating strategy simple and flexible.

■ Plan ahead for what you are willing to give up. Know your bottom line or BATNA (Best Alternative To A Negotiated Agreement). This represents the point you turn down their offer and stop negotiating.

■ Create the right ambiance for a win-win negotiation. Try to put yourself in the other party's shoes. Think about what they really need. Stress the need for agreement from the outset and only engage in constructive arguments.

■ If you are negotiating in a foreign country be prepared to fit in with their style of negotiating. Planning is crucial. Learn about the customs, values and practices of the people you are going to negotiate with.

■ Set the negotiations up so there won't be time pressures on anyone. If the other party try to bring up a completely new issue, then call for an adjournment. Also, if you are making no progress on a very difficult point, suggest you come back to it later.

■ Identify who the decision-maker is. Make sure you know who you're talking to. But don't be intimidated by status.

■ Control your emotions when negotiating. Don't give yourself away. Hide short tempers and frustration and never walk out in a rage. Never show fear or anger in face of intimidation. Remember, it's not personal. As soon as emotion enters into the negotiation you are likely to lose.

Be assertive, not aggressive, Focus on issues, not emotions.

■ Be the best listener you can be. Wait for the other party to finish their proposal before responding. Listen to the tone of voice as well as the words.

■ Watch out for body language that might give you some indication of how the other side is feeling or indicate a shift in position.

■ When you've made an important concession, you should point it out and emphasise that each concession is a serious loss for you. Don't concede ground unless you receive something in return.

■ After you've closed the deal, don't go on talking. Shut up. Stand up. Shake hands. And leave.

BE POLITE, BE PERSISTENT AND KEEP YOUR FOCUS

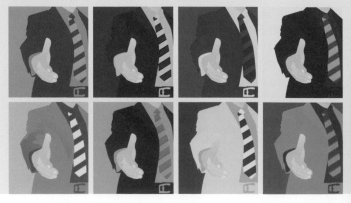

GRAMMAR: phrasal verbs

6 Find the highlighted phrasal verbs in the advice sheet that mean:

1 mention / introduce a topic
2 get information
3 show your feelings
4 let go / lose
5 explain / highlight
6 arrange / organise
7 refuse
8 return
9 work well with others in a group
10 continue
11 be quiet
12 rise to your feet
13 be careful because of danger

7 Read the language reference on page 154, then look at the phrasal verbs and answer the questions:

Stand up…

… you should point it out…

This represents the point you turn down their offer…

1 Which phrasal verbs are transitive and which are intransitive?
2 What is the difference in the structures of the phrasal verbs?

8a Choose the best answer, a), b) or c). There may be one or two correct answers.

1 With transitive phrasal verbs, if the *object* is a noun we can put it:
   a) between the verb and the particle
   b) after the particle
   c) before the verb
2 With transitive phrasal verbs, if the *object* is a pronoun we can put it:
   a) between the verb and the particle
   b) after the particle
   c) before the verb

8b Find other examples of transitive phrasal verbs in the advice sheet. Some may not have a direct object.

GRAMMAR TIP

With transitive phrasal verbs:
- We cannot put an adverb between the verb and particle or between the particle and object.

I turned reluctantly down the offer ✗
I turned the offer down reluctantly ✓
Reluctantly, I turned the offer down ✓

- We cannot put a relative pronoun immediately before or after the particle.

That's the offer which down I turned ✗
That's the offer which I turned down ✓

9 Put the words in brackets in the correct order to complete the sentences:

1 I was in a hurry so (I the out problem quickly pointed)
2 The Chairman wants the meeting in the morning , so (I've ten it set for up o'clock)
3 That's the colleague (gave last smoking who up week)
4 The topic was controversial so (I it up carefully brought)
5 Unfortunately, it was the secret (which found out I had)
6 Golf was too expensive so (I gave immediately up it)
7 She made me a good offer but (I've turned down it)

10 In pairs, take it in turns to answer the following questions.

1 Have you ever turned a job down?
2 Have you ever filled in a form and then regretted it?
3 What is the best thing you have set up?
4 Have you ever found out an important secret?
5 Did you fit in well with your classmates when you were younger?
6 Do you like to have your mistakes pointed out to you?
7 Have you ever given anything up?
8 Do you know when to shut up or do you tend to go on talking?

SPEAKING

11 Work in pairs to prepare for negotiation. Remember to try to see the situation from the other person's point of view.

Sales Representative: turn to page 159.

Sales Manager: turn to page 161.

SITUATION

Kenneth and Ingrid Carter own a company called Marine Instruments. They have recently developed a marine product, an alarm device which helps sailors to locate a member of their crew who has fallen overboard. They need finance to launch the product and to cover their initial marketing costs. They have contacted two investment firms who may be able to help them: Neptune Investments and Ariel Capital. Both firms provide capital and advice for start-up companies and in return expect to share in the profits of the company. This is usually in the form of a percentage stake (shareholding) in the company. Neptune and Ariel like to invest in companies run by enthusiastic, motivated people who have exciting products to develop.

Kenneth and Ingrid have arranged to meet Neptune Investments first. Neptune directors will question Kenneth and Ingrid about their product, and if all goes well, will negotiate a deal with them.

Details of the marine product are given below.

1   Read the situation and the description of the product. Then, in pairs, discuss the following:

1   What kind of companies do the investment firms finance?

2   How do the investment firms get a return on their money?

3   How does the MLSD save lives?

4   Do you think the MLSD is a marketable product? Give reasons for your answer.

2   If you were directors of one of the investment companies, what questions would you ask the inventors of the device? Make a list.

3   **3.9**   Kenneth and Ingrid meet directors from Neptune Investments. Listen to Part 1 and make notes on the points below.

- unique features of the MLSD
- patents
- tests
- production
- target consumer
- plans for the future

MLSD (marine life-saving device) helps to locate and search for crew members who have fallen overboard from a boat or yacht. The device is attached to the clothing of crew members. If someone falls into the sea, it automatically emits an signal which gives the exact location of the person who has gone overboard to someone on the boat. It also sends a signal to other boats in the area. As a result, crew members who fall into the water can be quickly recovered either by their own boat or other boats which are nearby.

KEY LANGUAGE: setting the agenda, responding to offers

4a **3.10** Listen to Part 2 and answer the questions.

1 What financial terms do Kenneth and Ingrid offer Neptune?

2 Why do the two sides fail to make a deal?

4b Complete the gaps in the extracts below. Then listen and check.

1 **N1:** Let's talk about the agenda for this afternoon. I propose we discuss three specific _____ : the amount of our _____ in your business, the _____ you can offer us and other _____ you're working on.

Kenneth: _____ OK to me.

Ingrid: Yeah, that's _____ .

2 **N2:** Well, I'm sorry, but that's not _____ . Investing half a million for a 15 per cent stake wouldn't _____ us.

3 **Ingrid:** If I can come in here, let me remind you of the ____ you'll get from investing in our device. Don't forget it's a ____ product, and several marine associations have _____ it. Also, it's got an international _____ .

4 **N1:** Maybe. But we're not _____ about the terms you offer. We're not _____ to invest in the project unless you improve your offer.

Kenneth: How about if we _____ you a bigger stake, would you be _____ to give us $500,000?

5 **Kenneth:** _____ we give you a 20 per cent stake for the full amount. What do you say?

N1: I'm sorry. We were _____ for a much higher stake.

Kenneth: Well, that's our final offer. It looks as if we can't _____ a deal.

5a The extracts above demonstrate four different ways of responding to proposals. Match each extract 1–5 to function a–d below.

a) accepting a proposal

b) using persuasive arguments

c) rejecting a proposal

d) bargaining

5b Which sentence in the extracts refers to the points that will be negotiated?

TASK: negotiating a contract

6 Having failed to make a deal with Neptune Investments, the two inventors have now set up a meeting with two directors from Ariel Capital. They are ready to negotiate a contract, providing they can agree on the terms.

Group A: turn to page 158.

Group B: turn to page 161.

7 Begin the negotiation. Try to make a deal that will satisfy both parties.

8 Now work as one group and discuss the following questions.

1 What strategy and tactics did you use in your negotiation? How successful were they?

2 How do you feel about the outcome of the negotiation? Was everyone happy with the result? If not, what went wrong?

OTHER USEFUL PHRASES

Making concessions

We're prepared to … if you'll …

We'll increase our offer provided you / as long as you …

Suppose we … would you be willing to…?

Accepting an offer

Fine! OK! Right!

Sounds good to me.

OK, that's acceptable to us.

Rejecting an offer

I'm afraid it's not acceptable.

Sorry, but we can't agree to that.

We were hoping for / expecting …

STUDY SKILLS: making a business presentation

1 In groups, discuss the following.

1 What makes a good presentation? Make a list of guidelines for presenters.

2 'A presentation is a performance.' Do you agree? Give reasons for your answer.

3 What kinds of presentations are common in business?

2 Introduction This is used to welcome your audience and explain the structure of the talk. Complete the gaps in the introduction with the words or phrases in the box. In pairs, practise saying the introduction.

> After that   By the end of my talk   Finally
> First of all, I'll comment   I'll be happy to
> answer   The purpose

Good afternoon everyone, my name's Rachel Chen. I'm Marketing Director of First Service, a maker of sports equipment. ¹_____ of my presentation is to familiarise you with our exciting new product, our *Winner 100* tennis racket. ²_____ briefly on the results of some research we've done. Next, I'll describe the unique features of the product. Then, I'll give you a profile of our target consumer. ³_____ , I'll talk about our plans for launching the product. ⁴_____ , I'll summarise my key points and make a proposal for future action. ⁵_____ , you should have enough information to start planning how you'll sell the new racket. ⁶_____ any questions when I've finished my talk.

3a Body of the presentation Use signalling language to structure your information. Match the functions (1–8) to the signalling language used in the sentences (a–i) below.

1 Giving an example

2 Introducing the subject

3 Finishing one subject

4 Analysing a point

5 Referring to a visual aid

6 Summarising

7 Starting another subject

8 Answering a question

9 Concluding

a) **First of all, I'll** talk briefly about the research we carried out.

b) **OK, I've told you about** our research and explained why we needed to produce a state-of-the-art racket.

c) **Moving on now to** the *Winner 100* range …

d) **For instance,** all the players in our focus group reported increased power.

e) **What does that mean for our marketing?** It means our product has a unique selling point.

f) **I'll come back to that point later,** if I may.

g) **To illustrate my point,** I'll show you a film of professionals playing with a Winner racket.

h) **I'd now like to recap.** I explained why we need to launch a new racket …

i) **Thanks very much everyone for coming to my presentation. Any questions?**

3b In pairs, practise saying the signalling language.

4a Conclusion Look at the following descriptions of how to conclude a presentation. Which do you think is most suitable for the presentation in Exercise 2?

a) Restate the main point but say it a little differently.

b) Finish with an impressive quotation.

c) Sum up, make a recommendation, thank your audience.

d) End by telling a human interest story.

e) Say something that reminds the audience of your original objective.

f) Conclude with a positive statement which encourages the audience to take action.

g) Say something inspiring which will stick in the audience's mind.

4b Write a short conclusion to the presentation. Use one of the ideas in Exercise 4a or choose your own.

5 Practise making a presentation about a new piece of sports or fitness equipment which your company has just launched. Answer any questions that your colleagues wish to ask.

WRITING SKILLS: a tactful business email

6 In small groups, discuss the question below.

Why is it necessary to take extra care with the language you use when sending emails at work?

7 Read the feedback on a presentation by Karl Meyer, a new sales manager. Rank the complaints according to how serious they are.

Here are some typical comments from the feedback forms:

1 'He arrived late and was very nervous. I don't think he'd prepared his talk properly.'

2 'I was sitting at the back of the room. None of the back row could hear what he said.'

3 'What a boring voice! I switched off after a couple of minutes. And I wasn't the only one.'

4 'He didn't seem to have any plan for his talk. It was like an improvised monologue, no structure at all.'

5 'He forgot to mention the most important thing, the unique selling points of the new product.'

6 'He read most of his presentation. There wasn't much eye contact. He had no rapport with his audience.'

7 'His powerpoint didn't work properly. He got his slides mixed up and looked really embarrassed. He kept apologising, which annoyed me.'

8 'I asked some straightforward questions, but he couldn't answer them. How can I sell the product if I can't answer my customers' queries?'

9 'He ran out of time, so he raced through the last ten minutes of his talk.'

10 'It was one of the worst presentations I've ever attended!'

8a Paraphrasing Match paraphrases (a–f) of some of the complaints in Exercise 7 to the original complaints (1–6).

a) A member of the audience mentioned that your voice was rather low.

b) It was suggested that you arrived late and seemed a little nervous.

c) Varying the tone and pitch of your voice would improve the delivery of your presentation.

d) Unfortunately, you failed to mention the unique selling points of the product.

e) Several participants felt that your talk lacked a clear structure.

f) It's probably not a good idea to read a presentation because you need to keep eye contact with your audience.

8b What words or phrases in each paraphrase help to express the participants' opinions in a tactful way? Try to explain how the words/phrases do this.

8c Paraphrase complaints 7–10 from Exercise 7 so the opinions are expressed in a tactful way.

9 As Karl Meyer's boss, write a tactful email to him, giving feedback on his presentation and advising him on how to improve his performance.

Dear Karl,

I've received some feedback from members of the audience who attended your recent presentation to our local distributors. Unfortunately, there were some negative comments about your presentation …

10 Compare your answer with the model answer on page 168.

12 Science and nature

12.1 SCIENCE FICTION

My spirits were elevated by the enchanting appearance of nature.
From *Frankenstein*, by Mary Shelley (1797–1851) English author

SPEAKING

1 Discuss these questions.

1 What are hot topics in science and nature today in your country / in the world? Do these topics appear in any novels or films?

2 Do you ever read science fiction books or watch science fiction films? Why / Why not?

3 What do you know about science fiction?

LISTENING

2a Look at the posters on these pages of three science fiction films that are based on books and answer the questions.

1 Do you know any of these films, or the books they are based on? What are they about? If you don't know them, what do you think they might be about?

2 How does each poster try to appeal to its audience?

3 Which is the most effective? Most artistic? Most attractive?

2b `3.11` Listen to three descriptions. Match them with the posters.

2c Listen again and try to remember as much as possible, without writing anything down. Then compare with a partner. Then check Track 3.11 on page 190.

READING

3a Read an extract from one of the three novels. Which one do you think it comes from?

3b In pairs, discuss these questions.

1 In your view, who is the narrator?

2 Who is Rheya, do you think? What is her relationship with the narrator?

3 Where do you think they are?

4 What do you think has happened in the narrator's life since he last saw Rheya?

5 Why do you think she looks both 'serious' and 'surprised'?

6 Why do you think the narrator thinks of throwing something at her?

7 Do you think the narrator is really dreaming?

8 What do you think happens next?

VOCABULARY: science and nature subject words

4a Put the words in the box into one of the four categories.

Geography and Geology   Physics and Chemistry
Biology and Zoology   Astronomy

| blossom   carnivorous   germinate   jellyfish |
| mercury   meteor   orbit   parasite   pollination |
| polythene   ridge   volcano |

4b Try to add more words to the categories.

SPEAKING AND WRITING

5a In pairs, think of a brief scenario for a science fiction novel or film. Discuss the characters, setting, narrative, etc. Then tell another pair about your scenario.

5b In one paragraph, write up the scenario you thought of in Exercise 5a.

For a long time, I lay there peacefully gazing back at her. My first thought was reassuring: I was dreaming and I was aware that I was dreaming. Nevertheless, I would have preferred her not to be there. I closed my eyes and tried to shake off the dream. When I opened them again, Rheya was still sitting opposite me. Her lips were pouting slightly – a habit of hers – as though she were about to whistle; but her expression was serious. I thought of my recent speculations on the subject of dreams.

She had not changed since the day I had seen her for the last time; she was then a girl of nineteen. Today, she would be twenty-nine. But, evidently, the dead do not change; they remain eternally young. She went on gazing at me, an expression of surprise on her face. I thought of throwing something at her, but, even in a dream, I could not bring myself to harm a dead person.

I murmured: 'Poor little thing, have you come to visit me?'

The sound of my voice frightened me; the room, Rheya, everything seemed extraordinarily real. A three-dimensional dream, coloured in half-tones … I saw several objects on the floor which I had not noticed when I went to bed. When I wake up, I told myself, I shall check whether these things are still there, or whether, like Rheya, I only saw them in a dream.

'Do you mean to stay for long?' I asked. I realised that I was speaking very softly, like someone afraid of being overheard. Why worry about eavesdroppers in a dream?

The sun was rising over the horizon. A good sign. I had gone to bed during a red day, which should have been succeeded by a blue day, followed by another red day. I had not slept for fifteen hours at a stretch. So it was a dream!

Reassured, I looked closely at Rheya. She was silhouetted against the sun. The scarlet rays cast a glow over the smooth skin of her left cheek and the shadows of her eyelashes fell across her face. How pretty she was! Even in my sleep my memory of her was uncannily precise. I watched the movements of the sun, waiting to see the dimple appear in that unusual place slightly below the corner of the lips. All the same, I would have preferred to wake up. It was time I did some work. I closed my eyelids tightly.

I heard a metallic noise, and opened my eyes again. Rheya was still sitting beside me on the bed, still looking at me gravely. I smiled at her. She smiled back at me and leant forward.

64

65

LISTENING

1 In pairs, discuss the following questions.

1 What do you have with you today that is made of plastic?

2 There are claims that plastic is a blight upon our lives. Why?

2a ▮3.12▮ Listen to a video blog. Make notes on the blogger's main points.

2b Which of these points did / didn't you know before?

READING

3 Skim the text below and answer these questions.

1 What is the subject of the text? What is the writer's basic opinion?

2 How would you describe his attitude?

3 Where do you think the text comes from?

4 Read the text again. Identify the key points in each paragraph. How do they relate to the video blogger's points?

5 Which of these points would undermine the scientist's argument?

1 The production of plastic from oil requires large amounts of energy.

2 Toxic chemicals leech from plastic into the environment.

3 Its comparatively low weight reduces fuel consumption during transportation.

4 The decomposition of biodegradable plastic produces CO_2.

6 With whom do you most agree, the video blogger or the scientist? Why?

SCIENTIFICA

Newsletters

A I've had it up to here with all the rubbish that tree-huggers like you spout about plastic, particularly on as informed a site as this **one.** Anyone would imagine that the discovery of this wonder material marks the lowest point in human civilization. Well, it **doesn't.** Thankfully, we're no longer living in the stone-age, so let's make the most of the **plastic one**.

B There's no point denying that plastic is a miracle **material** that's more versatile, more durable and more effective than any other **substance.** We've made more advances thanks to its invention than we ever **did before,** too **many for** me to bother listing here. You'd have to be bonkers to deny that. It would be nearly impossible to live without it. Try **doing so;** you won't manage to for long.

C What about the materials plastic has taken the place of? They're hardly eco-neutral, and **extracting** and **producing** them is just as bad. How much energy goes into **making** glass? **Mining** releases all kinds of poisonous **substances** into the environment, **chemicals** like mercury. All told, do plastic-based materials cause any more problems than any **others**? I **reckon not,** and they're a whole lot more useful.

D The oil argument is often wheeled out by the anti-plastic brigade, turning a blind eye to the fact that we get most plastic from a by-product of the oil refining. So, plastic is actually made from what would otherwise go to waste. How green is that?

E As for the claims that not all plastic can be recycled, well, point of fact – all types of plastic **can be.** The problem isn't the **stuff** itself; it's how we deal with it. If we wanted to recycle every last bit of it, we **could. Will we** in the future? I hope **so.** Anyway, bio-degradable plastic (from corn, not oil!) is coming on in leaps and bounds, so, soon, the waste issue may be a non-issue. On top of that, plastic makes up little more than 5 per cent of the rubbish in your bin; that's the **same** as glass.

F So, why does plastic get all this bad press? Quite simply, you can see it and it's unsightly. Well, I'm sorry, but, of all the types of pollution, the **visual sort** doesn't figure too highly on my list of threats to us. There are many dangerous invisible pollutants going into the sea that we should worry about, but **don't** because we can't see them. And besides, does it matter if a seagull builds its nest out of bits of plastic? I think **not.**

G Now, while this may be a bit of a rant, it's not an ill-informed **one,** as I'm a polymer scientist working in environmental technology. So, let's all sing 'Happy Birthday' to our flexible friend, polythene.

VOCABULARY: informal phrases

7a Find the informal words or phrases in the text which have the same meaning as the neutral phrases below.

1 unable to tolerate more (paragraph A)

2 environmentally concerned people (para. A)

3 talk incessantly (para. A)

4 to expend time and effort doing something (para. B)

5 insane (para. B)

6 referred to and presented (para. D)

7 a group of people against synthetic materials (para. D)

8 an uncontrolled or aggressive argument (para. G)

7b Complete the example sentences below by using the informal language in Exercise 7a. Make any necessary changes.

1 You must _____ to want to stay here with the hurricane coming.

2 I've _____ with that racket. Turn that music down!

3 It's good to have a good _____ every now and again; it helps clear the air.

4 I can't _____ to do the washing up. Let's do it when we get back.

8 Find other examples of colloquial vocabulary in the text and make those examples more formal.

GRAMMAR: cohesion 2 (substitution and ellipsis)

9a Match the types of substitution 1–5 with examples a–e below.

1 Lexical substitution: replace a word with a synonym, or near-synonym.

2 Nominal substitution: replace a noun / noun phrase with a word such as *one*, *ones*, the *sort*.

3 Verbal substitution: replace a verb / verb phrase with *do* or *do so*.

4 Clausal substitution: replace a whole clause with *so* or *not*.

5 Ellipsis (zero substitution): completely omit the repeated item. This often happens after words like *other*, *all*, *some*, *not*, *enough*.

a) Are plastic-based materials any worse than any others we use industrially?

b) There's no point denying that plastic is a miracle material that's more versatile, more durable and more effective than any other substance.

c) Does it matter if a seagull builds its nest out of bits of plastic? I think not.

d) Now, while this may be a bit of a rant, it's not an ill-informed one.

e) We've made more advances thanks to its invention than we ever did before.

9b Look at the bold examples in the text. Which words have been replaced or omitted?

➡ Language reference and extra practice, pages 156–157

10 Rewrite the sentences using the substitution techniques. More than one answer may be possible.

1 Is plastic a wonder material? I thought it was a wonder material until I watched the video blog.

2 Poor heat resistance is a weakness of biodegradable plastic, and its lack of strength is another weakness of it.

3 It is important to re-use plastic bags. If you re-use them you are actively reducing waste.

4 Chemical leeching may be a problem caused by plastic, but I'm not sure it is a serious problem.

5 We manufacture so many things out of plastic. We manufacture carpets and clothes. We manufacture components for cars and computers. How could we live without it?

SPEAKING

11 In small groups, discuss the following:

1 What do you and your country do to limit the use and consumption of plastic? How effective are these measures?

2 How would you have to change your lifestyle in order to live for a month without buying anything made of plastic?

3 What other materials have caused great change in the world?

WRITING

12 Choose one or two of the paragraphs from the text. Rewrite them in a formal register.

1a Make a list of as many insects and similar creatures as you can in one minute. Compare with a partner. What do you know about them? Discuss their differences. Do you like/dislike them?

1b Read this quote. What do you think it means?

'If the bee disappeared off the surface of the globe, then man would only have four years of life left.' Attributed to Albert Einstein

A WORLD WITHOUT BEES

ALISON BENJAMIN AND BRIAN McCALLUM

2a Read the blurb (A) from this book cover. How does it try to interest you in the book?

A

From London to Los Angeles, from Slovenia to Taiwan, honeybees are dying. In America, one in three hives was left lifeless at the beginning of 2008; in France, the death rate might be 60 per cent. In Britain, a government minister warns that honeybees could be extinct within a decade.

If or when the world loses its black-and-yellow workers, agriculture will collapse. Civilisation itself might be the next victim. A third of all we eat, and much of what we wear, relies on pollination by honeybees.

What is behind the catastrophe? Viruses, parasites, pesticides and climate change have all been blamed. Some accuse beekeepers themselves of working their charges to death by shipping their hives thousands of miles every year to different monoculture sites, all in the name of agribusiness profits. In this fascinating book, two keen amateur apiarists investigate the claims and counterclaims with the scientists and beekeepers in Europe, America and beyond. And they ask the question that will soon be on everyone's lips: is there any possible way of saving

2b Which of these words describe the blurb?

apocalyptic   apocryphal   apologetic   apoplectic

3a Which parts of the book do you think these extracts (B–E) come from? Choose from the list below.

1   In the beginning was the buzz (Introduction / Chapter 1)

2   The enemy within (Chapter 7)

3   A world without bees (Chapter 10)

B

The mountains of southern Sichuan in China are covered in pear trees. Every April, they are home to a rare sight: thousands of people holding bamboo sticks with chicken feathers attached to the end, clambering among the blossom-laden branches. Closer inspection reveals that children, parents and even grandparents are all pollinating the trees by hand. It is a ritual they have been following for more than 20 years, ever since pesticides killed their honeybees.

C

Apis mellifera, or the western honeybee as she is more commonly known, has been revered for thousands of years for her ability to make a sweet substance that delights the human palate. The earliest record of humans' use of honey is a cave painting in Valencia, Spain, depicting a man climbing a cliff to rob a swarm of wild bees. It dates back at least 10,000 years, to just after the last ice age, and the love affair has continued ever since.

D

Is this what the honeybees are telling us? That our industrialised farming with its monocultures, pesticides and increasingly unreasonable demands on honeybees themselves is not sustainable? With their limited resistance to poisons and pollutants, are they the canary in the coal mine warning us that if our lifestyles are killing them, we are not far behind?

E

By the early 19th century, honey was no longer the standard sweetening agent in Britain. The arrival of cheap sugar meant there was no need for every household in the land to have a hive in the garden. But as industrialisation expanded, the beehive, symbol of both hard work and the acceptance of the social order, still featured in Victorian society. Many buildings of the time had bees in their decoration, like Manchester's neo-gothic town hall.

3b In which section of the text (A–E) do we read about the following? There may be more than one possible answer.

1   the function of honeybees as an early warning system

2   an example of bees no longer performing their role as pollinators

3   the possible contribution of beekeepers to the current crisis

4   the name entomologists use for the western honeybee

5   a change in diet

6   an example of the way bees provide us with more than food

7 a change in the way of keeping bees

8 the fact that the authors of the book do not keep bees as a living

9 the use of bees in art

10 the metaphorical meanings we attribute to bees

3c What do you think about the argument of this book? Do you know of any similar problems?

VOCABULARY: collective nouns

4a Complete the groups of people, animals or things below with the collective nouns in the box.

| flock herd pack ~~swarm~~ |
| shoal bunch group set |

a swarm of wild bees

1 a _____ of grapes, flowers, keys

2 a _____ of wolves, hounds, cards

3 a _____ of elephants, cattle, cows, deer

4 a _____ of fish

5 a _____ of sheep, goats, birds, geese

6 a _____ of assumptions, conditions, values, problems, tools, chairs

7 a _____ of chemicals, islands, hotels, children, admirers

4b Use one of the phrases from Exercise 4a to complete these sentences.

1 One of the things we really wanted to see on our safari was _____ .

2 While diving around the reef we saw some beautiful _____ .

3 People were selling _____ by the roadside.

GRAMMAR: nominalisation

5a Look at the two sentences and complete the rule.

1 The *arrival* of cheap sugar meant that there was no need for every household to have a hive.

2 When cheap sugar *arrived*, it meant that there was no need for every household to have a hive.

We can make _____ from other parts of speech, very often from _____ , sometimes from adjectives. We call this process 'nominalisation'.

deny – denial, argue – argument, fair – fairness

5b Find other examples in the extracts where a nominalised form is used instead of a verb. How could you express the same ideas using the equivalent verbs?

➡ **Language reference and extra practice, pages 156–157**

5c Put these words in the correct order to make sentences using nominalisation.

1 diseases by America failed many the attempt life-threatening to keep out

2 railway honeybees be responsible for the trans-Siberian could the disappearance of many

3 of is Argentina world's exporter honey major the

4 of embankments, and nesting sites roadsides the loss and public areas is the result of flowers of excessive mowing

GRAMMAR TIP

- We often use nominalisation in more formal situations, e.g. in formal writing.

- In nominalisation, make a note of which prepositions are used.

  the arrival of   the ability to   an increase in

- We sometimes form a nominalisation from a verb with a similar meaning.

  Prices go up *every week.*

  There's an increase *in prices every week.*

5d Complete the pairs of sentences with a noun and any other necessary words.

1 The weather was getting better.

   There _____ the weather.

2 She got over her illness very quickly.

   She made _____ her illness.

3 He'll go into all the details later.

   He'll give _____ the details later.

4 The bombs went off all night.

   There _____ all night.

SPEAKING

6 In small groups, discuss the following.

1 Bees can symbolise hard work and the acceptance of the social order. What do other insects/animals symbolise?

2 Do you think that the way we farm is changing now, or will change in the future?

3 Do you eat organic food? Why / Why not?

4 Which other insects / animals could be extinct within a decade? What kind of impact would this have on humans?

5 What could you do to protect insect or animal life where you live?

SITUATION

Ask the Panel is a current affairs and social issues discussion television programme in which a mixed panel of experts, commentators and members of the public discuss questions posed by the audience. Recent programmes have covered topics of law, the media and healthcare. This week the topic is 'science and society'.

1 In groups, look at the topics under discussion on this edition of *Ask The Panel*. What do you know about these subjects?

Nuclear energy	Animal conservation
Genetic engineering	Climate change
Cloning	Illegal poaching of animals
Animal vivisection	The moral duty of science

2a Read the profiles of the members of the panel on this week's show.

Indira Patel: The former chair of the National Academy of Science, and a frequent media expert on science matters

Bill Patterson: A high-profile member of Earthwatch, an environmental pressure group

Molly Chang: An investigative journalist who recently exposed malpractice in the chicken farming industry

David Perez: A school science teacher for 20 years

2b **3.13** The first question posed to the panel is 'Should genetic engineering (in particular the genetic modification of plants and animals that we eat) be halted due to the potential for unforeseen future dangers that it might cause for us and the planet?' Who do you think might make the following points? Listen and check.

1 We can't trust the companies engaged in GM food research.

2 GM crops hold out the prospect of being able to feed the world's population.

3 We can trust the scientists and the companies concerned.

4 Research should continue, but with the correct safeguards and controls.

5 The problem is that the dangers cannot be predicted through research.

6 It is currently possible to feed the world, but politics and business prevent this.

3 Do you agree or disagree with the speakers?

KEY LANGUAGE: referring to what other people have said

4 Complete the gaps in the following extracts from the discussion by using one pair of words (a–f). Listen again and check.

a return what   d pick up
b as said   e understand correctly
c what said   f claimed suggesting

1 Well, _____ Indira _____ , this research certainly shouldn't be halted.

2 _____ David _____ about current safeguards might sound reasonable…

3 If I _____ you _____ , you're saying that science based businesses can't be trusted.

4 Could I just _____ _____ on something that Indira said about feeding the world's population …

5 She _____ that genetic engineering will enable us to feed the world, _____ that that wasn't currently possible …

6 Perhaps we should _____ to _____ the original question said, which was that there are unforeseen dangers …

5 Look at these different versions of the extracts in Exercise 4. Which one in each pair is correct?

1 a) Well, as Indira mentioned, this research certainly …
  b) Well, as Indira's words, this research certainly …

2 a) The things that David made about current safeguards …
  b) The points David made about current safeguards …

3 a) If I see you correctly, you're saying that science-based businesses ...
  b) If I follow you correctly, you're saying that science-based businesses …

4 a) If I could just comment on something that Indira said about feeding …
  b) If I could just say about something that Indira said about feeding …

5 a) She stated that genetic engineering will enable us to feed the world, implying that …
  b) She claimed that genetic engineering will enable us to feed the world, of the suggestion that …

6 a) Perhaps we should go back to what the original question said …
  b) Perhaps we should deal what the original question said …

TASK: taking part in a panel discussion

6a You are a guest on *Ask the Panel*. Read your role play cards.

Student A: turn to page 159.
Student B: turn to page 160.
Student C: turn to page 162.
Student D: turn to page 163.
Student E: turn to page 159.

6b Take it in turns to be the chair of the panel. Discuss the questions in the order indicated on the producer's notes below.

Producer's notes – Question running order
1 Is nuclear energy the solution to the energy crisis in the world and should all countries be able to develop nuclear power?
2 Is it right to continue testing both medicines and cosmetics on animals?
3 Do the dangers of cloning outweigh the advantages? If so, should all research into this area be halted?
4 As animals have always become extinct throughout the history of world, do humans really have a responsibility to save animal species from that danger?
5 Should scientists ignore the moral and social implications of their research, so that they can concentrate on pushing the boundaries of human knowledge without restriction?

OTHER USEFUL PHRASES

Chairing a discussion

Right, let's get the discussion under way. The question is …

Let's see what someone else thinks. David?

What's your view?
Do you have an opinion on that?

Anything to say to that?

What's your response to that?

If I could just bring David in here.

I think we're going round in circles here. Shall we move on to the next question?

It's time to move on I think. Let's look at the next question.

SILENCE
EXAMINATION IN PROGRESS

STUDY SKILLS: examination skills

1 Exam vocabulary Complete the gaps in the sentences with the words in the box.

> candidates   cheat   compulsory   cross out
> invigilator   legibly   revision

1 It is crucial to start your _____ for the exam early.

2 Your handwriting doesn't have to be perfect, but you are expected to write _____ . If you make a mistake, _____ the wrong answer neatly and write the correct one.

3 In section A there is a choice of questions, but the questions in section B are _____ .

4 The _____ will be looking out for _____ who try to _____ .

2 In pairs, discuss the following questions.

1 Think about exams you have done in the past. What went well? What could you have done better?

2 Do you find them stressful? If so, how do you try to manage the stress?

3 Exam culture The points below are all generally true of international English language examinations. Are they true or false for most examinations in your country?

1 Once the exam has started, if you need any help, you have to put up your hand and ask an invigilator. But they cannot tell you the answers to any questions!

2 You cannot talk to any other student; this will be viewed as cheating. Cheating is an extremely serious offence. If you cheat, your exam will not be marked.

3 In an essay question, you must answer the question that has been set. You cannot write everything you know about a topic, or discuss a vaguely related topic.

4 If there is a word limit, you must keep to it.

5 At the end of the exam, you must stop writing the moment the invigilator tells you to do so.

4 Preparation Here are some vital questions you should ask yourself if you're preparing to take an English language exam. Add one or two more questions.

1 How many marks are there for each section or question?

2 How long can I spend on each of the reading passages/texts?

3 In the listening exam, how many times will I hear the recording?

5a `3.14` Listen to a discussion between a student and a teacher. What kind of exam is Teresa going to take? What kind of tasks will it involve?

5b Listen again and write down the points of advice the teacher gives.

5c Write your own top five tips for taking exams.

WRITING SKILLS: a personal statement

6 What do you understand by a 'personal statement'? When might you need to write one?

7a You want to apply for an Advanced Communication Skills course at a London university. One section of the application form asks you for more information. Discuss your answers to the following suggestions with a partner.

1 the reasons why you want to do the course

2 your background, including previous studies

3 what you are currently doing

4 your English level and details of any English language exams you have taken

5 any work experience you have

6 your interests, hobbies, etc.

7 your future plans

7b Read the personal statement on page 131. What topics from Exercise 7a does the writer cover in each paragraph?

Name: **Monica Paganin**

Nationality: **Italian**

I am applying for this course because, although I feel I have a good level of written English, I need to improve my speaking skills. I am interested in learning how to give good presentations and to participate effectively in group discussions. My pronunciation is very heavily influenced by Italian and I would like to be more like a native speaker. I know this will be difficult, but it's my dream! One of my cousins studied at your university two years ago; he had a very positive experience and recommended the course to me.

I have studied English for ten years at a private language school in my city. About three years ago, I took the Cambridge First Certificate exam and passed with an A grade. I believe I am now at advanced level and I aim to take the CAE or IELTS exam soon. Can you advise me about that?

Concerning my background, I was actually born in India (my parents were working there for an NGO*) but I have lived in Italy since the age of three. I grew up in a small town on the west coast, and this was a very significant experience for me, first stimulating my love of the sea.

When I was 10, we moved to Padova (Padua in English) – an ancient university city near Venice – and I went to high school and university here. At school, I did well in science subjects and went on to study Marine Biology at university, graduating last summer. My dissertation was on the ecological effects of the tidal barrier being built to protect Venice and it was well-

received. I strongly believe that our future lies in the seas and we must do everything we can to understand and protect them. After all, Earth isn't called the blue planet for nothing! I very much want to make my own positive contribution to that goal. Next year, I hope to start work as a researcher in the Marine Environment Research Centre. If I am not successful, I may go abroad to do a Masters, for which English will be very important.

I am a qualified diving instructor, and in my summer vacations I have helped in seaside holiday camps for disadvantaged children, taking on a wide range of responsibilities, from planning activities to consoling homesick children! This has taught me soft skills such as listening to others attentively, teamwork and leadership.

In my free time, as well as diving, I enjoy many other water sports (e.g. swimming, water polo). I also like reading, especially novels by Paulo Coelho and Haruki Murakami. My greatest love, however, is travelling and experiencing foreign cultures and civilisations. While I am attending the course, I would also like to take the opportunity to visit museums and galleries, and generally soak up the rich cultural life of a great city.

I consider myself an enthusiastic and conscientious student, who will benefit from – and participate actively in – the classes. Everyone says English is important because it is the global language of communication, but for me it is also a beautiful language which I love learning!

*Non-governmental organisation

8 **The statements (1–8) below are often true of good personal statements. Are they true of Monica's? If so, why?**

1 It is convincing, and suggests the writer is committed and enthusiastic.

2 It shows that the writer is prepared to offer something – not merely take what they want for their own ends.

3 There are no contradictory pieces of information. It does not get itself into a tangle.

4 There are no obvious gaps in terms of coverage. No important parts of the writer's life are missing.

5 The statement has a personal dimension and the writer's voice comes through.

6 A lot of time and care has been taken over the writing.

7 The language makes the writer sound intelligent, without being pretentious.

8 There is a strong conclusion.

9 **Conclusions** **The conclusions to the personal statements below were written by international students who wanted to study in a UK university. Choose the best word (in italics) to complete the sentences.**

A If my application is *successful / rewarding / acknowledged*, I aim to *snatch / clutch / seize* the opportunity to take an active part in a *medley / variety / miscellany* of academic, cultural and social activities during my university life.

B In the future, I want to *play / partake / participate* a role in the development of my country of origin which, over the last *many / few / plenty* years, has been in a difficult situation and now needs good administrators. I could give back what I will *gain / attain / reap* from the UK, and help my country develop its economy and *struggle / clash / fight* corruption.

10 **You are going to apply for a course in an English-speaking country. Write the personal statement that will accompany your application. Write about 400 words.**

Public opinion counts ...
become part of the panel on the public participation chat show

Two years ago, the people of the town of Modbury decided to ban plastic bags. In the show on 18 June, we will be discussing the decision. How do you feel about it? Does it go far enough? Whether you agree with the anti-plastic stance taken by Modbury or not, we want to hear your views. Respond to the article below by phone or email (details under the article) and we will select six members of the public to join the show.

1 Modbury is a typical small town in the south of England with a population of about 1,600. Typical, that is, apart from the fact that there are no plastic carrier bags in the town. None. Plastic bags have been well and truly dumped!

2 The removal of the plastic bags was the brainchild of Rebecca Hosking, Modbury resident and documentary-maker. Filming a documentary in the Pacific Ocean, Rebecca was horrified at the effects of discarded plastic bags on the wildlife off Hawaii. Amongst other things, she saw seabirds fatally entangled in plastic bags that don't biodegrade. When Rebecca returned to her home town, she discussed this problem with people, including the shopkeepers, and everyone supported her suggestion to make the town plastic bag free.

3 But for Rebecca's concept, Modbury would still be an unremarkable little place. Now, however, shoppers take re-useable cotton bags shopping with them, or they buy biodegradable cornstarch ones in the shops. The shopkeepers now wrap their goods in paper. To prove that the townsfolk are not only committed to reducing plastic waste, they organised a mass beach clean-up last year. Dozens of volunteers came to the beach on the appointed day to 'clean it up', taking the rubbish that visitors throw away and recycling it. And the greatest part of that rubbish was ... no, not plastic bags, but plastic bottles.

4 Becoming the first town in Europe to ban plastic bags, Modbury is now reaping the rewards of fame – reporters and camera crews from newspapers and TV channels across the world are flocking to this mild, unassuming town to find out its secret. And, contrary to some of the initial reports, it is neither a radical, hippy-influenced slice of bohemia, nor is it a town of hypocrites driving gas-guzzling 4x4s. It is a normal town, trying to live life in a slightly different way. As one resident put it: 'We're ordinary people, but we want to make just a little difference.'

GRAMMAR

1a Read the article above quickly. What is the purpose of the text?

1b Which of these statements do you think apply to Modbury? Read the text again to check your answers.

1 It's a lively town.
2 It has a selection of small shops.
3 Tourists visit the town and area.
4 The people in the town are all 'eco-warriors'.
5 The people are happy to have lots of film crews in the town.

2 What do you think about Modbury's ban on plastic bags? Do you agree with it?

3a Now read the article again. Find and underline the following grammatical features.

• two alternatives to *if* (introduction, paragraph 3)
• three phrasal verbs (paragraphs 3 and 4)
• two occurrences of substitution (introduction, paragraph 3)
• two nominalisations (introduction, paragraph 2)
• five non-finite clauses (paragraphs 2, 3 and 4)

3b Now rewrite these sentences, using one of the features in Exercise 3a for each one.

We were fascinated by how James described the campaign.

We were fascinated by James' description of the campaign. (nominalisation)

1 Lucy – what have you picked up from the ground? Discard it immediately!
2 We wanted to encourage more people to join our group so we put an advert on the local Internet forum.
3 I've packed the children's clothes in the blue suitcase and our clothes in the other suitcase.
4 The club members suggested that we donate some money to Greenpeace and we agreed with donating some money.
5 If Theresa hadn't been so enthusiastic, we would all have given up.
6 While Alex was living in the jungle, he realised that he hated being alone.
7 If you don't know the phone number of the organisation, why don't you look on the Internet to discover it?
8 The soldier staggered away from his company. He was fatally wounded.

4a **3.15** Listen to Simon responding to the article. Note down at least three features of spoken English that you hear. Then check your answer with the Track 3.15 on page 191.

4b Make a few notes of your opinions on the issue, then tell your partner. Try to use at least three features of spoken grammar.

VOCABULARY

5 Use the clues to find words connected with music and performing.

1 The person who creates dance routines for a ballet, or dance group.

2 A number of people who work together in a dance or music group.

3 A group of people who sing together.

4 The place where a performance happens.

5 _____-packed = very funny

6 A change in the medium of a work of art, e.g. from a novel to a film.

7 A style of music with lots of drums and bass guitars, e.g. rock music.

8 A person who is extremely good at his/her instrument, or skill in general.

6 Read this letter to a newspaper and decide which phrases in the box can replace the underlined words.

admission   boom and slump   confusion
(our) income and expenditure   level off
mortgages and loans   rocket
takeovers and mergers

Dear Sirs
It now seems that the whole world is in a recession and there is no ¹acceptance of guilt or responsibility by the banks. They used their – no, *our* – money incredibly foolishly while governments seem to fall further and further into ²disarray. And while the banks are more concerned with ³buying other banks or joining together, we all have to monitor even more carefully ⁴what we earn and what we spend. Well, I've lived long enough to know that house prices will ⁵stabilise and high street prices will start to ⁶increase sharply. The ⁷fall and rise cycle of the economy will continue, so the banks had better start giving ⁸money to buy homes and for other reasons again, or they will soon be facing the anger of their customers!

KEY LANGUAGE

7a **3.16** Listen to part of the programme *Public opinion counts.* Which of these phrases do you hear? Tick the first box.

1 And as for … ☐ ☐

2 As Simon said … ☐ ☐

3 But then again … ☐ ☐

4 By and large … ☐ ☐

5 I propose that we discuss … ☐ ☐

6 I reckon that … ☐ ☐

7 If I could just pick up on something that Simon said about … ☐ ☐

8 Let's talk about … ☐ ☐

9 Perhaps we should return to what Simon said … ☐ ☐

10 What Simon said about … ☐ ☐

7b Listen again. Are the phrases you hear informal (I), setting the agenda (S) or referring to what other people have said (R)? Write I, S or R in the second boxes.

8 Continue the discussion in groups of three or four. Make a few notes on your opinion of Modbury, of plastic bags and food packaging, then discuss them in groups. Try to use some of the phrases from Exercise 7a.

LANGUAGE CHECK

9 Each of these sentences either contains a mistake or could be improved. Correct the sentences, then look at the pages to check your answer.

1 Most children learn quickly, giving the right kind of attention. (page 105)

2 I rushed to the post office yesterday, only found it had already closed. (page 105)

3 We've got to leave now, if or not you're ready! (page 115)

4 I'll send the sample by email today, assume you're happy to receive it electronically. (page 115)

5 It was the beach near Modbury up which they cleaned. (page 117)

6 The government decided to cut back on health spending. That they decided to cut back on health spending lost them the election. (page 125)

7 If you want me to hoover the bedrooms, I'll hoover the bedrooms after I've cleaned the kitchen. (page 125)

8 We all decided that we had to close the shop. What we decided made us very sad. (page 127)

LOOK BACK

10 Find the exercises in Units 10–12 where you …

• read an extract from a listings magazine (Unit 10)

• study some aspects of the grammar of spoken English (Unit 10)

• write part of a screenplay (Unit 10)

• learn some common business combinations, e.g. noun + *and* + noun (Unit 11)

• look at some words that are often confused (Unit 11)

• revise the grammar of phrasal verbs (Unit 11)

• listen to an extract from a novel (Unit 12)

• do a role play of a panel discussion (Unit 12)

GRAMMAR

G1 The continuous aspect

Use the continuous aspect to talk about:

- an action or situation which is/was in progress at a particular time.
  He was researching into gene therapy at the time.

- an unfinished action or situation.
  He **had been working** in the lab when I met him.

- a temporary action.
  I**'m using** Jo's laptop while mine is being repaired.

- a trend, changing action or situation.
  Scientists say the weather **is getting** hotter.

We use the present continuous to talk about actions or situations currently in progress.
> They**'re conducting** a series of experiments into genetic mutation at the moment.

We can also use the present continuous to describe future arrangements.
> I**'m giving** the lecture on Thursday.

We use the past continuous to talk about an ongoing action in the past, often unfinished.
> I **was working** on the genome project the whole of last year.
(The project hadn't finished by the end of the year ✓)

We use the present perfect continuous to talk about an ongoing action or situation in the past that is still continuing into the present, or has just finished but has a result in the present.
> The doctor **has been waiting** for you for ages.
> I**'ve been running to get** here on time. That's why I'm out of breath.

We use the past perfect continuous to talk about an ongoing action or situation in the past that is still continuing up to another time in the past.
> The researchers **had been focusing** too narrowly – that's why we stopped them.

We use the future continuous to talk about temporary actions in progress at a particular time in the future.
> We**'ll be working** on the project all next week.

G2 The perfect aspect

Use the perfect aspect to look back from one time to another.

Present perfect

This looks back from now to a time before now. It often focuses on completed actions or situations.
> We**'ve already interviewed** ten people for this post.

The present perfect continuous focuses on the duration of the action.
> We**'ve been interviewing** all morning.

Past perfect

The past perfect looks back from a time in the past to another time before that.
> She**'d applied for** ten jobs before she got this one.

The past perfect continuous focuses on duration.
> She**'d been applying** for jobs for months before she got this one.

Future perfect

The future perfect looks back from a time in the future to another time before that.
> Lucas **will have finished** the job by 6.00p.m.

The future perfect continuous focuses on duration.
> Lucas **will have been working** on it for three hours by then.

Other forms

The perfect has an infinitive form: *to + have +* past participle.
> I expected you **to have completed** the questionnaires by now.

The *-ing* form is *having +* past participle.
> **Having arrived** at the laboratory, we were shown to Professor Dalton's office.

KEY LANGUAGE

KL Stating requirements

Essential

It's absolutely essential that ...
The (candidate) must have (done) ...
They'll have to have (done) ...
Candidates have to be able to ...
That's/X is a pre-requisite / an essential requirement.

Desirable

(I imagine) it would be helpful to have (done) ...
It'd be a good thing if he/she had (done) ...
It would be an advantage if he/she had (done) ...
That/X would probably give them an edge.

VOCABULARY

V1 Issues in education

assessment, critical thinking, curriculum, dumbing down, elitism, informed decisions, interpersonal skills, knowledge base, plagiarism, rote learning, streaming, traditional teaching

V2 Idioms

all-rounder, dark horse, egghead, high-flier, know-all, loose cannon, showoff, smart alec, team player, whiz-kid

V3 Suffixes (adjectives)

accomplished, affectionate, allergic, ambitious, analytical, educational, electrical, famous, fictional, grammatical, passionate, persuasive, photographic, powerful, psychological, skilful, successful, superstitious, toxic

Extra practice

1

G1 **1** **Complete the sentences with the verb in brackets in the correct continuous form.**

1 Mercedes _____ (work) as a teaching assistant since she arrived here two years ago.

2 I _____ (try) to finish my assignment all through the plane journey, but it was too turbulent.

3 The rearranged lecture _____ (take place) next Friday at 5.00 p.m.

4 Working conditions in the factory _____ (improve) before the new management started.

5 The whole family _____ (stay) with Ralph's parents until the building work is completed.

6 The security guard _____ (lock) the office when the burglars forced their way past him.

7 I know I failed the test because I _____ (not concentrate) in Professor Williams' lectures.

G2 **2** **Choose the correct answer.**

1 By the time the strike at the car plant was over, several of the workers *already found / had already found* new jobs.

2 Alan will have *negotiated / been negotiating* deals with the US for 40 years when he retires.

3 That office block *has been / was* empty since.

4 They have *closed / been closing* the production department for five days already this month.

5 We really wanted *to have / having* finished all the work by now.

6 The company had *recruited / been recruiting* graduate trainees for over 20 years when the scheme was ended.

G1, 2 **3** **Complete the text with verbs from the box below in the correct form.**

be become (x2) found generate incorporate lay off look for sell trade

I ¹_____ a particular book on the Internet recently and found it on Amazon, and I started to wonder how the online bookshop ²_____ the giant that it is today. Amazon ³_____ books since 1994, when Jeff Bezos ⁴_____ the business.

It started out very small, but after it ⁵_____ in business for a year, a $100,000 investment was used to make the website more user-friendly. By 1999 it ⁶_____ $16m, and until that point it ⁷_____ only in books. But then things began to go wrong and by the end of 2001, the company ⁸_____ over 1,000 staff. Not one to give up, Bezos opened the Amazon market to other traders, and became successful once more. More than just a bookshop, Amazon ⁹_____ features into its website such as user reviews, and within a very short time now it ¹⁰_____ one of the main sellers of other goods, such as CDs, household goods, electrical goods, and so on. What a success story!

KL **4** **Read the advert and complete the sentences below.**

> ## University of
> ## West Hampton
>
> The Languages Department
> currently has a vacancy for a lecturer in English Language Studies.
> The successful candidate must:
> - be a native or bilingual speaker of English
> - have a first degree in English or Linguistics
> - have a postgraduate qualification in a related subject
>
> The following are also desirable:
> - knowledge of at least one other language
> - experience in the higher education sector
> - interest in the development of the English language
>
> Terms and conditions on application.

1 _____ the applicant speaks English fluently.

2 _____ studied English or linguistics.

3 _____ completed a postgraduate degree.

4 _____ could speak another language.

5 _____ worked in higher education.

6 _____ were interested in the development of the English language.

V1 **5** **Complete the sentences with words or phrases from V1.**

1 The subjects studied in a school/college are called the _____ .

2 If you reproduce other people's work and claim it as your own, you are guilty of _____ .

3 TV broadcasters are often accused of _____ because programmes aren't intellectual enough.

4 _____ is often criticised because it does not encourage independent thinking.

5 It is necessary in a language course to have frequent _____ to measure students' progress.

6 Some schools practise _____ , that is, they have groups of different abilities for some subjects.

V2, V3 **6** **Find an expression in V2 or an adjective in V3 which describes the following:**

1 something which is very poisonous _____

2 someone who can bring you round to their views or desires _____

3 someone who will be successful in their chosen field _____

4 someone whose immune system over-reacts to a particular substance _____

5 someone who is very emotional and believes strongly in things _____

6 someone who is loving and caring _____

GRAMMAR

G1 Articles

Use the indefinite article (*a/an*):

- to introduce something for the first time.
  Madagascar is **an** island off the coast of southern Africa.

❗ If we refer to a specific person or thing, or the number is important, we use *one*, not *a/an*.
Only **one** student failed the final exam.

Use the definite article (*the*):

- to refer to something mentioned before.
  (Madagascar is **an** island off the coast of Africa.) **The** island is well-known for ...

- to refer to something obvious from the context (common knowledge).
  Can you pass me **the** pepper?

- to refer to something unique.
  Doesn't **the** moon look beautiful tonight?

- with a superlative phrase.
  It's **the** best holiday we've ever had!
  The south coast of the island is too quiet for me.

- with the names of some countries and geographical features.
  The islands are in **the** Pacific Ocean.

Use the zero article (no article):

- with general plural and uncountable nouns, and abstract nouns.
  Islands often attract tourists because of the number of beaches in a small area.
  Conservation is an important issue now.

- with people's names and continents, countries, cities, mountains and lakes.
  Turkey is the only country to straddle two continents: **Europe** and **Asia**.

G2 Modal verbs: present and future

Ability / possibility

Use *can/be able to* for ability / possibility.

People **can** swim from this beach.

We **won't be able to** save Balandra Beach.

Permission / requests

Use *can, could* or *may* for permission, *can* and *could* for requests.

Can I borrow the car tonight? Yes, you **can**.

Could you hold my bags for a moment?

Likelihood / deduction

Use *can, could, may* or *might* to express a likelihood in the future.

The country **may/might/could** be moving towards tourism.

❗ But don't use *couldn't* to talk about a general possibility in the future; use *might not*.
~~The weather could not be good tomorrow.~~ ✗
The weather **might not** be good tomorrow. ✓

Use *can, could, might* or *must* (but not *mustn't*) to express the level of certainty about an action.

Antonia **might** be in her office.

She **can't** be there – she went out earlier.

No, she **must** be there. Her coat's here.

Advice / obligation / prohibition

Use *should* or *ought to* for advice.

You **should / ought to** go to bed earlier.

Use *should, must* or *have to* for obligation.

We **should** arrange our visas soon.

Must and *have to* are stronger than *should*. *Have to* is used for rules and obligation from 'outside'.

You **have to** pay this fine within two weeks.

Prohibition is negative obligation. We use *can't, shouldn't* or *mustn't* for this.

We **can't** go in there – it's for staff only.

Mustn't is stronger than *shouldn't*.

You **shouldn't** make a lot of noise on the beach and you **mustn't** leave any rubbish behind.

KEY LANGUAGE

KL1 Stating your position

I'd like to make my position very clear.

X is an absolute priority / is not negotiable.

It's vital to have X if you want to ...

It simply isn't possible to ...

KL2 Clarification and understanding

If I understand you ...

It seems you will/won't ....?

What exactly do you mean?

I understand where you're coming from ...

OK, you've been very clear about ...

VOCABULARY

V1 Travel collocations

ancient monument, baking temperatures, boutique hotel, budget airline, carbon footprint, gastronomic delights, last-minute deal, organised excursion

V2 Multi-word verbs

avoid getting ripped off, get away from it all, get back to nature, go off the beaten track, let your hair down, live it up, lounge around by the pool, soak up the atmosphere, steer clear of the tourist traps, take in the sights

V3 Conservation

biodiversity, emissions, endangered, irreversible, renewable, urban sprawl

V4 Words from Lesson 2.3

flawless, idyllic, stark, turquoise, unobtrusive, whacking

G1 **1** Complete the gaps in the text with *a/an* or *the*, or just leave the gap if no article is required.

'Last year I had ¹_____ very different holiday; some friends and I went on ²_____ 'yoga retreat' on ³_____ south coast of ⁴_____ France. ⁵_____ retreat itself was fascinating – it consisted of about ⁶_____ fifty huts for two people behind a really peaceful, quiet beach. We had three hours of yoga every morning on ⁷_____ beach and then we went for ⁸_____ walks in ⁹_____ hills behind the coast in the afternoon, or just relaxed. ¹⁰_____ instructor who took us for yoga was fantastic – so knowledgeable. ¹¹_____ holiday was only a week but I felt both calm and invigorated when I got back. It's certainly ¹²_____ most relaxing holiday I've ever had!'

G1 **2** There is one error with an article in each sentence. Identify the error and correct it.

1 A lot of people are becoming more interested in the eco-tourism these days.
2 I'm not sure if Karen's here at the moment. Hold on a minute, and I'll check if she's in a kitchen.
3 I didn't realise you wanted to go on the excursion too. I only booked a ticket.
4 We stayed in a great hotel in Florida. While a hotel was in a built-up area, it was very quiet.
5 People are travelling less because a lot of the package holidays are more expensive this year as a result of the rise in fuel costs.
6 We've been saving up for years to go on a really special holiday – we want to go to Galapagos Islands.

G2 **3** In each sentence, two of the choices are correct and one is incorrect. Circle the correct ones.

1 As we become more aware of climate change, more people *can / may / might* choose not to fly because of the environmental damage.
2 The play has started. You *can't / mustn't / don't have to* go in until there's a convenient break.
3 My pen's run out of ink. *Can / Will / Could* I borrow one of yours?
4 'Suki's on holiday in the Canaries this week.' 'That *isn't / can't / mustn't* be true – she's got an interview on Friday.'
5 It's very likely that Murray will win a major tennis tournament soon but it *may / could / might* not be this year.

KL **4** Complete the dialogue with Key language phrases.

A: I booked a holiday with you last month, but I'm afraid I can't go now. I'd like a refund.
B: That's a shame. When is the holiday for?
A: The flight leaves on Tuesday.
B: Oh, I see. If ¹_____ correctly, you want your money back for a holiday departing in five days?
A: That's right.
B: Well, I'm afraid that isn't possible.

A: I don't understand. What ²_____?
B: I'm saying that it ³_____ at this stage.
A: Oh, it ⁴_____ give me a refund. Is that correct?
B: I can't give you a refund. You'll have to go to your insurance company.
A: Insurance?
B: You don't have insurance? But it's ⁵_____ insurance when you book a holiday.

V1, 4 **5** Complete the advert with words and phrases from the box.

> ancient monuments   baking temperatures
> flawless   gastronomic delights
> organised excursion   turquoise

Land of ¹_____ ***like the Pyramids and the Sphinx.***

Two weeks in Egypt this summer from as little as 400 euros – one week by the ²_____ sea on the Mediterranean coast and another sampling the ancient history of Cairo and the ³_____ of its restaurants.
Or, if you prefer, a three-day ⁴_____ down the Nile with the ⁵_____ service of our tour guides – what better way to escape the ⁶_____ in July and August.

V2 **6** Which idioms are defined below?

1 to avoid places where there are a lot of visitors
2 to go somewhere which doesn't attract a lot of people
3 to relax at the hotel, sunbathing and swimming
4 to visit famous places
5 not to pay extortionate prices
6 to have a good time and lose your inhibitions

V3 **7** Match the words in V3 with these definitions.

1 not possible to change something back to what it was before
2 an area spreading out in an untidy and unattractive way
3 the variety of plants and animals
4 under threat of extinction, usually used for species
5 gases, often dangerous, sent into the air, e.g. in a manufacturing process
6 easily replaced, i.e. because there is a large supply, or something that replaces itself

Language reference

GRAMMAR

G1 Subordinate clauses

A sentence consists of one or more clauses. These may simply be two main clauses, joined by *and*, *but* or *or*.

> The contract was signed by all parties **and** the meeting ended.

The contract was signed and *The meeting ended* are two main clauses.

A sentence often consists of a main clause and a subordinate clause, joined by a subordinating conjunction such as *when*, *because*, *although*, *if*.

> Many people couldn't get to the conference **because** the train drivers were on strike.

When subordinate clauses begin sentences, they are often separated by commas.

> If you're ever in Geneva, let's visit CERN.
> Let's visit Cern if you're ever in Geneva.

Commas are not used before 'that' clauses

> It's quite natural that you should be concerned about the LHC experiments.

A main clause can stand by itself. In this example *Many people couldn't get to the conference* makes sense on its own.

A subordinate clause can't stand by itself: *because the train drivers were on strike* only makes sense when the main clause completes the meaning.

Subordinate clauses are dependent on a main clause; they often express a notion that explains or completes something in the main clause, e.g. a reason or a condition:

* cause/reason (*because*, *as*, *since*)
* result (*so*)
* condition (*if*, *unless*, *provided*)
* purpose (*to*, *so that*)
* time (*before*, *when*, *while*)
* relative (*who*, *which*)
* reported speech (*that*)

G2 Modal perfect

A modal perfect is a modal verb + *have* + past participle.

Use *must/can't/couldn't have* + past participle to express certainty about something in the past.

> He **must have paid** his bill – I've got all the money.
> She **can't have arrived** – her coat isn't here.
> Marcel **couldn't have written** this = his English isn't good enough.

! The opposite of *must have done* is *can't/couldn't have done*. It expresses impossibility.

We use *may/might/could have* + past participle to express a degree of possibility in the past.

> They **might have cancelled** the class – there was no one there.
> I **could have finished** my degree but I was too lazy.

We use *should/ought to have* + past participle to express past necessity or criticism.

> You really **shouldn't have missed** the exam.
> We **ought to have called** your family in advance – they might not be in.

This can also express regret.

> I **should have taken** the job they offered me; I'd be a director by now.

We use *needn't have done* to say that we did something, but it turned out not to be necessary, or there was no obligation.

> I booked the tickets in advance but I **needn't have done** so as there were lots of empty seats.
> 'I've brought an umbrella for you too.' 'Oh, you **needn't have done** that. I've got my own.'

! Compare with *didn't need to*. When we use this, we don't know whether the action happened or not. We **didn't need to book** tickets as the concert wasn't very popular.

KEY LANGUAGE

KL1 Stating objectives

Our main objective is to ...
One of our main goals will be to ...
Your priority is to ...
We aim (also) to ...
That/X should be a key objective.

KL2 Giving strong advice

It would be advisable for you to ...
I think you ought to ...
It's essential to ... / It's vital that you ...
I'd strongly advise you to ...
I strongly recommend you to ...
I urge you to ...

VOCABULARY

V1 Dependent prepositions

ability to, fascination with, great at, love of, passion for, proud of, reluctance to

V2 Adjectives of character

aloof, charismatic, cultured, devious, dogmatic, emotional, hospitable, meticulous, pragmatic, self-effacing

V3 The diplomatic world

cultural awareness, diplomatic immunity, international conflict, overseas posting, summit meeting

G1 **1** **Combine the sentences in each case to make one sentence with two clauses. Use the linking word given and make any necessary changes.**

1 Alex joined the diplomatic service. She wanted to live in different countries. (so that)

_____

_____

2 The people were very disillusioned. The election turnout was extremely low. (because)

_____

_____

3 The most successful candidate was the young woman. She had the best qualifications. (who)

_____

_____

4 I left university last June. I didn't get a permanent job until April this year. (but)

_____

_____

5 The police searched for some conclusive evidence. The suspect was questioned. (while)

_____

_____

6 The people in this city are very welcoming. You must respect their desire for privacy. (provided)

_____

_____

G2 **2** **Read the situations and then complete the sentences using a suitable modal perfect.**

1 Robert has never had very much money. He doesn't have a very good job and he hasn't got many qualifications. Suddenly he started spending a lot of money and buying expensive things, and then it stopped.

  a) He _____ got a better job because he isn't well qualified, and because the spending stopped.

  b) He _____ come into money somehow.

  c) He _____ won the lottery.

  d) He _____ inherited money from a relative.

  e) He _____ spent it all so fast – he _____ saved some for the future.

2 You are going to a concert with some friends and you want to eat first. Your friend Jo is late so you find a restaurant, but don't have time to eat much because you're late for the concert. You rush to get there, only to find that the concert is cancelled.

  a) Jo _____ arrived late – she knew we wanted to eat.

  b) We _____ rushed to get to the concert after all.

  c) We _____ spent more time over the meal and enjoyed ourselves more.

  d) The concert hall _____ sent a message to our mobile phones.

  e) Someone in the band _____ fallen ill suddenly to cancel the concert at short notice.

KL **3** **Complete each gap in the dialogue with one word only.**

A: We want to run a new course on cultural awareness. Our main [1]_____ is to get the students to appreciate differences.

B: That's very laudable. I think you [2]_____ to consider the content carefully, though.

A: Oh, yes. We [3]_____ to read a lot about it over the summer.

B: And I'd [4]_____ advise you to tread carefully – people get upset about this kind of thing.

A: We know. One of our main [5]_____ will be to reduce people's over-sensitivity. We want to get some good guest lecturers in.

B: Yes, that should be a key [6]_____ . Well, good luck!

V1, 3 **4** **Complete the sentences with a word from each list.**

A: cultural, fascination, international, overseas, proud, reluctance

B: awareness, of, postings, relations, to, with

1 My father was in the diplomatic service and had lots of _____ _____ to interesting places.

2 I've always had a great _____ _____ insects.

3 Many American people have a _____ _____ travel outside their own country.

4 Living in a multicultural environment, it's important to have good _____ _____ .

5 It's fine to be _____ _____ one's country and its achievements, without being jingoistic.

6 In today's globalised world, _____ _____ are more important than ever.

V2 **5** **Complete the puzzle with adjectives. Use the clues to help you.**

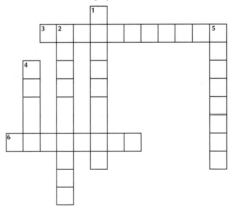

1 someone who is sensible and practical

2 friendly, welcoming and generous

3 pleasant and attractive

4 cold and distant, not friendly

5 interested in art, music, literature, etc.

6 someone who is self-_____ does not push themselves forward

GRAMMAR

G1 Cohesion 1 (linkers)

There are two different types of linkers: the conjunctions we use to link two sentences or clauses, e.g. *and*, *when*, *if*, and the adverbs we use to make a link across two sentences, e.g. *in addition*, *then*, *however*.

These conjunctions and adverbs perform a number of different functions.

notion	conjunctions	adverbs
funtion additive	and	as well as (this), furthermore, in addition, moreover, similarly
contrastive	although, but, even though, while, whilst, whereas, yet	even so, however, in contrast, nevertheless, nonetheless, on the other hand, otherwise
causal	as, because, since	as a result, consequently, for this reason, therefore
temporal	after, as, as soon as, before, since, until, when, while/whilst	after that, meanwhile, subsequently

Notice the difference between the use of the conjunctions and the adverbs:

Sonja was rarely ill **even though** she ate junk food and took little exercise.
Sonja ate junk foods and took little exercise. **However**, she was rarely ill.

Linking adverbs are often used in more formal situations than conjunctions.

We decided to have a meeting to get to know one another **while** they were putting up the exhibition.
The exhibition was being constructed when we arrived. **Meanwhile**, we held an introductory meeting.

G2 Future forms with *to be*

to be + **adjective/adverb + infinitive**

We use the following phrases to suggest certainty that something will happen: *to be bound to, to be certain to, to be sure to*.

Sunita **is bound/certain/sure to** pass her exams – she's studied so hard.

If we are less certain, we use *to be likely to*.

Ryan **is likely to** specialise in heart surgery, but he isn't sure yet.

We use *to be due to* when we expect something to happen at a particular time.

The plane **is due to** land at half past six.

We use *to be about to* when we know that something is imminent.

Lucy is over nine months pregnant – she's **about to** have the baby.

to be on + **noun** + *of* + **-ing form**

We *use to be on the point of/on the verge of* + *-ing* form when something is imminent; it is similar to *to be about to*.

We can't stop the procedure now – the surgeon **is on the point of operating**.

to be + **infinitive**

We use *to be* + infinitive in a formal context to talk about decisions, obligations and requirements.

The meeting **is to be held** in the boardroom and Janine **is to take** the minutes.

This can be used for prohibitions in the negative.

The patient **is not to be given** anything by mouth.

It can also be used for events that are fixed.

Interest rates **are to come down** to 2 per cent.

This structure is not used in informal conversation.

KEY LANGUAGE

KL Justifying your opinions

One reason I favour X / doing X is …
So, you can see that this …, can't you?
By this, I mean that …
That is exactly the kind of thing …
If we do X, people will inevitably …
The fact that X happens means that Y is fully justified.
While I accept that X would be …, it'd also be …
You may well ask …

VOCABULARY

V1 Health collocations

blood pressure, chest pain, flu virus, heart attack, heart surgery, high salt intake, immune system, infant mortality, life expectancy, maternity ward, Omega-3 oils, premature ageing, tanning salon

V2 Health care

alternative medicine, clinic, conventional medicine, doctor, doctor's surgery, general practitioner (GP), have a check-up, have an operation, have a scan/X-ray, hospice, hospital, lack of funding, long waiting lists, outdated equipment, palliative care, paramedic, pharmacist, pharmacy, post-operative infection, preventive medicine, to see the doctor, specialist, surgeon

V3 The language of emotion

antagonised, disillusioned, disorientating, elated, exasperated, exhilarating, inspiring, invigorating, rejuvenated, relieved

Extra practice

G1 **1** Combine the sentences in each pair with the linker in brackets.

1 Jamie called for an ambulance. The ambulance arrived ten minutes later. (after)

_____

_____

2 Sarah qualified as a doctor. She never worked in medicine. (although)

_____

_____

3 I'm on holiday the first week of June. I can't attend the conference. (as)

_____

_____

4 My classmates got jobs very quickly. It took me six months to get a job. (whereas)

_____

_____

5 Joe met Maria three months ago. He has been very happy for three months. (since)

_____

_____

6 There aren't enough people at the meeting. We can't take any votes. (since)

_____

_____

2 Complete these sentences to make them more formal. Use a linking adverbial.

1 My family all came to my graduation and my tutor came too.
My family attended _____

_____

2 The doctors won't operate on Mr Jacobs because he is hugely overweight.
Mr Jacobs is extremely _____

_____

3 We were delayed for an hour on the bus while the procession went past.
The procession passed _____

_____

4 Although I'm interested in alternative medicine, I prefer to visit my GP for serious problems.
I'm interested in alternative medicine. _____

_____

G2 **3** Replace the words in italics with a suitable future form. Make any other changes necessary.

1 These painkillers _should not be taken_ by children.
2 Your father _will definitely_ like your present. He's fascinated by vintage cars.
3 _We're expecting our first guests to_ arrive at the church at about 3.30p.m.
4 His plane _will land at any moment_ – look, you can see it in the sky.
5 _It's probable that Paul will bring_ the baby over at the weekend.
6 Visitors _should report_ to reception upon arrival.

KL **4** Match the sentence halves.

1 The fact that your GP refers you
2 That is exactly the kind of thing
3 One reason I favour putting this to the vote
4 While I accept that a high salt intake is unhealthy,
5 So, you can see that
6 If we change the rules again,

a) it's something I enjoy.
b) I've told you to avoid on numerous occasions.
c) we can't be of any more assistance, can't you?
d) is a sign that he is prepared to admit he doesn't know.
e) the people will inevitably call us indecisive.
f) is that we need to know that our members agree.

V1 **5** Complete the sentences with one word from each list.

A: blood, chest, immune, infant, life, premature
B: ageing, expectancy, mortality, pain, pressure, system

1 _____ _____ is higher now in developed countries than it has ever been.
2 Constant exposure to the sun can result in _____ _____ of the skin.
3 You shouldn't take your _____ _____ reading when you are under stress.
4 Taking a vitamin C tablet every day helps to boost the _____ _____ .
5 Older people need to take _____ _____ seriously as it could indicate heart problems.
6 Simple treatments like rehydrating children with stomach upsets can reduce _____ _____ .

V2 **6** Find the following in V2.

1 six practitioners: _____

_____

2 five places: _____

_____

3 three diagnostic treatments: _____

_____

4 three problems with a health service: _____

_____

V3 **7** Choose an adjective for each situation.

How might you feel when ...

1 you haven't found a job after 30 interviews?
2 your blood test shows no serious problems?
3 you passed all your exams with an A grade?

How would you describe …

4 a lecture by someone who is successful in a field you're interested in?
5 a cold shower on a really hot day?
6 a city you don't know where all the streets look the same?

GRAMMAR

G1 Future in the past

We sometimes need to talk about the future but from a point in the past. For example:

two days ago: I**'m going to buy** a laptop tomorrow.
today: I **was going to buy** a laptop yesterday ...

was/were going to

Use this when the future action happened.
When I last saw Ginny, she **was going to** start her new job the next day.

But we often use it with actions that did not happen.
Michael **was going to** study law at Oxford before he had the car accident.

We can also use it to make excuses.
We **were going to** get in touch but we've been so busy.

was/were to

Use *was/were to* in formal contexts to talk about decisions, obligations and requirements (see *is/are to*, Unit 4), usually for actions that were not fulfilled.

The ministers **were to** meet at the Paris Fashion Show, but it was cancelled after the bombs.

would

Use *would* when the action definitely happened.
Madonna's childhood was quite poor, but she **would** become one of the richest women on the planet.

We can also use phrases with nouns and adjectives that express the future (see Unit 4) with *was/were*.
They **were due to** catch the 11.20 train. I don't know if they did.
Marcus **was bound to** be chosen for the job.

G2 Emphatic structures

There are several ways of changing the word order of a sentence in English to make it more emphatic.

Inversion

Inversion means changing the position of the subject and verb to put the verb first. This is common with a number of negative adverbs, e.g. *not only, no sooner, never, scarcely, at no time, little*.

No sooner had the doors opened than the customers flooded in the shop.
Never in my life have I been so offended!

Little did Val know that Colin had already planned the holiday.

Note that when we use inversion with present or past simple, we have to use the *do* auxiliary.

Fronting

Fronting involves putting an element at the beginning of the sentence that does not normally go in that position, e.g. adjective complements, adverbials.

Interesting she may be; pleasant she isn't.
Out of the woods the deer shot, in total panic.

Cleft sentences

A cleft sentence means splitting one clause into two. We do this to emphasise part of the sentence. There are two types of cleft sentences:

It-clefts emphasise the object of the clause. So, to emphasise *her dreadful behaviour* in this sentence:
I really object to her dreadful behaviour.

we can make *her dreadful behaviour* into a separate *it*-clause:
It's her dreadful behaviour (that) I really object to.

Wh-clefts emphasis the verb of the clause. To emphasise *would like* in the following sentence, we can make it into a separate *wh*-clause.
We'd like to inspect your kitchens.
What we'd like is to inspect your kitchens.

With *wh*-clefts, we use *to be* to link the two clauses.

If the verb in the original sentence is in the present or past simple, we form the *wh*-cleft with *do/did*.
The companies maximise their profits.
What the companies do is maximise their profits.

KEY LANGUAGE

KL Discussing hypothetical ideas

Suppose we did have a café, wouldn't that ...?
It'd mean that we'd have to ...
I'm not sure how (feasible) that would be.
If we were to ..., we'd ...
I was wondering if we might ...
We'd need to ..., otherwise we'd ...
(Surely,) It'd be better to ...
If we did X, but still ..., we'd ...
There'd be a chance to ...
Admittedly, that'd mean ...

VOCABULARY

V1 Consumer collocations

advice, boom, choice, confidence, demand, goods, issues, price index, products, society, spending, trends, watchdog

V2 Compound adjectives formed with nouns

big-name, eye-catching, fashion-conscious, hand-made, high-quality, jet-black, time-consuming, world-renowned

V3 Suffixes (nouns 1)

activity, consciousness, convenience, obsession, popularity, sustainability, violation

G1 **1** Choose the correct form of the future in the past. In three cases, both are correct.

1 The letter said that all new recruits *were going to / were to* report to reception on arrival.

2 The guard shouted at us to hurry as the train *was bound to / was about to* depart.

3 The Minister *was to / was due to* address the committee first thing in the morning.

4 Alice *was going to / would* join the Dior fashion house but she decided against moving to Paris.

5 It was clear from the outset that Noel *would / was to* become the President's successor.

6 Once Nadal had been knocked out, everyone felt that Federer *would probably / was likely to* win the tournament.

2 In pairs, discuss your answers. What's the difference in meaning between the forms in the three sentences where both are correct?

G2 **3** Match the beginnings and endings of the sentences.

1 No sooner had the shops stocked Miyake's new perfume

2 What Issey Miyake did

3 It was a really fresh new scent

4 It was exploitation in the fashion industry

5 It was Ben Francis who

6 Damning though Ben Francis's report was,

7 Not only do certain companies accept exploitation,

a) that Ben Francis wrote about.

b) was release a really popular perfume.

c) wrote about exploitation in the fashion industry.

d) than everyone was wearing it.

e) but some also seem to endorse it.

f) exploitation in the fashion industry still goes on.

g) that Issey Miyake released.

4 Complete the second sentence so that it has a similar meaning to the first.

1 The staff had no idea that the company was going to close.
Little _____

2 Steve ran the London Marathon in a rabbit costume.
What _____

3 My accountant alerted me to the tax problems.
It was _____

4 Her application was truly awful, but they offered her the job.
Awful _____

5 The humidity is really difficult to bear.
What _____

6 The humidity is really difficult to bear.
It _____

KL **5** Use the prompts to write sentences expressing hypothetical ideas.

1 *I not sure profitable that be.*

2 *There be chance attract new customers.*

3 *I wonder I redesign window display.*

4 *If we employ only graduates we still need train them.*

5 *Suppose we have weekly meetings that create sense of involvement?*

6 *We need clear ideas with Head Office they not approve funding.*

V1 **6** Complete the collocation for each definition.

1 consumer _____ = the level of satisfaction with the economy, demonstrated in how much is spent

2 consumer _____ = list of prices of products to show increase/decrease in the cost of living

3 consumer _____ = questions/topics which concern consumers

4 consumer _____ = the kind of things that consumers buy

5 consumer _____ = the range and variety of products available for consumers

V2 **7** Replace the words in italics with a compound adjective. Make any other changes necessary.

1 Don't complete new forms for every student; it *takes too long*.

2 *Famous* golfer Tiger Woods announced his participation in the US Open today.

3 He has a *very noticeable* tattoo on his left shoulder.

4 Her eyes are amazing – they're *as dark as you can imagine*.

5 Tissane chocolates are *crafted personally* by our own chocolatier, Pierre Didier.

V3 **8** Complete the puzzle with words from V3.

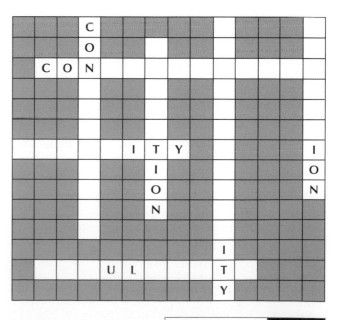

GRAMMAR

G1 The passive: form

We form the passive with a form of *be* + past participle. We can use the passive in most tenses:

> The company **was started** in 2008.
> A prototype **will be produced** next year.
> Two hundred people **have been invited**.

We can use the passive in the present and past continuous, but we avoid other continuous forms:

> His behaviour **is being monitored**.
> Your proposal **was being considered** along with several others.

We form the infinitive of the passive with *to be* + past participle.

> We expect the work **to be finished** within the next three weeks.

There is a perfect form of the passive infinitive: *to have been* + past participle.

> The students were hoping **to have been awarded** their degrees by now.

We form the passive of *-ing* forms with *being* + past participle, for example after prepositions.

> We congratulated her **on being promoted** to sales director.

! Intransitive verbs cannot be made passive.
~~The train was arrived on time.~~ ✗

G2 The passive: use

There are several reasons for using the passive. Some are simply because the agent is:

• obvious from the context.
> The law has been changed.

• unknown or unimportant.
> My laptop was stolen at the airport.

! If we want to give the agent, we use **by**:
> You will be contacted **by** customer services.

The passive is sometimes used to avoid naming the agent, perhaps to avoid blame or responsibility.

> The keys seem to have been mislaid.

We also use the passive to manipulate the order of information in text. (In English we prefer to start a new sentence with a something that has already been mentioned). The passive can help us do this.

> This new software is revolutionary. ~~Apex Solutions designed it.~~ ✗
> This new software is revolutionary. **It was designed by Apex Solutions.** ✓

We can choose to put longer subjects at the end of a sentence by using the passive.

> The new software was designed **by a developer at Apex Solutions who had previously worked for Microsoft.**

The passive is also used in processes:

> The mixture was heated to 100 degrees.

G3 Causatives

We use both *have* and *get* (more informal) + past participle to say that we didn't do something ourselves, but 'caused' another person to do it:

> We **had our photos taken** after the ceremony.
> I **got my hair cut** at Stella's last week.

Or it can be something we don't want to happen:

> I **have my bag searched** every time I go through Customs at the airport.
> My husband **got fired** from his job yesterday.

(This last example is similar to a passive.)

We can use *make* + infinitive without *to* when we force another person to do something:

> My boss **made me stay** late at the office.

We can use this in the passive, but then we need *to*:

> We **were made to explain** our movements in great detail.

We use *let* + infinitive without *to* when we allow another person to do something:

> Did Mark **let you pay** for your meal?

We do not use this in the passive. Instead, we use *(not) allowed to*.

> The children **are usually allowed to** go home early on the last day of term.

KEY LANGUAGE

KL1 Persuading

I think the facts speak for themselves, don't they?
The total number of ... is 4.1 billion, yes, 4.1 billion.
It's incredible what this ... can do.
I'm sure you'd agree mobile phones are an extraordinarily versatile piece of equipment.

KL2 Giving examples

Let me give you an amazing statistic.
I'd like to give you one other striking example ...

VOCABULARY

V1 Technology words

behind the times, breakthrough, cutting-edge, ground-breaking, hi-tech, innovative, low-tech, new fangled, obsolete, old-hat, outdated, outmoded, pioneering, redundant, retro, revolutionary, state-of-the art

V2 Dependent prepositions

account for, contribute to, expansion in, impact on, lead to, result in, rise in, stem from

V3 Idioms and phrasal verbs with *get*

get off to a flying start, get on (with someone) like a house on fire, get on your nerves, get somebody down, get the hang of something

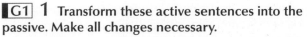
G1 **1** **Transform these active sentences into the passive. Make all changes necessary.**

1 Technicians at our Milton Keynes factory assemble all the parts.

2 CCTV cameras are always monitoring us in this office.

3 Builders equipped the building with cutting-edge technology.

4 We require you to include all relevant documents with the application form.

5 Would you mind our cameraman recording your presentation?

6 We expected them to have made the final decision by now.

G2 **2** **Choose the best options (a or b) from (1–8) below to complete the text.**

I had an interview in the most incredible building yesterday. It's the new Department of Defence headquarters, and ¹_____ . It's a high-rise building and ²_____ . On arrival, ³_____ to the 'security suite', where ⁴_____ and ⁵_____ against government records. Once that is done, ⁶_____ for an appropriate level of security. From then on, when you go to particular departments, you just look into the camera as ⁷_____ , and it opens automatically. If a door is not security-sensitive, ⁸_____ .

1 a) an architect who specialises in hi-tech systems designed it
   b) it was designed by an architect who specialises in hi-tech systems

2 a) it towers over the surrounding office blocks
   b) the surrounding office blocks are towered over by it

3 a) a guard meets visitors and takes them
   b) visitors are met and taken

4 a) someone scanned their eyes
   b) their eyes are scanned

5 a) an official checks the images
   b) the images are checked

6 a) officials issue a pass
   b) a pass is issued

7 a) you approach a door
   b) a door is approached

8 a) body heat alone activates it
   b) it's activated by body heat alone

G3 **3** **Rewrite the sentences, using the word in brackets and without changing the meaning.**

1 Our managers let us wear shorts in the office because of the heat. (allowed)

2 The authorities confiscated our cameras at the airport. (had)

3 The gunmen forced us to hand over our valuables. (made)

4 The suspect was allowed to leave the police station after the interview. (let)

5 The college secretary is typing up Jack's thesis for him. (getting)

KL **4** **Complete the text with the phrases below.**

Ladies and gentlemen, I'd like to present our new household robot. We launched Robomate in the US last year and so far we have 25,000 units. ¹_____ Robomate can do – cleaning, hoovering, tidying – you name it. ²_____ that this is an extremely useful piece of equipment, vital for the elderly and disabled. ³_____ of what it can do – it can retrieve post and newspapers from the doormat, so better than a dog, eh? And the price of this little wonder? It's $10,000, ⁴_____ ! ⁵_____ , don't they?

a) yes, only $10,000

b) I'm sure you'd agree

c) It's incredible what

d) I think the facts speak for themselves

e) I'd like to give you another striking example

V1 **5** **Complete the sentences with an appropriate word or phrase from V1.**

1 Hawkings' work on cosmology was really _____ and paved the way for more research.

2 Surely you don't use a personal stereo any more? That's so _____ .

3 With the arrival of new, _____ diagnostic technology such as PET scanners, older tools such as simple X-rays are likely to become _____ in the not-too-distant future.

4 A lot of kitchen equipment today, such as toasters, come in really _____ designs.

5 Make sure you invite Andrew to the meeting; he often comes up with very _____ ideas.

6 Mum and Dad are so _____ sometimes. Honestly, they think that a DVD player is a _____ gadget!

V2, 3 **6** **One preposition in each of these sentences is incorrect. Find it and correct it.**

1 We'd like you to contribute at our magazine on a weekly basis.

2 That new advert on the radio really gets in my nerves.

3 We got down to a flying start on the very first day.

4 The mood in the office doesn't really account about the number of staff who have left.

5 The new software installed in the computers has really had an impact to their speed.

6 That report on the bombing in Iraq really got me up.

GRAMMAR

G1 Quantifiers

Use quantifiers before a noun to indicate the amount or quantity of the noun. A few quantifiers describe precise quantities, e.g. *both, no*. Most, however, describe vague quantities, e.g. *some, several, many, much, (a) few, (a) little*.

Note how they are used:

+ singular countable noun	+ plural countable noun	+ uncountable noun
no, either, every	no, any, both, (a) few, a lot of, some, several, many, most, all	no, (a) little, a lot of, some, much, most, all

To talk about things in general use quantifier + noun.
 We received **several packages** this morning.

To talk about something specific use quantifier + *of* + *the/my/our/these* etc. + plural noun.
 We received **several of the packages** you'd sent.

! With *all* and *both*, we do not need *of*:
 We received **both/all the packages** you'd sent.

! We don't use *no* + *of the*. We have to use the pronoun *none*:
 None of the letters arrived.

Sometimes we use quantifiers + noun/pronoun as subjects. Most are followed by a plural verb.
 Most of the volunteers **are** available.
 All the books **have** been signed by the author.

Note that *every, much* and *little* are followed by a singular verb:
 Every delegate **is** expected to attend.

With *no* and *none*, we can use either a singular or a plural verb:
 None of the students **was/were** prepared.

G2 Conditionals

These are the most common conditional forms:

Zero conditional

If + present, present / imperative

Use this for actions that happen every time a condition is fulfilled, and for instructions.
 If you **press** F1, the help menu **appears**.
 If the alarm **sounds**, **leave** the room at once.

First conditional

If + present, will/can/may/might/should + infinitive

Use the first conditional to talk about real possibilities, and for promises, warnings, etc.
 If it**'s raining** tomorrow, we **won't go** to the beach.
 If you **come** here again, I**'ll call** the police.

Second conditional

If + past, would/could/might + infinitive

Use the second conditional to talk about an unlikely possibility in the future or an unreal situation in the present or future, and to give advice.
 If I **got** the job, I**'d have to** move away.
 If we **had** more money, we **might stop** work.
 If I **were** you, I**'d finish** my degree.

Third conditional

If + past perfect, would/could/might + have + past participle

Use the third conditional to talk about unreal situations in the past, i.e. situations that are contrary to the facts, to express regrets and to criticise others.
 If I **hadn't been talking** on my mobile, the police **might not have stopped** me.
 If you **hadn't argued** with my mother, we **would have had** a nice evening.

Mixed conditionals

We use the clauses from the second and third conditionals to talk about present or past results of unreal situations.

i) *If + past perfect, would/might/could + infinitive*
 If he **hadn't left** me, I**'d** still **be** happy now.

ii) *If + past, would/might/could + have + past participle*
 If I **loved** him, I **wouldn't have left** him.

KEY LANGUAGE

KL1 Approving ideas

Sounds like a great idea!
I think it's a really good suggestion.
It's a good project, in my opinion.

KL2 Expressing doubts

I'm not too keen on this one.
I can see some real problems.
Will it really work?
I just don't think it's feasible.

KL3 Offering counter arguments

It could be a very expensive option.
But (X) might not be such a big problem.
Some of the projects must be for the long term.
It may not cost as much (money) as you think.

VOCABULARY

V1 Idioms with *hand*

a safe pair of hands, give someone a hand, hand in hand, have a hand in, have (got) your hands full, my hands are tied, on hand, time on your hands, turn your hand to anything

V2 Words from 7.2

contemporary, crescent, humanitarian, pilgrimage, providence, reluctantly, renowned

V3 Irregular plurals

criteria, phenomena, hypotheses, analyses, theses

G1 **1** Read the report. Find nine errors with quantifiers and correct them.

Creative writing course –
end-of-year report

This year's presentation of the course has been the most successful so far.

Results
- All of students passed the course and exam
- Most them (33/40) achieved a grade 3 or better
- Few (9/40) passed with a grade 1

Both the course tutors agrees that the results reflect the aptitude of the students. They agreed that most of this year's group have put in much hours and deserved their excellent results.

Student feedback
Only a little end-of-year feedback forms have been received so far (further information to follow). Of the students who have responded, several has commented that this course is the most interesting they have taken so far. Every student who have responded has praised the tutors for their knowledge and enthusiasm for their subject. No of the respondents so far feel that the course is too difficult.

G2 **2** Choose the correct meaning for each conditional.

1 If I were you, I wouldn't bother to read her latest novel.
  a) I think you should read the book.
  b) I don't think you should read the book.
2 We would have got you a ticket if they hadn't all sold out.
  a) We got you a ticket.
  b) We didn't get you a ticket.
3 The rubbish collectors don't see the bin if you leave it in the garden.
  a) They never see the bin in these circumstances.
  b) They sometimes don't see the bin.
4 If the flight to Dubai was delayed, we'd have to wait 24 hours for our connection.
  a) We think the flight will be delayed.
  b) We don't think the flight will be delayed.
5 The course won't take place if we don't have enough enrolments.
  a) We need a certain number of students for the course to take place.
  b) We can run the course with any number of students.
6 She'd probably have a job by now if she'd finished her teaching qualification.
  a) She has a job.
  b) She doesn't have a job.

3 Complete the conditional sentences with the correct form of the verbs in the brackets.

1 I _____ (join) an amateur operatic club if I _____ (can) sing better, but my voice isn't great.
2 The personnel department _____ (not overlook) you if we _____ (have) your details on file, but we don't appear to have them.
3 It's quite easy. If you _____ (put) the coins in and _____ (press) the green button, the machine _____ (print) the ticket.
4 We _____ (not sell) our old hi-fi if you _____ (tell) us that you wanted to keep it!
5 It's about time for a career change, so if the hospital _____ (offer) me that job, I think I _____ (take) it.

KL **4** Complete the monologue with phrases (a–f).

'Thanks for your presentation of the new organic cosmetic range. Personally, I think [1]_____ , but I have some reservations. First, [2]_____ with the pricing structure. It [3]_____ for our usual market, which doesn't spend a huge amount on cosmetics. [4]_____ to expect our customer base to switch to a product that's 20 per cent more expensive, so we need to explore a different market. But [5]_____ such a big problem as we sell into some very upmarket stores. Yes, I like this idea and think we should research it further. [6]_____ . What do the rest of you think?'

a) could be a very expensive option
b) I can see some problems
c) It's a good project, in my opinion
d) that might not be
e) it's a really good suggestion
f) I don't think it's feasible

V1 **5** Replace the words in italics with an idiom with *hand*. Make any other changes necessary.

1 Can you *help me*? I can't do this alone.
2 It's obvious that Richard *was involved in* this project!
3 Look, *I'm not very busy*. Let me finish that report.
4 Let's ask Gemma to help. *She's really versatile.*
5 I'm afraid *I'm can't do anything for you because of my position.* You could talk to Personnel.
6 Yes, I've got one of the driving licence applications *quite near*. Here we are.

V2 **6** Match the words from V2 with the definitions.

1 unwillingly; not wishing to do something
2 concerned with improving things for people living in poverty or other bad conditions
3 very famous, known and admired for something
4 a visit to a particular place for religious reasons
5 belonging to the present time
6 a street with a curved shape

GRAMMAR

G1 Verb patterns + -ing/infinitive

When one verb follows another, it may appear in the infinitive or -ing form.

verb + infinitive without *to*

Few verbs are followed by the infinitive without *to*, mainly modal verbs, verbs of perception (e.g. *see, watch, hear*), *help, make* and *let*.

> We **saw** the President's plane **land**.
> The police **made** the protestors **move back**.
> My boss **let** me **leave** work early today.

Note the passive of *make* and *let*.

> The protestors **were made to move** back.
> I **was allowed to leave** work early today.

! With verbs of perception the -ing form is used when we perceive only part of the action.

> We **saw** the house **burning**.

verb + (object) + infinitive

Many verbs are followed by the infinitive with *to*, often verbs of wants, desires, recommendations, e.g. *want, need, agree, appear, promise*. There are also many that have an object, e.g. *want, allow, advise, invite, recommend, urge, tell*.

> The editor **promised not to run** the story.
> We **invited the minister to appear** on the show.

verb + (object) + -*ing* form

Some verbs are followed by the -ing form, often verbs of liking/disliking, e.g. *like, enjoy* or verbs of thought, e.g. *consider, imagine*. Most of these can have an object.

> I **can't stand having** to wait for people!
> Can you **imagine being** trapped in a lift?
> The school **doesn't mind students bringing** their own lunch.

verb + (object) + preposition + -*ing* form

Many verbs are followed by a preposition. If another verb is used after the preposition, it is in the -ing form.

> The director **succeeded in raising** the money for the documentary.
> They **criticised the editor for printing** lies.

verb + -*ing* or infinitive

Some verbs can be followed by either the infinitive or the -ing form, with little change in meaning, e.g. *begin, continue, like*.

> I **continued to work/working** as though nothing was wrong.

G2 Prepositional verbs

Prepositional verbs always have an object (a noun, a pronoun or an -ing form), and the object always follows the preposition.

> The child **had broken into several houses** before he was caught.
> This is a tricky problem. Let me **look into it**.
> Barry can't **get over being** made redundant – he just isn't coping at all.

Adverbs of manner and degree can come between the verb and preposition, but not immediately after the preposition.

> We need to **deal quickly with** this issue. ✓
> ~~We need to **deal with** quickly this issue.~~ ✗

These adverbs, and most others, can come at the end of the clause.

> We need to **deal with** this issue **quickly**.
> Please **look into** the problem **immediately**.
> I **got through** the course **eventually**, on my third attempt!

KEY LANGUAGE

KL Being cautious

We need to think this (one) through.
If you don't (get the facts straight), he could (take us to court).
If X is the case, we could be in hot water/trouble.
X is a very sensitive issue.
If we get our facts wrong, it'll have a bad effect on our reputation.
It's just speculation on our part.
We need to hold fire on this one.
It could land us in court.

VOCABULARY

V1 The media

bias, broadsheet, chequebook journalism, circulation figures, deadline, libel laws, media coverage, off the record, popular press, pose a question, privacy, ratings wars, scoop, soundbite, source, speculation, spin, tabloid, viewing figures

V2 People in the media

anchor, columnist, correspondent, editor, paparazzo, producer, publicist, publisher, reporter

V3 Idioms with *keep*

keep a close eye on (something), keep a low profile, keep an open mind, keep track of (someone/something), keep your fingers crossed, keep your wits about you, keep in with

Extra practice

G1 **1** Complete the sentences with the verbs in brackets in the correct form.

1 Working on a newspaper, I really enjoy _____ (see) the publication process from start to finish.

2 The newspaper urged its readers _____ (not vote) in the forthcoming European election.

3 The corporation will continue _____ (broadcast) controversial programmes.

4 With your health problems, you really need to consider _____ (not spend) seven days a week in the office.

5 The travellers were made _____ (empty) their bags on the airport tarmac.

6 Is everything OK with Kyle? He appears _____ (be) rather short-tempered today.

7 The minister was criticised for _____ (not reveal) the extent of the budget deficit.

8 Several paparazzi watched the two cars _____ (crash) into each other and did nothing to help.

G2 **2** Rewrite the sentences using a suitable prepositional verb from the box, and making any changes necessary.

come across	come up	deal with	get over
get through	look at	look into	look like

1 The error in your account has been noted. We will investigate it immediately.

2 Please observe the animal's behaviour very closely.

3 We're back and we survived the week at Aunt Doreen's!

4 Your investigators need to handle this delicate matter carefully.

5 Most healthy people recover from this illness with no adverse effects.

6 The editor's suggestion arose entirely unexpectedly – out of nowhere.

7 If you find my old reading glasses in the study, can you hang on to them?

8 Your sister resembles Cameron Diaz amazingly! It's uncanny.

KL **3** Match the beginnings of the sentences with the endings.

1 If we don't get our facts straight,

2 Let's think about the implications of this –

3 We need to hold fire on this

4 This is just speculation on our part

5 Have you covered every possibility here?

6 We could be in very hot water

a) it's a very sensitive issue.

b) We really need to think this one through.

c) the actor involved could sue us.

d) if what you say is really the case.

e) so we'd better not publish it.

f) until we've heard from our lawyers.

V1 **4** Complete the sentences with a word from A and a word from B.

A: chequebook, circulation, libel, off, popular, ratings

B: figures, journalism, laws, press, the record, wars

1 It's not easy for newspapers to print untrue stories about people because of the _____ _____.

2 Many people hate _____ _____, where victims or even criminals are paid to tell their story.

3 The _____ _____ always sells more than the broadsheets.

4 The journalist told me my remarks were _____ _____, then printed the whole interview.

5 Reality TV gets huge viewing figures and usually wins the _____ _____.

6 Some broadsheets have increased their _____ _____ by changing their format to a smaller size.

V1, 2 **5** Complete the text with suitable words from V1 and V2. Use one word only in each gap.

I started life as a journalist on a very low-quality ^{1}_____ newspaper in the 1990s. I hated it, because I felt it had no principles: the ^{2}_____ checked every report from his journalists and he would change them to make them more sensational if necessary. The articles were often based on ^{3}_____ rather than hard facts, and some of its reporters had no respect for people's ^{4}_____ , no matter who they were. The important thing was always to get the ^{5}_____ before the other newspapers, and to send a ^{6}_____ out with a camera to get the most salacious photos possible. Well, I stuck it for two years, but then I was lucky to get a job on a ^{7}_____ . I'm still there, and I'm now a regular ^{8}_____ , writing in depth about any medical stories in the news.

V3 **6** Replace the words in italics with an idiom with *keep*. Make any other changes necessary.

1 I'm quite a quiet person. I tend *not to draw attention to myself* when I'm with other people.

2 In this job you need to *be ready to think quickly and deal with problems* as soon as they arise.

3 Everyone is *waiting and hoping for a good result* after their exams.

4 I've always admired Charlotte because she *listens and accepts other opinions* on most topics.

5 Our local shopkeeper won't allow more than two schoolboys in the shop together. He has to *watch them carefully* all the time.

6 It's essential to *read and learn about* current affairs if you want to do this job properly.

GRAMMAR

G1 Adverbs of degree

Adverbs of degree can be used to either intensify or soften the meaning of the word they qualify. They can qualify verbs, adjectives or adverbs.

They always come directly before the word they qualify.

> The measures announced **hardly address** the problem at all.
> Your suggestion is **totally impractical**.
> This juvenile is **quite likely** to offend again.

Common intensifying adverbs of degree are: *very, really, extremely, totally, utterly, entirely* and *highly*. Of these, only *really, totally, utterly* and *entirely* can qualify verbs.

> The director is **extremely** angry at the situation.
> All the applicants were **highly** qualified.

Common softening adverbs of degree are *quite, slightly, fairly*. These do not qualify verbs.

> It's **slightly** inconvenient that you've changed the time of the lecture.

We do not use the same adverbs of degree to qualify all adjectives. We use different adverbs with gradable adjectives and ungradable adjectives.

Gradable adjectives represent points on a scale, e.g. *hot* and *cold*; ungradable adjectives represent the **limits** of the scale, e.g. *boiling* and *freezing*.

The table shows common adverbs of degree used with the different types of adjective.

adverbs used with gradable adjectives	adverbs used with ungradable adjectives
very, extremely, fairly, really, slightly	absolutely, entirely, really, totally, utterly

So we say *very important* but *absolutely essential, extremely tired*, but *utterly exhausted*.

Many adverb-adjective combinations are quite fixed collocations, e.g. *highly qualified, completely different, fully convinced*.

The adverb *quite* has different meanings according to whether it is used with a gradable or ungradable adjective.

> It's **quite important**. = It's fairly important.
> It's **quite essential**. = It's absolutely essential.

G2 Reporting using nouns

It is also possible to introduce reported speech with a noun, e.g. *claim*. The 'rules' of reported speech remain the same.

> Patrick **claimed** he **had come** into the country legally, but it wasn't true. (*claim* = verb)
> Patrick's **claim** that he **had come** into the country legally wasn't true. (*claim* = noun)

There are many nouns that can introduce reported speech, e.g. *accusation, advice, answer, argument, claim, complaint, denial, excuse, explanation, observation, point, remark, response, statement, suggestion*.

> I asked my tutor about my bad marks. **His explanation** that my work **showed** little independent research was fair, I suppose.

KEY LANGUAGE

KL1 Balancing an argument

Having said that, ... the law / it isn't solely about ...
Although we're here to ..., I think that ...
That's all fair enough but it's simply too ...
Certainly X is important, but I still think that ...
While accepting X, we mustn't / shouldn't ...
Admittedly, X would be ...
I see what you're saying, but ...

VOCABULARY

V1 Idiomatic verb phrases

bring something to a halt, draw attention to yourself, know something is amiss, make a scene, make a song and dance about something, mind your own business, shirk your responsibilities, take something for granted, wash your dirty linen in public

V2 Justice systems

care system, community service, (non)-custodial sentence, deter, deterrent, juvenile delinquency, punishment, rehabilitation, young offenders, youth court

V3 Noun conversion

best, catch, complain, do, find, hopeful, international, investigate, walk, white

G1 **1 Choose the correct word. In one sentence, both are possible.**

1 Don't forget to send that court report. It's *very / absolutely* important they receive it tomorrow.

2 I *entirely / extremely* agree with all your points.

3 The defendant has admitted the assault so it's *slightly / highly* likely he'll get a custodial sentence.

4 We should look carefully at the final candidate – she was *highly / very* qualified.

5 I know the manager shouted at you, but don't worry, he was just *slightly / extremely* concerned about the deadline.

6 What do you think about the new project? I *really / very* believe that we should sponsor it.

7 This medication must be taken for fourteen days and it's quite *important / essential* that you finish the course or they won't be effective.

8 Let's not have an argument now. I'm *really / utterly* exhausted after work.

9 Losing those documents is *fairly / extremely* annoying, but we've got copies so it's not really a problem.

10 You're in serious trouble, so think *very / totally* carefully before you answer this question.

G2 **2 Complete the reported forms of the quotes.**

1 'I didn't steal the bike!'
   Sam denied that _____ , but it wasn't true.

2 'Your music is really loud.'
   Our neighbour complained that _____ , and she was quite right.

3 'I'll be on time tomorrow, honestly.'
   Janet insisted that she _____ , but it was ill-founded.

4 'We should close early today.'
   Our manager suggested that _____ , which was a relief.

5 'Lucy's put on a lot of weight.'
   Mark remarked that _____ , which was cruel.

3 Now change the sentences in Exercise 2 to use a suitable noun, e.g. Sam's denial that ...

1 Sam's denial that _____

2 Our neighbour's _____

3 Janet's _____

4 Our manager's _____

5 Mark's _____

KL **4 Complete the dialogue with KL phrases or parts of phrases.**

A: Can we talk about the proposed detention centre now? A lot of us are unhappy about that.

B: Well, [1]_____ to discuss general community issues, I think we should leave that until the relevant planning officer is available.

A: Mmm, I [2]_____ , but we really want to make our views known, and express our concerns.

B: I understand, and [3]_____ , but it's simply too early to get into discussion.

A: Yes, it's early and that's precisely why we want to discuss it now. [4]_____ is important, but can't we register our misgivings now?

B: OK, what are your misgivings?

A: Well, we really don't want criminals in our village.

B: That's a valid view, and [5]_____ opinions like these, I'm sure you'll understand we at the council mustn't listen only to your views ...

V1, 2 **5 Complete the text with words from V1 or 2.**

We've had a lot of problems with [1]_____ delinquency in our area. Young people hang around on street corners and cause problems. Only last week I saw two lads breaking things in my neighbour's front garden. I didn't want to make a [2]_____ but I equally didn't want to [3]_____ my responsibility to my neighbour. I complained to them about their behaviour, but they of course told me to [4]_____ my own business, so I called the police. The officer said that even if he arrested them, a [5]_____ would only give a [6]_____ sentence, such as [7]_____ , which in his opinion was no [8]_____ at all to other young people.

V2 **6 Find words and phrases in V2 that mean the following.**

1 imprisonment   _____

2 a criminal under the age of 18   _____

3 punishment that prevents further crime
                                     _____

4 punishment of working (unpaid), e.g. street cleaning
                                     _____

5 reforming offenders   _____

6 judicial process for young people _____

V3 **7 Complete the sentences with an appropriate noun.**

1 It's a lovely day. Let's have a _____ in the park after dinner.

2 Over 500 young _____ come to audition for the new *Pop Stars* show.

3 My daughter's boyfriend is handsome, successful and kind. He's a very good _____ .

4 I'll do my _____ to sort out your problem, but you may need to call in a computer expert.

GRAMMAR

G1 Non-finite clauses

A non-finite clause contains a non-finite verb, i.e. a verb that has no indication of person or tense.

Arriving late, we failed to find a hotel.

In this example, the non-finite clause is *arriving late*, and the non-finite verb is *arriving*. A non-finite verb usually relates to the subject of the main clause (*we*), and we know the time/tense from the verb in the main clause (past).

Non-finite clauses express different relationships with the main clause, e.g. time, reason, condition, result. In this case, it is reason:

Because we arrived late, we failed to find ...

There are three main types of non-finite clause.

Present participle clause

In these clauses the non-finite verb is active.

The company reduced its overhead, **cutting 60 jobs**. (i.e. with the result that it cut 60 jobs)

Present participle clauses can also replace relative clauses.

Did you hear the fox **calling in the garden** last night? (i.e. the fox that was calling)

Past participle clause

In these clauses the non-finite verb is passive.

Handled carefully, this glassware should last a lifetime. (i.e. if it is handled with care)

This type of clause can also replace a relative.

The police have identified the driver **killed in the crash**. (i.e. the driver who was killed)

Infinitive clause

An infinitive clause is formed with *to* + infinitive. It usually expresses a purpose or result.

They installed dim lighting **to improve the ambience in the shops.**

We came home early (only) **to find that everyone had left.**

This can also replace a relative.

Walcott was the only player **to score a goal.**

When an infinitive clause expresses purpose, it can come before the main clause.

To improve the ambience in the shops, they installed dim lighting.

! Note that non-finite clauses are usually used in formal writing.

G2 Spoken English

Spoken English differs from written English in a number of ways, and to the extent that we talk about the grammar of spoken English.

These are the most common features of spoken English:

1 overlaps – two speakers talking at the same time, usually when one interrupts another in order to say something

2 listener responses – supportive comments such as *Really?*. *Go on, I know what you mean*

3 hesitation and use of sounds such as *er*, *um*

4 repetition of words and phrases

5 discourse markers such as *well*, *you know*, *I mean*, *like*, which give a speaker time to organise his/her thoughts

6 simple clause structure, adding clauses to each other, often independent clauses with *and*, *but* and *or* (also called the 'add-on strategy'), or simple dependent clauses introduced by a conjunction such as *because* or *if*

7 ellipsis – omitting grammatical words such as pronoun and articles

8 reformulations – when a speaker starts a sentence but then either can't finish it or changes to say something else, or express him/herself in a different way

KEY LANGUAGE

KL Informal phrases

That is, ...
And as for ...
But then again, ...
Oh, and before I forget ...
Anyway, ...
I reckon (that) ...
You know, ...
By and large, ...
... that kind of thing.
So, all in all, ...

VOCABULARY

V1 Performance reviews

adaptation, bill, choir, choreographer, company, trio, venue, virtuoso

V2 Compound adjectives

award-winning, awe-inspiring, bass-heavy, British-born, female-featuring, laughter-packed, out-of-the-way, Rambert-trained, star-studded

V3 Academic verbs

consume, distribute, enable, erode, identify, indicate, reinforce, vary

G1 **1** **Choose the correct form of the verbs.**

1 *Playing / To play* with the Berlin Philharmonic was James' lifetime ambition.

2 *Playing / Played* his first performance with the Berlin Philharmonic, James' felt he'd reached the pinnacle of his career.

3 *Playing / Played* by a virtuoso, the violin is truly the king of instruments.

4 We hurried to get to the theatre on time, only *found / to find* the performance had been cancelled.

5 *Found / Finding* by a nurse on the hospital steps, the baby was named Florence.

6 Luke dropped the course on the technology of music, *to find / finding* it too difficult.

2 **Rewrite the underlined part of the sentences, using a non-finite clause.**

1 The theatre raised its ticket prices <u>so that it could fund the renovation</u>.

_____

2 <u>When we arrived at the hotel</u>, we discovered that they'd given us a suite.

_____

3 We bought the tickets on e-Bay, <u>then we found that we had paid twice as much as our friends</u>!

_____

4 The organisers will identify and destroy <u>tickets that have been produced illegally</u>.

_____

5 Do you remember the name of the actor <u>who was playing that role at the time</u>?

_____

6 Mario was the only student <u>who thanked me for the extra tuition</u>.

_____

7 Because the show proved to be a success, <u>it was given an extended run at the Royal Theatre</u>.

_____

8 <u>If you water these plants regularly</u>, they will provide tomatoes for several months.

_____

G2 **3** **Look at the parts of the dialogue in italics (1–8), and match them with the features of spoken English below. (Ignore the gaps.)**

overlap ____   listener response ____   hesitation ____

repetition ____   discourse marker ____   ellipsis ____

add-on strategy ____   reformulation ____

A: I've just been reading this article about the Internet changing entertainment completely, ¹*you know, like*, we download movies and a) ____.

B: ²*Mmm*, not sure what I think about that really, I mean, I download movies sometimes, but I still watch them on ³*TV* ...

C: *Yeah, and at the cinema.* b) ____ , I still watch them at the cinema. It's a better and, ⁴*er*, more complete experience.

B: That's right. But I c) ____ that a lot of people watch movies on their laptops, I mean, ⁵*if they want to be* ... it's just convenient.

C: Sure, but it's such a small screen, and d) ____ watching movies on MP3 players, well ...

A: ⁶*Go on*.

C: Well, ⁷*it's* ... it's just ridiculous! They're so small, e) ____ is, you can't get any nuances from the image ⁸*because it's too small, and it's easy to be distracted and the sound isn't great* ...

A: Good point, but f) ____ , surely the point of MP3 players is that the sound is very good.

C: Oh, I don't know. I just know I prefer the big screen!

KL **4** **Match a–f in the dialogue with these words/phrases.**

1 reckon   2 then again   3 that kind of thing
4 anyway   5 that   6 as for

V1, 3 **5** **Replace the underlined words with words with similar meanings from V1/3.**

Last night's performance of the Maidenhead Youth Ensemble was a marvel and has served to ¹<u>support</u> this newspaper's view that we need to invest more in the arts movement for the young. The ²<u>group</u> consists of a small orchestra, but a large ³<u>band of singers</u>, and the ⁴<u>programme</u> included a superb solo by the young piano ⁵<u>genius</u> from Marlow, Adrian King, whose interpretation of Rachmaninov is second to none. The ⁶<u>place</u> for the concert was a local church, which made for a very atmospheric evening, and the acoustics ⁷<u>made it possible for</u> us to appreciate the solos as much as the full ensemble pieces. With groups like this it is possible to ⁸<u>pick out</u> stars of the future, like young Adrian, and that is where local arts council funds should be channelled.

1 _____   2 _____   3 _____   4 _____
5 _____   6 _____   7 _____   8 _____

V2 **6** **Complete the sentences with compound adjectives.**

1 The bill for tonight at the comedy club promises a _____ evening.

2 What I don't like about rock music is that it's very drum- and _____ .

3 Don't miss the opportunity to see this _____ film – it well deserved its six Oscars.

4 The circus performer's abilities on the high wire are truly _____ and have to be seen.

5 The _____ singer, raised and educated in London, could perform with any of the soul greats.

6 The performance is what we have come to expect from this spectacular, _____ ballet dancer.

GRAMMAR

G1 Alternatives to *if*

There are several different expressions that we can use in conditional sentences other than *if*.

unless

Unless means *if not*, but we can only use it in 'real' conditions, not in imaginary conditions where the result is contrary to known facts:

I'll get you a ticket **unless** it's too expensive.
~~I'd stay here unless I got a good job abroad.~~ ✗
~~They'd join us now unless they were so busy.~~ ✗

provided/on the condition that, as long as/assuming

We usually use these conjunctions with the first conditional. They suggest that a condition is necessary.

I'll lend you the car **provided (that)** you bring it back this evening.

We often use *but for* with the third conditional. It is a preposition so has to be followed by a noun.

But for her quick thinking, we would have had a serious accident. (= If it hadn't been for ...)

supposing, what if, in case

We use these mainly with the second conditional to speculate about imaginary conditions. They are quite informal.

Supposing you could take a month off work, where would you go?

We use *in case* to suggest a course of action in a possible situation. It is different from if:

I'll take an umbrella **in case** it rains. (= I don't know if it will rain, but I'll take an umbrella.)
I'll take an umbrella **if** it rains. (= in the situation where it is raining, I'll take an umbrella.)

We use *even if* to emphasise a condition or to suggest that it's unexpected.

Even if I passed my exams, I still wouldn't go to university. (I probably won't pass the exams.)

Whether or not introduces two possible conditions. We can use the phrase together or split it:

I'm going to become an economist, **whether or not** you think it's a good idea.
I'm going to become an economist, **whether** you think it's a good idea **or not**.

G2 Phrasal verbs

Phrasal verbs consist of verb + adverb particle. They can be transitive or intransitive.

Intransitive phrasal verbs

Intransitive phrasal verbs do not have an object (and can therefore not be passive). They are often used in instructions and commands.

Stand up. Come back. Watch out for the foxes.

Transitive phrasal verbs

These have an object. A noun object can either come between the verb and the particle or after the particle.

I feel obliged to **turn down your offer**.
I feel obliged to **turn your offer down**.

However, a pronoun object has to come between the verb and the particle.

I'm sorry that I had to **point it out** to you. ✓
~~I'm sorry that I had to point out it to you.~~ ✗

Note where we can place adverbs.

Please **fill this form in** carefully. ✓
Please **fill in this form** carefully. ✓
~~Please fill this form carefully in.~~ ✗
~~Please fill in carefully this form.~~ ✗
~~Please fill carefully this form in.~~ ✗

In relative clauses, the adverb cannot come before the relative pronoun, unlike prepositional verbs.

It was your suggestion **which I took up**. ✓
It was your suggestion **up which I took**. ✗

KEY LANGUAGE

KL1 Setting an agenda

Let's talk about ...
I propose we discuss ...

KL2 Responding to offers

Sounds OK to me. / Yeah, that's fine.
Well, I'm sorry. That's not acceptable.
We're not happy about (the terms you offer).
We're not prepared to (invest in) ... unless ...
I'm sorry, we were looking for (a much higher stake).

VOCABULARY

V1 Business and economic terms

assets and liabilities, boom and slump, creditors and debtors, imports and exports, income and expenditure, mortgages and loans, profit and loss, supply and demand, takeovers and mergers

V2 Confusing words

affect – effect, creditors – debtors, debt – loan, discrete – discreet, principle – principal

V3 Suffixes (nouns 2)

abolition, abstention, admission, clarification, collision, confusion, decision, donation, elimination, extension, instigation, permission

Extra practice

11

G1 **1 Complete the mini-dialogues with an alternative to *if*. More than one may be possible.**

1 Can I leave early to pick up my son?
– Yes, _____ that you finish the urgent work.

2 Are you going to apply for the job?
– Yes, _____ it would mean that I'd have to move. I don't want to move again.

3 _____ you could invite anyone at all to dinner, who would it be?
– Oh, Nelson Mandela, no question!

4 That agent hasn't called, and I have to go now.
– Leave the details with me _____ he calls later.

5 You can go to the club this evening _____ you're back by 11.00p.m.
– OK, thanks, Dad.

6 How will you vote in the meeting?
– Against. I don't think we should sell, _____ they offer the full price.

7 I think Smiths may offer you your old job back.
– They needn't bother. I wouldn't go back there _____ they offered to pay me double!

8 It was lucky that the airport official was there.
– Yes, _____ his help, we might have missed the flight.

G2 **2 Write the words in the correct order to make sentences with phrasal verbs. There may be more than one correct order.**

1 smoking my father up recently gave

_____

2 that road the potholes for in out watch

_____

3 the offer down you'd turn politely better

_____

4 information interesting that's – found out who it?

_____

5 when played up the national anthem is stand

_____

6 very efficiently the meeting up set assistant your

_____

7 the issue bring which want that's I up to

_____

8 it you the agenda fit in can to?

_____

KL **3 Complete the dialogue with a KL phrase or part of a phrase.**

A: Are we all here? Good. OK, first, I ¹_____ the budget for the new magazine.

B: Yeah, ²_____ .

C: Actually, we'd like to suggest a different order.
³_____ about the schedule first, as in Design, we're ⁴_____ the timescale you're proposing.

A: OK, the schedule, then. We've proposed a deadline for copy on the 15th of each month, and then a disc to printer date of the 29th.

C: Well, I'm sorry, ⁵_____ . We can't design a 192-page magazine in two weeks.

A: I realise it's tough, but it's a current affairs magazine, so we have to produce it quickly.

B: Well, we appreciate that, but we were ⁶_____ a much longer turnaround, say 28 days. Can we look at getting closer to that ...

V1 **4 Complete the sentences with the two terms in brackets in the correct order.**

1 (*income and expenditure*) I check my personal accounts each month to ensure my _____ isn't higher than my _____ .

2 (*supply and demand*) It's essential to reduce manufacturing output when _____ outstrips _____ , and spare output can't be sold.

3 (*imports and exports*) A successful economy is likely to have higher levels of _____ than _____ .

4 (*creditors and debtors*) Some people say the secret to a successful business is to demand payment from your _____ within 30 days but pay your _____ only after 60 days.

5 (*boom and bust*) For every economic _____ , there's likely to be a depressing _____ round the corner.

6 (*mortgages and loans*) The company has huge debts, both in the form of _____ on its properties and _____ for purchasing expensive equipment.

V2 **5 Choose the correct word.**

1 I really need to pay off my credit card *loans/debt*.

2 I've forgotten to bring my calculator. Can you *borrow / lend* me one?

3 I'd advise you to be *discreet / discrete* about this project – it's confidential.

4 I'm afraid the question of funding didn't *arise / rise* in the meeting.

5 The *affects / effects* of slavery lasted well beyond the 19th century.

6 We're pleased to announce the appointment of Mike Richards as our new *principle / principal*.

V3 **6 Complete the words from their definitions.**

1 the giving of money or goods
_ _ _ _ _ ion

2 a crash between two vehicles
_ _ _ _ _ _ ion

3 the official ending of a law or system
_ _ _ _ _ _ ion

4 not voting for or against something
_ _ _ _ _ _ _ ion

5 being officially allowed to do something
_ _ _ _ _ _ _ ion

6 the removal or destruction of something
_ _ _ _ _ _ _ _ ion

GRAMMAR

G1 Cohesion 2 (substitution and ellipsis)

When we construct a text, whether spoken or written, we use a number of devices to ensure that we avoid repeating things too much and also to ensure the flow of the text. Two of these are substitution and ellipsis.

Substitution

This means replacing one word or phrase with another. The most common form of substitution is substituting a pronoun for a noun (nominal substitution).

John's arrived. **He**'s in the living room.
We take **plastic** completely for granted. The **material** has been with us for 75 years now and it is here to stay. This **wonder stuff** has so many uses …

We often use different nouns for the same thing in order to avoid repetition (lexical substitution).

We can also use words like *one*, *ones*, *the sort* to substitute nouns.

This course is too expensive. I need to find a cheaper **one**.

If we want to avoid repeating a verb or a verb phrase, we use the auxiliary *do* (verbal substitution).

I need to write up the experiment but I'll **do** it tomorrow. (do = write)

We can use *so* or *not* to replace whole clauses, with *do* or with other verbs (clausal substitution).

They said we were required to complete the form, and we **did so**. (= completed the form)

Can we afford to ignore this problem? I think **not**. (= I think we can't afford to ignore this problem.)

Ellipsis

This means omitting something completely.

We can omit nouns after words like *some*, *the other* and comparatives.

He wants to go to one lecture and I want to go to **the other**.
We were offered two rooms and we chose the **bigger**.

In repeated verb phrases we can usually omit the main verb rather than repeat it.

'She shouldn't have apologised. It wasn't important.'
'I disagree. I think she **should (have)**.'

G2 Nominalisation

Nominalisation means using a noun rather than a verb or an adjective.

The committee **postponed** the meeting …
The **postponement** of the meeting (by the committee) …
The tiny baby was **perfect**. It astounded him.
The **perfection** of the tiny baby astounded him.

Nominalisation is common in formal writing. We use it for a number of reasons:

It can combine two clauses so is more economical.
The university decided to expand its physics department, which attracted greater funding. (
The university's decision to expand its science department attracted greater funding.

It can be used to avoid mentioning who does an action.
The government closed the mine and made 300 miners redundant. (The **closure** of the mine resulted in **300 redundancies**.)

It can be used to summarise a previous point.
Protestors have prevented traffic from moving through the centre again today. **This situation** cannot be allowed to continue. (this situation = protestors preventing traffic from moving)

Nominalisations are often followed by a preposition:
postponement of, arrival at, wait for.

KEY LANGUAGE

KL Referring to what other people have said

As (Steven) said, …
What (Steven) said about …
If I understand you correctly, you're saying …
If I could just pick up on something that (Steven) said about …
(Steven) claimed that …, suggesting that …
With regard to (Steven's) argument that …
Perhaps we should return to what (Steven) said, which was …

VOCABULARY

V1 Science and nature subject words

blossom, carnivorous, germinate, jellyfish, mercury, meteor, orbit, parasite, pollination, polythene, ridge, volcano

V2 Informal phrases

anti-plastic brigade, bonkers, bother, have something up to here (I've had it up to here), rant, spout (vb), tree-hugger, (be) wheeled out

V3 Collective nouns

a bunch of, a group of, a flock of, a herd of, a pack of, a set of, a shoal of, a swarm of

G1 **1** Read the text. Find and circle eight examples of substitution and five examples of ellipsis.

There's a lot of publicity about recycling these days and whenever I see some I wonder if it really does a lot of good. I'm all for helping the environment – of course I am – but sometimes I wonder whether all the different rubbish and recycling collections are really useful. I mean, we have a bin for household waste and one for green; we have a small bin for compost for our own garden and another that goes to council compost. We've got a box for glass, another container for plastic and a third for paper. But is all this rubbish really separated out once it's collected? Sometimes I doubt it. Then of course there's the waste that we're supposed to take to the recycling centre. I do this all the time, but then each time I go to the centre I wonder if I should have, because I use the car, and that just causes pollution ...

2 Improve these texts by changing repetitions either to use substitution or ellipsis.

1 Our local council has proposed fitting microchips in all our rubbish bins. The microchips detect if the wrong type of rubbish is put in the bins. Residents would be really angry if the council put microchips in the bins, and residents have said they would refuse to comply with the proposal.

2 Apparently, incinerators are the best way of getting rid of non-recyclable rubbish so the council wants to install an incinerator here. The problem with incinerators is that incinerators can produce toxic fumes and obviously people living nearby don't like the fact they produce toxic fumes.

G2 **3** Rewrite the sentences, using a noun form of the underlined word.

1 The images have been computer <u>enhanced</u>, which makes them much sharper.

_____

2 We were amazed that Selina <u>recovered</u> so fast from the illness.

_____

3 The food here is <u>excellent</u>, making the restaurant good value for money.

_____

4 The hijacker <u>threatened</u> the flight attendant, which terrified the passengers.

_____

5 The factory is <u>capable</u> of producing 1,000 cars per week, which makes it very profitable.

_____

6 The President <u>arrived</u> and he was greeted by crowds at the airport.

_____

KL **4** Complete the gaps in the sentences.

'In *Questions Now*, we discussed climate change. We've had a lot of phone calls on this topic.'

1 If I could _____ on _____ Mr Davies said, it seems there have been no tests to check coastline erosion ...

2 Mr Davies _____ this was already happening, _____ that he had reliable information.

3 Perhaps we _____ to _____ the first speaker said, _____ connected with the warming climate.

4 With _____ the Minister's argument that we aren't prepared for the effects of climate change, ...

5 If I _____ you _____ , you're saying that you don't think climate change is a serious issue?

V1 **5** Find words in V1 to match these definitions.

1 cause a seed to grow/develop _____
2 long area of high land _____
3 meat-eating _____
4 organism that lives on another organism _____
5 path of, e.g. a planet in space _____
6 piece of rock that travels through space _____
7 silver-white poisonous metal _____
8 strong, light plastic _____

V2 **6** Rewrite the words in italic with an informal phrase.

A: You know, [1]*I really can't tolerate any more of* these [2]*aggressive arguments* you get in the press against taking the kids to school by car.

B: I know what you mean. I hate these people who [3]*talk incessantly* about parents causing congestion in the streets morning and evening, as if no one else goes out then.

A: Yeah, and they seem to think we're [4]*insane* driving the kids around. Don't these [5]*environmentally-concerned people* realise that we wouldn't [6]*expend time and effort* getting the car out if we didn't have to because of the distance?

V3 **7** Match the sentence beginnings with their endings and complete the ending with an appropriate noun.

1 Jonathan gave Sue a bunch of
2 We were lucky enough to see a herd of
3 Can you bring a spare pack of
4 That farmer has a large flock of
5 The cruise takes us around the whole group of
6 We need to get a new set of

a) _____ to go with the new dining table.
b) _____ to the games evening?
c) _____ for her birthday.
d) _____ in the mid-Aegean Sea.
e) _____ , and they're really vicious.
f) _____ on the safari.

INFORMATION FOR STUDENT A

Lesson 2.4 Exercise 6 (page 23)

Student A

Mayor

You lead the meeting.

You should ask:

- Ricardo Hernandez to state his position regarding the project and to explain the advantages of the project to the local Granville inhabitants

- the other members of the meeting to state their position, with their reasons

- if anyone has any questions they would like to put to Ricardo Hernandez.

Try to have a full and frank discussion. At the end of the meeting, say whether or not you will recommend the Council to support Ricardo Hernandez's project.

Lesson 11.4 Exercise 6 (page 119)

Group A

Lesson 4.2 Exercise 1 (page 40)

Student A

Read the profile of Michael Moore. What questions do you need to ask to find the missing information? Ask your questions and answer your partner's ones.

Michael Moore was born in [1]_____ in an industrial town called Flint in the USA. When he was 22 years old, he founded a local weekly newspaper, and he then went on to [2]_____. In 1989, he completed his first documentary film, called *Roger and Me*, which was about [3]_____ . He had to partly finance this film by selling his house, but eventually it received both [4]_____ , making over $7 million at the box office. [5]_____ began in 2002, when he released *Bowling for Columbine*, which is about guns and violence in American society. This film won [6]_____ and, at that time, became the highest grossing documentary of all time. He followed this up with [7]_____ , which is highly critical of the then US President, George W Bush. This film became the first documentary to [8]_____ , and it made even more money than *Bowling for Columbine*. His third great success was the film entitled [9]_____ , which is about the American health care system. When he showed this at the Cannes Film Festival in 2007, he famously received [10]_____ . In 2005, he was named by *Time* magazine as one of the world's 100 most influential people, and he hasn't stopped making films yet.

INVENTORS

Read the information and prepare for the negotiation. Decide: a) what your priorities are b) what concessions you can make c) what strategy and tactics you will use in the negotiation.
You want Ariel Capital:

Finance

to give you at least $500,000. In return, you will offer them a 30 per cent stake in your company. You do not want to give up control of your company.

Support

to provide and pay for a Managing Director to run the company during the first year.
to recommend an accountant who can look after the financial affairs of the company.
to offer on-going advice on any problems which will arise during the first year.
to agree to your partner being in charge of all the company's marketing.
to pay for a course on international marketing for your partner.
You are prepared to offer AC an additional 5 per cent stake in the business (35 per cent in total) if they will provide on-going management support and advice after the first year.

Facilities

to help you find factory space to produce the device in large quantities and to hire a supervisor to manage production of the MLSD.

Long-term planning

to help you build up your company so that eventually you will become the Chairman and Managing Director of a major international firm, offering a range of high tech products.

ACTIVITIES

Lesson 5.4 Exercise 5 (page 55)
Student A

You think All Seasons should target the under-35s.

Why? How would you attract these people to the stores? What new facilities would be good to have? What would make All Seasons a destination store for them?

All Seasons would have to sell more up-to-date fashion. How could this be achieved? Would it be better to sell disposable fashion at low prices or quality clothes at higher but reasonable prices?

In general, you think the store should change direction radically, rather than offer special ranges aimed at particular groups

What would the disadvantages be of targeting the family market, or the over-40s?

Lesson 4.4 Exercise 6 (page 45)
Student A

SKIN CANCER

Skin cancer caused by too much exposure to the sun: UV radiation damages skin cells, leading to premature ageing, possibly cancer – can be fatal. Fair-skinned people are most susceptible.

Skin cancer facts
- second most common cancer amongst people aged 20–39
- skin cancer rates rising dramatically: increased number of foreign holidays, excessive use of sun beds
- more male sufferers than female; men less likely to visit their doctor to check skin problems

Ways to lessen the risk of getting skin cancer
- avoid direct sun, especially between 11 a.m. and 3 p.m.
- avoid burning in the sun; use T-shirt and hat
- children need extra protection
- use high factor sunscreen
- report changes to your skin – such as moles that change shape – to your doctor

Lesson 12.4 Exercise 6a (page 129)
Student A

A senior member of the National Academy of Science

You are intensely pro-science and believe that its purpose is to expand human knowledge and to advance human society.

Look at all the discussion questions, and prepare your points of view.

You are chair for the discussion of the first question.

Lesson 12.4 Exercise 6a (page 129)
Student E

A member of Earthwatch, an eco-pressure group

You want science to work to benefit the world as a whole, and that it should not harm or exploit the natural world.

Look at all the discussion questions, and prepare your point of view.

You are chair for the discussion of the fifth question.

Lesson 11.3 Exercise 11 (page 117)
Student A

You are a Sales Representative who has recently done very well. You recently became salesperson of the year. You think you should have:
- a 10 percent salary raise
- a top-of-the-range new company car to impress your clients
- to work two days a week from home (for phone sales)
- more time for training courses and staff development

Negotiate with each other and try to get a good outcome. Begin by putting yourself in the other person's shoes.

Lesson 12.4 Exercise 6a (page 129)
Student B

A member of the public – a taxi driver

You are generally positive about science and the improvements it makes to our lives.

You are chair for the discussion of the second question.

Lesson 4.2 Exercise 1 (page 40)
Student B

Read the profile of Michael Moore. What questions do you need to ask to find the missing information? Ask your questions and answer your partner's ones.

Michael Moore was born in 1954 in an industrial town called [1]_____ in the USA. When he was 22 years old, he [2]_____ , and he then went on to work as a journalist for other political journals. In 1989, he completed [3]_____ , called *Roger and Me*, which was about the effect on his home town when local industries moved their factories abroad to cut costs. He had to partly finance this film by [4]_____ , but eventually it received both critical and financial success, making over [5] $_____ at the box office. His most successful period began in 2002, when he released *Bowling for Columbine*, which is about [6]_____ . This film won an Oscar for the best documentary film and, at that time, became [7]_____ . He followed this up with the film *Fahrenheit 9/11*, which is highly critical of [8]_____ . This film became the first documentary to win the Palm D'Or award at the Cannes Film Festival, in France, and it made even more money than *Bowling for Columbine*. His third great success was the film entitled *Sicko*, which is about [9]_____ . When he showed this at the Cannes Film Festival in 2007, he famously received a 20 minute-long standing ovation from the audience. In 2005, he was named by *Time* magazine as [10]_____ , and he hasn't stopped making films yet.

Lesson 11.1 Exercise 7 (page 113)

Your decisions	(this year)	(next year)	
Education and training	_____	_____	%
Defence (army, air force, etc.)	_____	_____	%
Law and order (police, prisons and the legal system)	_____	_____	%
Infrastructure (roads, railways, etc.)	_____	_____	%
Health care	_____	_____	%
Investment in industry (subsidies)	_____	_____	%
Environment (e.g. recycling, traffic reduction, etc.)	_____	_____	%
Social services (for children/the elderly/ the unemployed, etc.)	_____	_____	%
Public service jobs	_____	_____	%
Arts and Culture	_____	_____	%
International development (reducing world poverty)	_____	_____	%

Lesson 5.4 Exercise 5 (page 55)
Student B

You think All Seasons should focus on the family market, and not worry about teenagers and young adults. Why?

How would you attract these people to the stores? What new facilities would be good to have? What would make All Seasons a destination store for them?

All Seasons would have to sell more up-to-date fashion. How could this be achieved? Would it be better to sell disposable fashion at low prices or quality clothes at higher but reasonable prices?

You think it would be a good idea to have special ranges aimed at particular groups, e.g. young mothers and small children.

What would the disadvantages be of targeting teenagers and young adults, or the over-40s?

Lesson 2.4 Exercise 6 (page 23)
Student B

Ricardo Hernandez

Try to persuade members that your project will be good for the island.

- You will invest one billion dollars in the project.
- The investment will generate $200,000 annually for the island.
- It will create 650 new jobs.
- It will bring 400 per cent more tourists to the island each year.
- It will raise the profile of Granville Island internationally.

You can offer:

- to build a primary school, shops and 100 houses for local residents.
- to protect the environment where possible. You will have to cut down mangrove trees to clear the area, but will replant mango trees in other parts of the island.

Lesson 11.3 Exercise 11 (page 117)
Student B

You are the Sales Manager and boss of the salesperson. You want to keep your salesperson of the year, but the company as a whole has had a difficult year. You think:

- the company can only afford a 4 percent increase in salary
- the salesperson should have a standard model car like everyone else
- working from home should be limited to one day
- there is no budget for training at the moment

Negotiate with each other and try to get a good outcome. Begin by putting yourself in the other person's shoes.

Lesson 11.4 Exercise 6 (page 119)
Group B

ARIEL CAPITAL NEGOTIATORS

Read the information and prepare for the negotiation. Decide: a) what your priorities are b) what concessions you can make c) what strategy and tactics you will use in the negotiation.
You want:

Finance

to offer finance in the range of $300,000–$500,000 in return for a stake of at least 40 percent. Ideally, you would like to have a controlling interest in the company (over 50 percent).

Support

to introduce a management structure in the firm by appointing a Managing Director, Financial Director, Marketing and Production manager within the first year.
to provide on-going advice and expertise to help the company to expand and become international.

Facilities

to outsource the production of the device either to a local firm or to an overseas manufacturer in China or India. This would reduce costs and increase profits on the product.

Long-term planning

to persuade the inventors to focus on inventing new high tech products to add to the firm's product range.
to grow the company until it is large and profitable enough to be sold – in 5–10 years' time.

Lesson 4.4 Exercise 6 (page 45)
Student B

HEALTHY EATING

Healthy diet reduces the risk of heart disease and cancer

'Superfoods' help fight serious illnesses, e.g. berries and tomatoes.

Food that contains Omega-3 oils helps maintain a healthy brain and memory, e.g. oily fish.

Facts about healthy eating habits

- less than 25 per cent of the population aged 12–64 eat the recommended five portions of fruit and vegetables per day
- Only 12 percent of children eat five or more portions of fruit and vegetables per day
- less than half of the population eat oily fish at least once a week

What is a healthy diet?

- at least five portions of fruit and vegetables each day
- plenty of fibre, such as cereals and wholemeal bread
- limited amounts of red and processed meats, e.g. ham, bacon
- food rich in Omega 3 at least once a week

Lesson 2.4 Exercise 6 (page 23)
Student C

Head of the Wildlife Society

You represent the conservationists, bird lovers, farmers and fishermen in the area.

You are totally against the project because:

- cutting down the mangrove trees and clearing the waterfront area will seriously affect fish stocks.

- The 80 different species of birds in the area will be threatened. The Virginia dove will become extinct.

- The rare turtle will no longer come to White Sands beach to breed

Find out:

- what Ricardo Hernandez will do to protect the environment

- if the ramblers will have access to the beach.

Lesson 5.4 Exercise 5 (page 55)
Student C

You think All Seasons should focus on the over-40s. Why?

How would you attract these people to the stores? What new facilities would be good to have? What would make All Seasons a destination store for them?

All Seasons would have to sell more up-to-date fashion. How could this be achieved? Would it be better to sell disposable fashion at low prices or quality clothes at higher but reasonable prices?

In general, you think the store should change direction radically, rather than offer special ranges aimed at particular groups.

What would the disadvantages be of targeting the family market, or teenagers and young adults?

Lesson 4.4 Exercise 6 (page 45)
Student C

PHYSICAL FITNESS

Regular exercise helps prevent obesity. Being overweight increases the risk of heart disease and some cancers.

Physical fitness facts

- 35 per cent of men and 41 per cent of women are inactive

- obesity causes around 12,000 cases of cancer each year

- physical activity has declined in girls by 46 per cent and in boys by 23 percent in the last five years

How much exercise should you do?

- Just 30 minutes of exercise, five days a week, will keep you healthy

- You must balance the energy you take in from food with the energy you burn through activity.

Lesson 12.4 Exercise 6a (page 129)
Student C

A journalist

You speak from a personal point of view, and you always question people's arguments closely – you like strong and healthy discussion.

Look at all the discussion questions, and prepare your points of view.

You are chair for the discussion of the third question.

Lesson 2.4 Exercise 6 (page 23)
Student D

Journalist

You represent the opinions of your readers. You are against the project.

- Over 60 per cent of your readers are against Hernandez's project.
- They believe that the natural beauty of this part of the island will be destroyed, resulting in fewer tourists visiting the area.
- Ramblers are particularly worried as they think Hernandez will stop them from exploring the area.
- Readers fear that access to White Sands beach will be restricted or that Hernandez will make people pay to go on some areas of the beach.
- Readers fear that Hernandez will lose interest in the resort once it has been built.

Lesson 12.4 Exercise 6a (page129)
Student D

A member of the public – a shop manager

You are generally sceptical of the claims made by scientists, particularly when they claim new developments will be safe.

Look at all the discussion questions, and prepare your points of view.

You are chair for the discussion of the fourth question.

Lesson 5.4 Exercise 5 (page 55)
Student D

You are the Chief Executive of All Seasons.

You would prefer to offer specialised ranges of products rather than to completely change market.

What would the advantages and disadvantages be of targeting the under-35s, the over-40s and the family markets?

What would make the stores more attractive to shoppers in those different market segments?

How could the clothes be more up-to-date?

You are concerned about finding suppliers in developing economies. Why?

Lesson 2.4 Exercise 6 (page 23)
Student E

Chamber of Commerce representative

You represent business people on the island. You support Hernandez's project.

Business people believe the project will:

- help to rebuild the island's economy following the damage done by Hurricane Barbara.
- solve the unemployment problem for young people.
- completely rejuvenate this part of Granville, which has been an under-developed area on the island for many years.

Business people would like Hernandez to:

- invest more in local community projects, e.g. build a library, a cinema or a youth club
- point out that human beings are more important than birds!

Try to persuade the Mayor to get the Council to approve Hernandez's project as soon as possible.

Lesson 9.2 Exercise 2 (page 92)

Age of criminal responsibility. (Below this age, children cannot be dealt with as criminals.)

7	Pakistan, Thailand, the USA
9	Philippines, Iran (girls only)
10	Ukraine, UK
11	Turkey
12	France, Poland
14	Germany, Japan, Italy, Russia, China
15	Iran (boys only)
16	Argentina

Lesson 7.1 Exercise 2 (page 70)

1 = in the dark
2 = on the outside
3 = if they are tinned tomatoes
4 = in the ground
5 = a leg (also a snail)
6 = one
7 = his horse was called Friday

Unit 6.5 Exercise 10 (page 67)

EAGLE NIGHT VISION BINOCULARS

4x42 binoculars
Extra long distance viewing for day time and night time.
Effective up to 300 metres.
42mm lens; high quality optical glass.
Colours: green, black and grey.
Infra-red illuminator for night vision.
Contrast and brightness can be adjusted.
Lightweight and waterproof. Protective rubber casing – very durable.
Fold up, so easily portable.
Can be mounted on a tripod.
Lifetime guarantee.
Many uses: covert surveillance, hunting, observing wildlife, etc.

Lesson 4.1 Exercise 5a (page 39)

MOVING TO THE COUNTRYSIDE. The environment is a key factor in determining our happiness. Noise and pollution don't do it any good at all. The rural idyll – clean air, peace and quiet – will increase your sense of well-being – but watch out for the birds' dawn chorus!

GETTING MARRIED. It's a fact – married people are happier, especially married men! Propose now.

GOING TO THE GYM. Yes, it's tedious, but physical activity can instantly boost your happiness levels. If you don't fancy building your muscles, at least build some exercise into your daily routine – a long energetic walk will do the trick.

SUPPORTING A GOOD CAUSE. There's no doubt that, in life, having a sense of purpose and helping other people lead to increased happiness. Join a charity organisation. Raise funds for disadvantaged children in developing countries or work for world peace. But you shouldn't set your sights too high all at once. Start small, with achievable short-term goals.

A RELAXING DAY FISHING. A day away from it all and great for tackling stress. And to be really happy, we have to keep our stress levels under control.

BEING SLIM. Maintaining a healthy weight is a key ingredient of health and happiness. But the road to happiness isn't lined with crash diets.

TAKING AN EVENING CLASS IN SOMETHING YOU REALLY WANT TO LEARN. How to kill two birds with one stone. You can learn a new skill, such as pottery, car maintenance or a foreign language, as well as realising a personal ambition. Both boost happiness.

GOING ON HOLIDAY WITH A GROUP OF YOUR BEST FRIENDS. Having a break will lower your stress levels but, more importantly, quality time with friends is essential for long-term happiness. But don't save it all up for a once-a-year jamboree.The more the better.

TIDYING UP YOUR ROOM, FLAT OR HOUSE. Create some living space by getting rid of all the clutter. It's not sexy work, but it'll be very satisfying and the sense of achievement is sure to raise your happiness levels.

WINNING A MILLION EUROS. The jury's out on this one. You'll definitely get rich quick. But will it make you happy? Some experts think no – full-stop. Others argue it will, but not in the short term – the impact on your well-being, they believe, takes one to two years to show up. The verdict? True happiness probably lies elsewhere.

Lesson 4.5 Exercise 2 (page 46)

Figure 1 The shift towards noncommunicable diseases and accidents as causes of death*

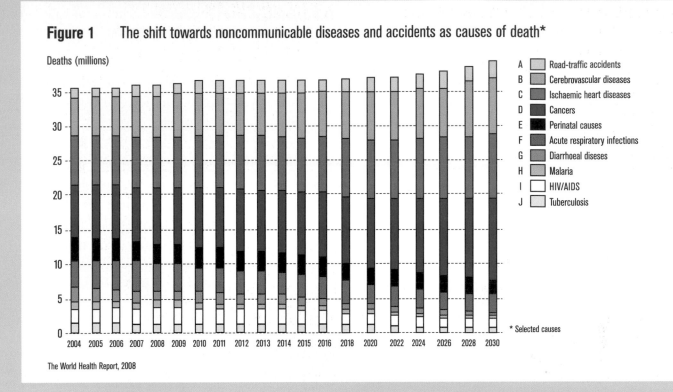

The World Health Report, 2008

Lesson 4.5 Exercise 16 (page 47)

Figure 2 The professionalization of birthing care: percentage of births assisted by professional and other carers in selected areas, 2000 and 2005 with projections to 2015

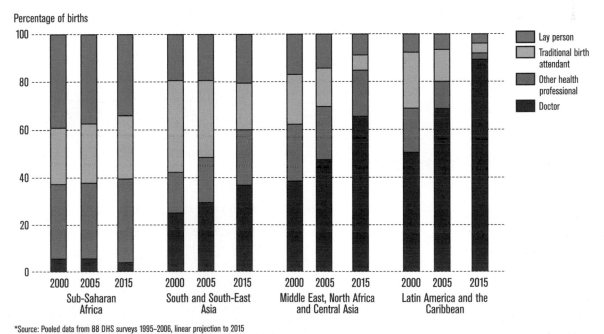

*Source: Pooled data from 88 DHS surveys 1995–2006, linear projection to 2015

The World Health Report, 2008

Lesson 1.5 Exercise 4 (page 14)

The diver

Characteristics

- [ ] You tend to jump in and have a go.
- [ ] You like to get things over with.
- [ ] You like to see if things work.
- [ ] You like to get onto the next thing quickly.

The dreamer

Characteristics

- [ ] You think a lot about the subject.
- [ ] You like to research things thoroughly.
- [ ] You put off practical aspects such as writing.
- [ ] You have no idea where time goes.

The logician

Characteristics

- [ ] You like things to make sense.
- [ ] You like to know the reasons behind things.
- [ ] You are organised in your approach to study.
- [ ] You enjoy tackling complex problems.

The searchlight

Characteristics

- [ ] You find everything interesting.
- [ ] You like to see the big picture.
- [ ] You have bits of information on lots of things.
- [ ] You find it hard to select what is relevant.

Unit 10.5 Exercise 4 (page 110)

- Make sure you know what the topic of the seminar is beforehand.
- Think about what you know about the topic - and what you don't know. Write down a few of the things you need to know more about.
- Read any relevant lecture notes you have. Read any material (articles, etc) your teacher has given you or recommended. Research the topic in the library, on the Internet, etc. Make notes of important points.
- Work out a position on the topic. What's your opinion? Are you for or against?
- Prepare some questions you can ask in the seminar.
- Consider working with another student from the same seminar group to discuss your ideas together. Or meet with other students to form a study group – you can practise participating in seminars to give you more confidence for the actual seminar.

Lesson 5.2 Exercise 3 (page 50)

To qualify for membership of the Chambre Syndicale de la Haute Couture, a fashion house must:

- make clothes for individual customers, involving at least one fitting
- employ at least 15 people in a workshop in Paris
- present a show twice a year to the press, comprising at least 35 runs, with both day and evening outfits.

Lesson 1.5 Exercise 3b (page 14)

Skills:
- interpersonal skills
- linguistic ability
- motivation to live abroad (cultural curiosity)
- tolerance for uncertainty and ambiguity
- flexibility
- patience and respect
- cultural empathy
- a strong sense of self (ego strength)
- a sense of humour

Lesson 6.1 Exercise 2 (page 58)

Quiz Answers

Q 1 Score 1 for each item

Q2 a) = 3   b) = 2   c) = 1

Q3 a) = 2   b) = 3   c) = 1

Q4 score 1 for each

Q5 a) = 3   b) =2   c) = 1

Q6 a) = 3   b) = 2   c) = 1

Q7 a) 2   b) 3   c) 0

Q8 a) = 1   b) = 2   c) = 3

18+ You are a real technophile, however you may be a slave to your machines!

10–17 You find technology useful but it doesn't rule your life.

0–9 You may be a bit of a technophobe. Some aspects of technology worry you, but you still get things done!

Lesson 6.4 Exercise 5 (page 65)

GENETIC TESTING

What it is

Genetic testing is used to test for genes that cause or make us vulnerable to disease. It allows medical people to diagnose people's likelihood of inheriting certain diseases. It can detect if a person has an increased risk of developing a genetic disorder.

Some of its uses

- To screen newborn children just after birth. In the USA, millions of babies are tested each year.
- To diagnose or rule out a specified genetic condition, e.g. breast cancer or cystic fibrosis.
- To test individuals who have a family history of a genetic disorder.
- To do tests for couples who risk having a baby with a genetic disorder.
- To find gene mutations (changes) linked with disorders that appear before birth or later in life.

Criticisms of genetic testing

- The results of tests are often difficult to explain and interpret.
- A positive result cannot establish the exact risk of developing a disorder.
- Many tests cannot detect all the genetic changes that cause a particular disorder.
- You may be genetically more likely to develop a disease, but this does not necessarily mean you will develop it.
- It's difficult to make tests which are reliable.

Benefits

1 Tests can provide a sense of relief from uncertainty.
2 They help people to make informed choices about their health care.
3 A positive result focuses people on preventing, monitoring and treating the disorder.
4 Some results can help people to make a decision whether to have a child or not.

ROBOTS

What are they

Robots are electro-mechanical systems. They can do some of the following things: move around, operate a mechanical limb, interact with their environment and show intelligent behaviour, for example, they can mimic the behaviour of humans and other animals.

Some of their uses

- They are used in commerce and industry to perform jobs more cheaply or with greater accuracy than human beings.
- They are used to do jobs which are too dirty, dangerous or dull for human beings.
- They are used in a wide variety of activities, for example to mass-produce goods, to perform functions in surgery and laboratory research, and to assist in space exploration.
- Domestic robots are becoming increasingly common in households to assist in cleaning and maintenance.

Criticisms of robots

- Some people are afraid that highly intelligent robots will take over and destroy the human race.
- Some missiles and bombs are like robots. They have artificial perception and make decisions autonomously. Some people fear humans are handing over decisions to machines.
- Some robots may become dangerous when acting unpredictably and harm human beings. Workers have been killed in accidents involving robots.
- Over-use of robots could cause large-scale unemployment.

Benefits

- Robots can help to make workers more productive.
- They can work longer hours without losing efficiency than human beings.
- They have led to cheaper mass-produced goods, for example in the field of automobiles and electronics.
- Their increased use has enabled people to have more time for leisure activities.

ELECTRIC CARS

What are they

Electric cars use electric power from battery packs in vehicles. The packs are rechargeable. Many car companies are developing electric cars. Well-known makes include the Tesla Roadstar and Reva, which is the top-selling electric car in Europe. Other carmakers, such as General Motors and Toyota are working on battery-powered vehicles that have small gasoline engines for recharging. These cars are called hybrid cars.

Where they are used

In many countries all over the world. For example:

- In Canada, they are allowed on city streets, but not on highways.
- In Israel and Portugal, French carmaker Renault and Nissan, its Japanese partner, are installing recharging and battery replacement networks nationwide. In Israel, they aim to put 100,000 electric cars on the roads by 2011.
- In the San Francisco Bay area (USA), they plan to make the area one of the world's leading centres for electric vehicles. The plan is to switch the transport system from being powered by traditional fossil fuels.

Criticism of electric cars

- Electric cars are not as quick or practical to recharge as other cars.
- Not really suitable for long-distance driving.
- There would be problems of refuelling in remote locations.
- Electric cars are not as safe as ordinary cars.

Benefits

1 Electic cars have lower carbon dioxide emissions.
2 They are less noisy than petrol driven cars.
3 They use renewable sources of power.
4 Technology improvements will enable their performance to match that of ordinary cars.

SURVEILLANCE AND IDENTITY TECHNOLOGY

What it is

Surveillance and identity technology is used by governments and police forces to monitor people's movements and communications. It may also be used by companies, institutions and individuals. The technology includes CCTV camera networks, DNA and biometric databases, biometric ID cards and the storage of electronic communications.

Some of its uses

- CCTV cameras monitor and record behaviour in public spaces.
- Police forces keep records of an individual's DNA in order to match people to DNA found at crime scenes.
- Mobile telephone companies and Internet Service Providers are required to keep all communications data for several years, so that the police can investigate who someone has been communicating with.
- Cameras monitor road and transport networks in order to deal more accurately and speedily with congestion and accidents.
- ID cards with key biometric information (fingerprints, iris details, possibly DNA) are issued to citizens in order to identify illegal immigrants and prevent ID theft and fraud.

Criticisms of surveillance and ID technology

- CCTV cameras do not actually prevent crime, they only identify criminals, and may also only push crime into areas where there are no cameras.
- CCTV cameras mean that people have lost personal privacy in public areas.
- The storage of personal electronic communications, and their access by the police, is indiscriminate and an infringement of rights to privacy.
- Police forces use cameras as a replacement for police officers walking the streets, but cameras are not as effective, nor as reassuring to the general public.
- There is the potential for this storage of information and surveillance to be used by governments in ways that go against the interests of the people. The government becomes too powerful.

Benefits

1 CCTV cameras help identify criminals and make people feel safer.
2 DNA databases are highly effective ways of identifying criminals. Many crimes have been solved solely because of this information.
3 Camera networks provide real-time information for those responsible for the safety of transport networks, and at large events and public gatherings.
4 Doors and locks that are activated by fingerprint or iris recognition allow companies and individuals to raise building security.

Lesson 8.5 Exercise 10 (page 89)

Rupert Murdoch. Born – Australia 1931. Studied Oxford University, England. Father owned regional newspapers. Age 22, he managed loss-making Adelaide News, soon made it profitable.

Built up a global empire, buying companies in all the media.

Created first national newspaper in Australia. Bought the UK newspaper, The Sun. Changed newspaper, introducing gossip articles and sensational stories + glamour photos of young women.

People accuse The Sun of being vulgar, in poor taste. 'I'm tired of snobs who tell us they're bad papers, snobs who only read newspapers no one else wants' Murdoch quote.

Bought newspapers in the US, satellite TV companies in the US, Britain and Hong Kong. Put his publications on-line. Bought the social networking site, MySpace.

Major purchase of US Dow Jones Group. Gave him control of famous US business newspaper, Wall Street Journal. Owns a movie company 20th Century Fox + Fox News (TV company) + classy UK newspaper, Sunday Times, + down-market tabloid News of the World (scandals, gossip about stars, etc).

Some observers say he has 'an aggressive management style'. Does his power threaten the independence of the newspapers he owns?

Murdoch quote 'I try to keep in touch with the details...I also look at the product daily. That doesn't mean you interfere. It shows you understand what's happening.'

Murdoch - the most famous and powerful media magnate in the world.

Often accused of 'dumbing down' some of the newspapers and TV channels he owns.

Some people say Murdoch is a 'workaholic'. He's still working at the age of seventy seven. 'It gives meaning to his life. That's what gives him pleasure.

Private life complicated. Married three times.

Great media interest when divorced his second wife, Anna, after 31 years marriage.

Three weeks later, married TV executive Wendi Deng, 36 years younger! Have two children.

Lesson 11.5 Exercise 10 (page 121)

Dear Karl,

I've received some feedback from members of the audience who attended your recent presentation to our local distributors. Unfortunately, there were some negative comments about your presentation.

In terms of your technique, some participants mentioned that you arrived late and that you seemed to lack confidence. They felt this was possibly because you had not fully prepared your talk. Also, some people in the back row had difficulty hearing you. One person complained that you rushed your presentation towards the end, another that you failed to make eye contact.
As far as the content of your talk is concerned, some people felt they were not informed about the unique selling points of the new product. Also, I understand that you had problems with the order of your slides. Finally, it seems that your answers to questions were not very convincing.

In view of the comments, I think you might find it useful to follow one of our short courses on Presentation Techniques in the near future.

Lesson 9.5 Exercise 10b (page 99)

Leblanc, C. (2009) The Great Depression: Key Facts and Figures
- following New York stock market crash (Oct 29, 1929) stock prices fell by 80% over 3 yrs → thousands of investors ruined. Some (mainly men) killed themselves (p8)
- in US, crop prices fell about 60%. Rural areas suffered badly - no alternative jobs (p12)
- 10,000 US banks wiped out by 1933 (p23)
- 1933 - 27% unemployment in Canada (p41)
- Newcastle, England: collapse of shipbuilding → 70% unemployment (p43)

Letchworth, B. (1999) The Effects of the Great Depression
- 'most serious economic depression of 20th C'. Affected rich and poor countries (p5)
- collapse of international trade (p11)
- loss of economic confidence - reduced spending levels (p13)
- Chile and Germany badly hit. Nearly 30% unemployment in Germany, 1932 (p109)
- led to political upheaval - growth of extreme left and right-wing parties. Germany: Nazis came to power 1933 (p124)

Samson, B (2004) The Great Depression in the USA
- large-scale fall in incomes and prices (p17)
- farming, mining and logging esp. badly hit (p32)
- 25-30% unemployment in 1932. People lost homes, cars, furniture (p46)
- high suicide rate during this period (p182)
- bankers very unpopular - seen as responsible for depression. Bank robbers (e.g. Bonnie and Clyde) acquired 'hero' status (p212)
- era 'produced at least one great work of literature': John Steinbeck's (1939) The Grapes of Wrath (p263)

Lesson 6.1 Exercise 2 (page 58)

Technology QUIZ

1 How many pieces of technology do you have with you at the moment (on your person / in your bag)?

2 How do you feel when you have to use a new piece of technology, e.g. a photocopier, car, camera etc?
a) excited
b) indifferent
c) anxious

3 You have a new electronic gadget. Do you:
a) read the instructions carefully before use?
b) learn how to use it by trial and error?
c) get someone to show you how it works?

4 Which of the following do you have?
a) a mobile phone
b) an MP3 player
c) a sat nav
d) a palmtop
e) a blog
f) your own website

5 Do you take photos with:
a) a digital camera?
b) a disposable camera?
c) a camera phone?

6 How do you feel about online shopping/banking?
a) It's great.
b) I do it sometimes but the security worries me.
c) I don't do it.

7 Do you read 'e-books'?
a) Yes, now and again.
b) Yes, all the time.
c) No, I prefer to hold a real book.

8 Which of the following best describes you technologically speaking?
a) set in your ways
b) moving with the times
c) at the cutting edge

Turn to page 166 to find out your score.

Lesson 1.1 Track 1.2

Presenter, Jim, Nancy, Bob

P: OK, thank you Miranda … and now I think we can go to our first caller… who is Jim, a salesman from Brighton. Hello Jim, what do you think?

J: Yeah … good morning. Well, I think all formal education is a waste of time and money. It's the 'university of life' that's important, you know, learning things the hard way by doing them and making mistakes. Experience, that's what counts, that's how you learn to make informed decisions, not by reading books. I mean obviously you need to be able to read and write. Numeracy and literacy and all that are important, but all those subjects like Chemistry and Geography, how useful are they in the modern world? They don't really help anyone's career prospects. Life skills, the things that really matter, can't be taught in schools.
All that learning stuff by heart which I had to do at school, rote learning, just like parrots, what a waste of time. School is full of show-offs and smart alecs who want to show how many facts they know, but you really learn by being out there in the world and making your own way. Everyone has the same chance in life, or at least they should have.

P: OK, thank you, Jim. And now I think we can go to Nancy in Cambridge… er, who is a university lecturer, I believe. Go ahead, Nancy.

N: Thank you. I have to say that I totally disagree with the previous caller. Education is about accumulating a body of knowledge which contributes to an individual's development and helps create a sense of identity. It's really the most important thing: a broad education with a strong knowledge base. Also, if you think about it, a high-quality education system contributes to the economy as a whole. The better educated the population is, the more people go to university, the more it benefits the whole country. Subject knowledge and the ability to use it, er, self-awareness and mental agility are all very important qualities which are developed at university. The experience of campus life is at the heart of creating all-rounders who have the capacity for independent study and can think for themselves. That's what education is all about.

P: OK, Nancy, thank you for your contribution. And, er, now can we go to Bob, a company director in London. Hello Bob, what's your view?

B: Good morning, I have to say I have a quite different view to the previous callers. Erm, for me, the problem with education in this country is that it doesn't teach the right stuff, that which is actually useful for the world of work. Education at all levels should be much more practical, er, less theoretical. As an employer, I'm not looking for academics and egg-heads. I want good team players who can write a decent letter or email, you know, people who have practical skills like meeting deadlines and the ability to prioritise tasks, people who are competent and who can be trained up. It's amazing the sort of stuff I see on application forms. I must say I see very little of the critical-thinking skills which people like, er, Nancy talk about. I think we need to go back to more traditional teaching methods. I don't think any of these modern techniques actually work.

P: Right, er thank you, Bob. Well plenty to think about there. Let's see what the panel think about what they've heard … er, Cristina, let me come to you first …

Lesson 1.3 Track 1.3

Interviewer, Vadim

I: Thank you Vadim. That was a very interesting presentation. Now, I know you're flying back to Russia this evening. Hopefully, we will have finished the interview by 3 o'clock, so you should have lots of time to catch your flight. I'd just like to start by checking some of the details on your CV. Can you tell us what you have been doing since you were awarded your Masters?

V: Well, since December 2008, I've been working as a financial analyst at the Bank of Foreign Trade in St Petersburg and the job has, erm, also included some marketing … including preparing market surveys.

I: OK. I'd like to come back to that in more detail later. Having read your CV, we'd like to know more about your internship and exchange programmes.

V: Sure. I've been on two exchange programmes: one in Finland and one in Germany. I studied mainly business subjects and also some Finnish, although the programme was in English. One of the subjects I studied was Marketing. The programme in Germany also included International Marketing but it was taught in German, so, if I'm honest, that was quite difficult for me. I studied German at school but I dropped it before I had taken any exams. Luckily, my English is fairly advanced and I have an 8.0 in IELTS, which is a really good score. I really enjoyed the exchange programme and my only regret is that I didn't study more German.

I: You mentioned your IELTS score. We know about that, but can you tell me what BEC Higher is?

V: Certainly. BEC is a Business English Certificate awarded by UCLES, you know, the University of Cambridge Local Examinations Syndicate and the highest award is the Higher Certificate.

I: Thank you. OK. Could you tell us about the internship?

V: Well, my internship was actually at the place I'm working now – the Bank of Foreign Trade – and luckily they invited me back to work for them.

I: Does that mean all your work experience, including your internship, has been in one place? Have you done any other work?

V: Well, I've had a number of holiday jobs. I've been a waiter and I've also worked as a shop assistant.

I: Right. I'd probably include that in your CV in future.

V: Sure. Thanks for that advice. I'd applied for a number of work placements before I got the one in the bank. I'd just like to add that I'm quite proud that I was offered a job after my work placement and I've really enjoyed working at the Bank of Foreign Trade. I'm very happy there. But I'm looking for a new challenge and the opportunity to use my English in Britain.

I: Right. Now before we go into your current job responsibilities in detail, I need to check one last thing. I'm sorry but I seem to have lost your references. Is it OK if we phone your referees?

V: Yes , no problem. I have their phone numbers.

I: OK , so why do you think you are suitable for this job?

Lesson 1.4 Track 1.4

Lisa, Howard

L: We've got three possible candidates for the internship at UNESCO. They all have slightly different strengths, so I think it may come down to who's best at interview. Shall we run through UNESCO's requirements for this internship?

H: Yeah, let's do that.

L: OK, well, the first thing is academic qualifications. It's absolutely essential that candidates are doing a postgraduate degree. In other words, a second university degree or higher.

H: OK, so having an undergraduate degree definitely isn't enough.

L: Exactly, they'll have to be enrolled in a Master's degree or already have one.

H: OK. What about languages?

L: Well, they must have an excellent knowledge of one of the working languages of the organisation – that means really good English or French – oral and written.

H: Right, so that's a pre-requisite.

L: Yes.

H: How about work experience?

L: Well, they don't mention that specifically, but it's obviously an advantage to have some work experience, preferably with an international organisation.

H: Yes, that's true. You haven't mentioned computer skills.

L: Well, candidates are expected to be able to use office-related software. That's fairly standard.

H: Anything else?

L: No, but we'll be looking for some evidence of a special cultural or scientific interest. It is UNESCO after all.

H: Yes, quite. By the way, how long is the internship?

L: Er, it must be between one and four months. So they're not that long.

H: OK. Shall we take a look at the candidates now?

Lesson 1.5 Track 1.6

Jan, Marco

J: I'm learning English because I love the language and I'm fascinated by the culture. When I was at school, I learned about Shakespeare and the Queen and the Tower of London, and I dreamed of coming to England. Now I'm in London and I want to improve my English so I can understand English books, like *Pride and Prejudice* and Sherlock Holmes, the classics, and follow all the English films and television. I go to the theatre here twice a month. It's wonderful to see a play by Shakespeare at the National Theatre. I want to become really fluent and speak like an English person.
I enjoy learning languages and travel a lot. I've visited several foreign countries.
I think I'm a good traveller because I try to fit in wherever I go. I've developed good cross-cultural skills, and because of this I always manage to integrate into the culture of the country I'm visiting.

M: What's motivating me to learn English? Simple. I work in the export department of an international clothing company. I'm attending an English course in my company to improve all my skills, so I can pass an English language proficiency test. If I pass the test, I'll get promoted and earn more money. That's my main motivation. I've never been good at learning languages, and I'm not particularly interested in English or its culture, but I am ambitious and very career-minded. I have to travel a lot in my job to visit suppliers, and I often need to communicate with customers in English. So, I'm also trying to improve the level of my English to become more fluent. It'll help me to do my job better. So, to answer your question, my main goal is to pass the language test and get a higher salary, but I also need to improve my English language skills to perform better in my work.

Lesson 1.5 Track 1.7

OK then, I've told you how to organise a covering letter and what to include in it. Now let me give you some advice.

First, focus on the employer's needs and show how your qualities and skills match what they're looking for. Try to avoid starting every sentence with 'I'. I mean you have to talk about yourself, but do try to vary the way that you do this.

Make sure you include all your 'selling points'. They're things you can offer which will really impress the employer. For example, you could say, 'I've had three years experience in the newspaper industry and was voted 'financial journalist of the year' in 2006. I speak Spanish and English and can take notes quickly in shorthand.' In other words, highlight your strengths and what you can offer the employer.

Now, be careful about the length of the covering letter. If you make it too short, you'll probably leave out important information and not 'sell yourself' properly. But if you make it too long, the reader may get bored and might not read it properly. Remember that some employers have to read thousands of letters every year, so the letter needs to be concise and persuasive.

And don't put the same things in every covering letter you write. Customise each letter, so that the qualities and skills you mention, your strong points, are targeted at the specific job you've applied for. You may include different points, depending on the job.

Finally, sign your letter and print your name under the signature.

Well everyone, that's all I'd like to say about covering letters. Good luck in your job hunting. I hope you've found this talk interesting and useful.

Lesson 2.2 Track 1.8

Part 1

G: Er, I became a conservationist, in part, because of my family background. My father was an agricultural scientist and travelled throughout the world. One of my brothers was born in Africa. I was born in, er, British Guiana and throughout our young life we, er, were constantly exposed to my father's pictures, particularly of Africa, which were … a strong effect on me. So the first reason, I think, is that it's the way I grew up and that attracted me to erm, my field and as a result of that I went to the University of Oxford to study zoology. I finished my first degree there. Er, after that, I was lucky enough to become a guide in the Galapagos Islands. I did that for about 18 months and as a result of that experience, which was really quite a life changing experience, I went to the University of Pennsylvania to study ecology and evolution. Er, that took me about six years to finish that and once I had finished that I embarked on a career almost immediately, moving straight into conservation biology and then subsequently into things like park management and research management and that's basically how I became a conservationist.

Lesson 2.2 Track 1.9

Part 2

I: What are the key threats from tourism to conservation areas?

G: I think the first thing to say about tourism is that in many situations it's a very positive thing. It can help conservation quite substantially but there are also many examples in the world, for example in the Caribbean, where tourism also causes other … causes problems and has direct impacts on the environment. Er, many of the reefs in the Caribbean have serious problems as a result of pollution from the large hotels. So, when you have massive development of tourism it can create substantial problems, er, for the wildlife in the particular area. There are other areas where tourism can also cause what are, you could say, are more hidden … have more hidden consequences. For example, in the Galapagos Islands where you have a growth in tourism, an explosion in tourism that has basically resulted in more planes and more cargo ships arriving in the islands and bringing with them what we call invasive species. These are species that are not from the Galapagos that cause serious problems for the Galapagos species. It's one of the major reasons why the Galapagos is in so much trouble at the moment. So, in summary I'd say that tourism can be positive but needs to be managed effectively to make sure that it remains positive, er, for the conservation of the areas to which people go.

Lesson 2.2 Track 1.10
Part 3

I: Should we stay away from conservation areas?

G: No, I don't think so. I think, as I've mentioned many of ... er, tourism can be very positive for conservation areas. I think it's more an issue of how we visit those areas. I think it's important for people to see other parts of the world and also to see these incredible sights that have become conservation areas, but I also think, er, it's very important to make sure that when you visit those areas you minimise your impacts and not just your direct impacts, so you don't take away anything from the island, well from the places you visit, you don't cause any problems for the wildlife and the places that you visit but you also become integrated into the local society.
And so the best forms of tourism are those forms of tourism that actually contribute to what we call sustainable development, which means you, that you, er, contribute by making sure that the companies you're going with are ... tend to be locally owned, they tend to employ local people, they intend to purchase items locally and be fully integrated into local society.
If you visit under those circumstances where you're both contributing to sustainable development of the area and contributing to conservation, I think you're having a positive impact.
If you're not visiting under those circumstances then I would suggest that you rethink your, your trip.

Lesson 2.4 Track 1.11

Will Granville Island have the finest golf course in the world in three years time? That's what everyone is talking about.

Ricardo Hernandez, Chief Executive of Hernandez Enterprises, has announced that he's made a provisional offer to buy the Roberts Estate and to develop it as a sports complex. This will be subject to the usual planning approval. Mr Hernandez plans to build a championship 18-hole golf course on the site. In addition, he intends to build a tennis complex, an Olympic-sized swimming pool, four blocks of timeshare flats, 40 villas and a 12-storey hotel. There would also be housing for hundreds of staff.

Mr Hernandez is certain to meet strong opposition to his plans. The 3,000-acre estate overlooks the sea and it's in a prime area of the island. It's ecologically sensitive because it's a favourite area for ramblers and also one of the few sites for the national emblem of our island, the Granville dove, one of our most endangered species.

To build the waterfront villas, Mr Hernandez plans to remove a large number of mangroves, which will undoubtedly affect fish stocks. Mangroves are vital for the eco-systems in the area. Another problem is that the estate is close to White Sands beach, which is a breeding ground for turtles. This beautiful beach has always been a major attraction for tourists. Environmentalists say the resort will discourage tourists from visiting the beach and will have a negative impact on the turtle population.

Will Hernandez's plan become reality? Who knows? Much will depend on discussions between interested groups and the Hernandez organisation.

Lesson 2.4 Track 1.12

Bradshaw, Hernandez

B: Let's talk about your plans for the golf course. I know that building this golf course is central to your plans, but would you be willing, if necessary, to scale down this part of the project?

H: Scale down? What do you mean exactly?

B: Well, would you be prepared to reduce the size of the course to a 9-hole course, instead of 18 holes? Of course, we'd only ask you to do that if it was absolutely necessary.

H: I'd like to make my position very clear about this, Ms Bradshaw. The size of the course isn't negotiable, I'm afraid. It simply isn't possible to shorten its length. It's my dream to build the greatest golf course in the world here on this island. But I can't go ahead if I have to build a shorter course. You see, it's vital to have a full-length 18-hole course if you want to attract the top golfers in the world to play here. Also,

I've commissioned a famous golf course architect to design the layout of the course. He certainly won't want to design anything that isn't championship length. I hope you see my point of view.

B: Mmm, I understand where you're coming from. So, it seems you won't compromise on that point. Right?

H: Exactly. A full-length course is an absolute priority. I couldn't go ahead without your agreement on that.

B: OK, you've been very clear about that. I just hope it won't prevent you from realising your dream.

H: I hope not too. But you know, there are other countries I can go to, if I'm turned down here! I don't want to, but if I have to, I will.

Lesson 2.5 Track 1.13

Marion, Erika

M: OK Erika, you have to write an essay about the effects of tourism on conservation but you don't know how to start, right?

E: Yes, I've read the essay title but I seem to be stuck at the moment. Just don't know how to get started.

M: OK, I think the best way forward for you is to do some brainstorming about the topic.

E: Brainstorming. Mmm, OK, how do you go about it?

M: Well, there are three approaches you could use, it's up to you which one you prefer.

E: Right. Can you tell me a bit about them, please?

M: Sure. The first way is a technique called 'Free-association', it's really good for generating ideas about a topic and developing supporting arguments. How does it work? Well, you list everything you can think about that relates to the topic, things you've learned in class, or from your reading, or simply ideas that come to you when you think about the topic. Even if the ideas don't appear to be very practical or realistic, you should still note them down. That's free-association.

E: Right, I've got that. What about the other approaches?

M: Some people need to see what they are thinking. And for them, 'visual thinking' is a good technique to use. It helps them to develop new ideas. This is how it works. In the centre of a bit of paper, you put some kind of picture, an image representing the topic. Then from the central image, you draw, say, five or six branches which move away from the centre. At the narrow end of each branch, you write a sub-topic of the main topic. Beneath each sub-topic, you can write data which supports your sub-topics. This way, you build up a map to help you organise your essay.

E: Mmm, interesting, but I don't think the technique's good for me, I'm not really a very visual thinker. How about the third approach?

M: This approach is called 'Question and Answer'. It's a relatively new technique and it can help you to come up with good ideas quickly. With this technique, you think of as many questions as you can about the topic, without worrying at this stage about the answers. The questions may help you to identify problems relating to your topic. You then choose the best questions and then are ready to start thinking about what the answers are. However, you may prefer to delay discussion of the answers to a later session. One of your questions might be: what is the relationship between the ideas I've noted down? This question could help you to work out a logical structure for the essay. OK?

E: Well thanks. I'll think about what you've told me and decide which technique to use for my essay.

M: That's it, Erika, choose a technique which works for you, one you're comfortable with.

Lesson 2.5 Track 1.14

As you know, many animals and plants face extinction because their habitat is being destroyed or they are being hunted by human beings. Take the example of the African elephant, the world's largest land animal. The elephant population of Africa has suffered a catastrophic decline in recent years. A century ago, there were millions of elephants, 20 years ago there were about one million, but today there may be as few as 400,000. The African elephant is an endangered species and will become extinct unless solutions are found to protect it.

Why is the African elephant population declining so rapidly? Well, most elephants have been killed for their ivory tusks, which are made into jewellery or souvenirs. The tusks and bones are often ground down to make medicines. Although the sale and trade of ivory and other elephant products is banned in a number of countries, many elephants are still shot illegally by poachers. Also, and this is a very important point, increasing populations has meant that human beings are encroaching on land that used to be the natural habitat of the elephant.

Lesson 3.2 Track 1.15

Many international organisations are known by abbreviations, or shortened forms of phrases. You usually say each letter separately, with the main stress on the last letter. So the International Olympic Committee, the organisation which organises the modern Olympic Games, is known as the IOC, with the stress on the final letter … C. Similarly with the IMF, the International Monetary Fund, the stress is on the F. The IMF being the international organisation that is meant to oversee the global financial system. Some abbreviations use the first letter of each word to form a new word. This type of abbreviation is called an acronym. Acronyms are pronounced as words rather than saying each letter. So, the United Nations Educational, Scientific and Cultural Organisation is known as UNESCO. UNESCO is a specialised agency of the United Nations which tries to contribute to peace and security by promoting international collaboration through education, science and culture. CERN, the world's largest particle physics laboratory, is another acronym. It originally stood in French for Conseil Européen pour la Recherche Nucléaire or the European Council for Nuclear Research. However, the name changed in 1954 when the word council was changed to organisation. However, this meant the new acronym would've been OERN which seemed rather awkward. So they decided to keep the original acronym CERN.

Lesson 3.3 Track 1.16

Most people can't begin to understand how you feel when you're sent from New York to Tokyo, to Abu Dhabi, to Moscow, without a real break. You get a strange feeling of helplessness, as if you're no longer in control of your life.

You see, when you arrive in each new place, you don't have any friends there. You feel insecure, isolated, not part of the local scene at all because you probably don't understand the culture very well. So, you gradually build up a life for yourself and then, just when you've done that, you're sent somewhere else where you have to start all over again.

It's important to be positive when your husband gets a new overseas posting. It helps to remember that although you were unhappy when you arrived in the last country where your husband was posted, er, you were in tears by the time you left because you knew you would miss so much of what you liked about that country.

Our most recent posting was to Moscow – we'd previously been in Saudi Arabia. It would have been helpful if I'd been to Russia before, when I was younger. My husband had been there several times before we got married, but I'd always spent my holidays in the US, and had only visited London and Paris during my vacations. I'd never been to Eastern Europe. Er, I found it really tough at first. It wasn't just the freezing cold weather in January, 15 degrees below zero and lots of ice on the pavements. I also felt er, really lonely at first. I know I should have learned some Russian before we went out there, but I didn't have time. I suppose I could have found a local Russian to give me lessons, but I just didn't have the motivation at that point.

It must have been at least a year before I felt happy in Moscow. I attended a cultural awareness course and I gradually began to understand Russian culture better, learned more Russian words, and made some wonderful friends. I created my own world, and as soon as I'd done that, we were sent to Canberra, Australia, for a new posting! So, to be honest, I guess I have mixed feelings about being an ambassador's wife.

Lesson 3.4 Track 1.18

UN Official, Chair

UN: You're worried about the image of your company, Mr Leiterman, I can understand that, but at this time, you need to be very clear about your objectives and how to achieve them.

C: I understand that. Of course, our image as a responsible company is important, but our main objective now is to develop a strategy to prevent the expansion of the oil flow.

UN: Of course, you're right. Your priority must be to contain the oil spill, so you'll have to act quickly and efficiently. It's vital that you have a realistic plan of action as soon as possible, I know you're working on that. But there's something else you should be doing …

C: Oh yes?

U: Well, it's a very difficult situation for you, I know. So I urge you to get as much outside help as you can to deal with it.

C: Of course, I realise that. I'm well aware we haven't got the expertise or the resources and labour to deal with the spill on our own. So, one of our main goals will be to involve the international community.

UN: You're right. It's essential to bring

in some international companies for the clean-up tasks, even though it could be very expensive. And it'd be advisable to get help from UN organisations as well as the governments of the countries which are most affected.

C: Yes, I'm counting on their support and financial help.

UN: There's another piece of advice I'd like to give you, Mr Leiterman. It would be very helpful to involve the International Maritime Organisation and MAP, the Mediterranean Action Plan group. That should be a key objective, as they'll have a lot of experience to offer you. And then there's the European Community, you'll need their help as well.

C: Yes, we can't do without the support of the EC, that's for sure. We aim also to set up meetings at regular intervals to monitor progress – we're agreed that good communications are an important objective for us. We want to keep everyone in the company fully informed about what we're doing.

UN: Absolutely. There's one other point I'd like to mention. I'd strongly advise you to set up an Emergency Action Committee as soon as possible. Your top management should be involved as well as the Ministers of the Environment in the countries along the coastline. I know you've been very busy since the spill and you haven't had much time to deal with the public relations side of things. But, you ought to organise a press conference in the very near future. I mean, as soon as you've devised a credible action plan. There are journalists from all over the world here and they're crying out for information from you. Of course, I can understand why you haven't made a statement yet …

C: Well, actually I'm just about to issue a short statement. But I only want to talk to the international press corps when I'm fully briefed on what actions we're taking. It's always a bad thing to hold a press conference before you have all the facts. You can get into a lot of difficulties that way.

UN: True! Look, I know you've got a lot on your plate, But all the same, I strongly recommend you visit the parts of the coastline that are most affected. It'd be good for your public relations and you might learn quite a lot from your visit.

C: Yes, that's a good idea, I'll try to organise a visit as soon as possible.

Lesson 3.5 Track 1.19

How do you become an active listener? Well, I'd say there are five things you have to do, five ways to behave, if you like, when you're listening to someone:

Firstly, pay careful attention to what they're saying. You must focus on the person speaking and not be distracted in any way. Make eye contact – that's very important. Listen and try to get the message they're sending you. Secondly, show the speaker that you are listening. Use your body language to do this. You can nod occasionally, and show by your posture that you're being attentive. You should look relaxed and receptive to what the person's saying. You can use verbal signals to show interest, by saying things like 'yes', 'uh huh', (really?) And so on.

Next, give the speaker feedback. You're focusing on the speaker rather than your own ideas, so you may need to reflect on what is being said and ask questions. For example, you may paraphrase what the speaker has said using phrases like 'So what you're saying is …' or 'if I understand you, you're saying …' or you may ask questions to check your understanding, for example, 'What exactly do you mean … ?' Or 'Have I got this right? You're saying …'

Having said that, it is important not to interrupt too often. Wait until he or she finishes. It's really annoying if you're trying to get across a message and someone keeps on interrupting you.

Finally, respond in a positive, constructive way. Show that you value the information you've received. Give your opinions, but don't be aggressive when doing so. Don't put down the person speaking, even if you don't agree with him or her. Respond in an honest and direct way.

Now then, if you put into practice the advice I've given you, you'll show that you're an active listener and this will help you to become a better communicator.

Review Units 1–3 Track 1.20

Ron, Jenna

R: I don't know about you, Jenna, but I think those last three candidates were pretty good.

J: Did you? I wasn't sure about the last one – Andrea McCartney. I thought it was very difficult to see where she was coming from. She didn't really show us much of herself, did she?

R: No, I suppose not. She certainly didn't push herself too much, and she seemed quite quiet, but is that a bad thing? I don't think she thought she was superior to us or anything.

J: No, no, no, I don't mean that. On the contrary, she might be a bit too sensitive, but also, she seemed a bit secretive, as though she might be trying to hide something. Well, I mean, I think we've got better candidates than her.

R: Mmm, yeah, perhaps you're right. I like the guy – what was his name, Will …

J: Will Davison. Yes, I agree, he was great. I felt that he'd fit in with us and work well with the team, and also that he could probably turn his hand to most things. He's got a really impressive CV.

R: Yes, and he knows this area of Turkey inside out.

J: Indeed. I also felt that he was very practical, you know, he would always know which would be the most sensible decision for the team, even if it wasn't his choice.

R: Yes, I know what you mean, and I think he wants to go a long way in the tourism business – he could be good for us. Do you think we should go with him, then?

J: Possibly, but I also liked the second candidate, the other woman, Kate Samson. She seemed so knowledgeable – well-read, interested in art and history, and that would be a great addition to the team.

R: That's true, and the fact that she can play several instruments was impressive, but I did have a couple of misgivings.

J: Oh? What were they?

R: Well, she made it perfectly clear that she's very intelligent and that she knows a lot, didn't she?

J: Well, maybe, perhaps you're right. Our clients wouldn't like someone who showed off their knowledge all the time. And, come to think of it, she didn't accept our views on a couple of things, did she? She was so certain that she was right.

R: Yes, I think she might be a bit inflexible for our team, and for our clients. So, Will Davison, shall we offer him the job?

Review Units 1–3 Track 1.21

Head, Nick, Jess

H: You wanted to see me about the school's use of resources, I gather.

N: Yes, that's right. The teachers all feel that the school's a bit wasteful.

H: OK. Can you be a bit more explicit?

J: Well, yes, there are three or four things, for example, we waste a lot of paper, and we feel that we could cut down on the electricity we use, you know, the heating's on all the time – it isn't necessary. It could be turned off mid-afternoon.

N: And it's essential that we consider the number of teachers who come to the school in cars …

J: And students.

N: Yes, and students. Perhaps a car pool would be a good idea …

H: Hang on a moment, let's look at these one by one, shall we?

N: OK, well, I think that the paper issue should be a key objective for us.

H: Go on …

J: The thing is, we issue students with paper and notebooks, and they just scribble on it and throw it in the bin.

N: And the same happens in the staff room and the office. We're throwing paper away all the time.

H: OK, so if I understand you correctly, you're saying that you think we should start recycling paper.

N: Exactly. We could have two bins in each classroom – one for waste and one for paper.

J: Yes, they do it in Germany – I've seen it, and also one for cans, and one for organic stuff like apple cores and …

H: Stop there a moment. You know, I'd strongly advise you to think carefully about this. First, how are you going to monitor the students? Are you going to stand and watch them put rubbish in the correct bins? Second, while I'm happy to consider your paper proposal, it simply isn't possible to provide bins for cans and organic waste too. Think about it – where would they all go in each classroom? There isn't space here.

N: No, OK, but it would be helpful to have a bin in the café for waste food.

H: Yes, I'll go along with that – a good idea. Let's go back to the paper issue. If we do agree to having special paper bins in each room, it's an absolute priority to work out who is going to be responsible for emptying them and taking the paper to the recycling place. I can't see the cleaners doing that, and you know our rubbish collection doesn't do paper separately.

J: The teachers have talked about that. If the cleaners could put the waste paper somewhere every evening, we'd take it in turns to take the paper to the recycling depot on our way home the next day.

H: So, it seems that you'll take full responsibility for disposing of the paper? Is that right?

N: Yes, exactly.

H: Well, I'm impressed. I can't say no to that, can I? I'll organise a paper bin for each room. Now, your next point.

Lesson 4.2 Track 1.22

Michael Moore has made his name by producing documentaries that are undeniably controversial in terms of both subject matter and film making style. A Michael Moore documentary doesn't give you a balanced analysis of the facts; instead it gives you his opinion, which is presented emotionally and supported by the facts that he chooses to show you.

In *Sicko*, he targets the United States' privatised healthcare system and the health insurance companies who put profit before care. He asks why, when more money is spent on healthcare in the USA than in any other country, is the system only ranked 37th in the world? The answer is that when people actually need their insurance companies to pay out some money, well these companies do everything they can to avoid paying for the treatment, which leads to people dying because they can't pay for the care that they need.

We meet people who have suffered at the hands of the insurance companies, and also former employees of these companies who actually received bonuses when they managed to avoid paying out money, which clearly underlines the profit motive that defines that privatised healthcare system.

Moore visits four other countries, er, namely Canada, France, the UK and Cuba, which all have state-funded systems of healthcare. Now while these comparisons are useful, Moore is guilty here of wearing rose-tinted spectacles. He presents these systems as if they are perfect because healthcare is available to everyone and because they don't have to pay for it when they need it, but he doesn't show us the problems that these systems have.

However, that criticism doesn't prevent the conclusion that this film certainly shows that the American healthcare system is seriously flawed and that something … something desperately needs to be done about it. Overall, this must-see film may not be a cure, but is a perceptive and worrying diagnosis.

Lesson 4.4 Track 1.24

Charlie, Nishi, Peter

C: Right, well, my proposal is that we launch a major campaign to reduce people's currently high levels of salt consumption.

N: Salt consumption?

C: That's right. Eating too much salt is a significant risk factor in developing high blood pressure, which causes nearly 200,000 deaths each year.

P: Okay, let's hear what you have to say.

C: Right, well one reason I favour this campaign is that almost half of the population eat more than the daily recommended amount of salt, which is 6 grams a day. So, you can see that this affects a large number of people, can't you? Secondly, changing salt consumption habits has a quick and tangible effect. By this I mean that within just four weeks of reducing your salt consumption, your blood pressure will be lower. That's exactly the kind of thing that people want to see – an immediate result of their actions. Basically, a simple and slight change to lifestyle can have a dramatic effect.

N: Fair enough, and quite convincing. Have you had any thoughts about the shape that the campaign could take?

C: Yes, I have. So, obviously, the main aim of the campaign is to get people to reduce their salt intake. Firstly, we need to make sure that people can find out how much salt they're consuming, and I think this means that we have to lobby the food industry for improved labelling on food packaging, and, secondly, we also need to press the food companies to reduce the salt content of processed foods – you know the kind of thing, microwave meals, crisps, etc. If we do these two things, people will inevitably be eating less salt, and also they'll be able to monitor their salt intake. Thirdly, we of course have to run a major publicity campaign to inform the public about the effects of salt. In this case, the fact that the problem's so widespread means a TV advertising campaign's fully justified. While I accept that that'd be expensive, it'd be the most direct way to reach such a large target audience. A key part of the strategy here would be to have a humorous approach to make the message memorable.

P: OK, and I guess you'd have a poster campaign as well, and an internet presence of some sort, wouldn't you?

C: Absolutely, and on the Internet we'll provide factsheets and have some blogs written by people who are reducing their salt intake. You know the kind of thing, weekly updates about the changes in their diet, how their health is improving, etc. Finally, the whole campaign would be tied together by our main campaign tool – Sid the slug!

N: Sid the slug? Do you mean an animated slug?

C: Exactly. You may well ask why a slug, and the answer is that salt kills slugs. And so Sid the slug will highlight that direct link between eating too much salt and the increased risk of fatal heart attacks. And also, this gives us the all-important humour that I talked about. We can have Sid being tempted by all those things which are high in salt, only to see him fall ill as a consequence. Or, we could have him turning his back on that kind of food, telling us why he always goes for lettuce over a packet of crisps. Of course, we'll need a slogan, perhaps, 'We're all Sid at heart'. I like that because it makes the connection with blood pressure. Oh, and on the website, Sid'll host the site and answer user enquiries and so on. So, what do you think?

Lesson 5.1 Track 1.25

Narrator, Mika Ando, Professor Ishikaua, Jun Tanaka, Lisa Sandler

N: Japan is one of the most highly developed consumer societies in the world. Japan loves brands. About 40 per cent of the world's sales of luxury brands are in Japan. Louis Vuitton sells more bags here than in any other country. Mika Ando has her own advertising agency 'TokyoMA', located in the trendy Omotesando district of central Tokyo. She explains why brands are so important to the Japanese.

MA: You have to look as if you come from a middle-class family. Erm, but one of the problems we have here, especially in large cities like Toyko, is that the value of land is astronomically high. So most people, even those with good jobs, live in very small apartments. So people want to show their status by means of clothes, shoes and bags. This is really where brand value comes from.

N: Critics of this consumer society – many of them Japanese – believe it's far too materialistic. But how did Japan get to this point? Professor Futaba Ishikawa is a historian from Ueno University.

PI: After the devastation and defeat of the Second World War, Japan was determined to rebuild. By the 1980s, it had become extremely successful at developing advanced manufacturing techniques in a wide range of industries – shipping, cars and electronics. The growth rate was phenomenal. Low interest rates led to booming land prices and a runaway stock market. Japanese had money to burn and were finding new ways to spend. In these bubble years, retail therapy became a natural thing to do. Consumerism became a sport, a hobby. These were times of excess. But it wasn't to last. Fundamentally it was a false economy and the spending excesses of the 1980s were brought to a sudden halt when the bubble burst in the early 1990s. The stock market crashed and banks were left with debts of billions of yen.

N: From the mid-1990s, however, Japan began to recover and conspicuous consumption bounced back. But not all consumers were equally influential. By the mid-noughties, one group in particular had emerged as the most important of all – young women aged between 18 and 30. They maintain their spending power by living off their parents. Jun Tanaka is a sociologist who is concerned by this phenomenon.

JT: Men's earnings have decreased so these days women don't want to get married. It would mean a lowering of their standard of living. This has profound implications for family life in Japan. What we're seeing now is a situation in which consumerism outweighs having children. It's actually more attractive to be a consumer than to have kids.

N: Lisa Sandler is an Australian journalist in Japan. She agrees with Professor Tanaka.

LS: A few years back new flats were being built and marketed specifically at this consumer group of young women. Some of them had special lifts for pets, as well as beauty salons in the basement.

N: The consequence of all this is a population that's ageing and shrinking. What are the solutions? Some Japanese are suggesting a move away from this rampant materialism to more traditional Japanese cultural values, with a greater emphasis on the family. But many Japanese fear that no-one is thinking seriously about the future. People are too focussed on the present. They just want to get on with some more retail therapy.

Lesson 5.3 Track 1.26

Narrator, Mavis Hambling

N: In India, in a hot, airless factory and for the sixteenth hour today, Amitosh carefully sews some tiny plastic beads on to the blouse he is making. No sooner has he attached one than he picks up the next from the thousands in the bag. The blouse bears the label of an internationally famous fashion chain. Amitosh, whose name means happiness, is only 10 years old.

In Uruguay, shockingly thin models parade down the catwalk, showing off the latest creations by top South American designers. Little do the audience realise that two models, the Ramos sisters, are missing today, as they both tragically died from extreme dieting and anorexia earlier this year.

In London, the cash tills ring incessantly as shoppers grab the latest bargain outfits to replace the ones they bought only a month ago. At no time are they aware of the effect this fast fashion is having on the environment.

M: Three different snapshots of the fashion industry, and in each one you have a victim. All of which begs the question, does the fashion industry do enough to be socially responsible? To discuss this, I have with me in the studio Sarah Maitland from Making Fashion Better and Diana Spooner from the Fashion Industry Association.

Lesson 5.3 Track 1.27

Mavis Hambling, Diana Spooner, Sarah Maitland,

M: So Diana, that's a fairly damning introduction to the workings of the fashion industry. You're not really going to defend it, are you?

D: Well, damning it may have been, but fair it certainly wasn't. I think you'll find that the fashion industry as a whole is taking steps to improve things.

M: Such as?

D: Well, to take the example of sweatshops. Almost all major fashion chains now make their suppliers and manufacturers sign agreements which detail the rules for fair employment, concerning everything from child labour to working hours.

S: If that's the case, how come we still keep hearing about the appalling conditions that workers face all over the world when producing products for multinationals? Surely it's because these agreements are not worth the paper they're printed on. It's the enforcement of these rules that fashion chains have to focus on, and companies are not doing enough on that front.

D: In defence of the industry, it's not easy to check working conditions in small remote factories all over the world.

S: Yet, they seem to be able to check the quality of their displays in their shops, all over the world. What the companies do is maximise their profits, not improve their workers' lives.

D: Yes, but remember, the suppliers are independent companies who have a contract with the fashion house. We can't be held so responsible for the way they treat their staff; technically they're not our workers.

M: OK, well, perhaps we should move on and deal with the whole size-zero question. Sarah?

S: Indeed, and not only is this about the health of the models, but also about the psychological health of young women all over the world. The continual use of very thin models leads to women having a very poor body image, and, I believe, directly leads to the ever-increasing prevalence of anorexia and unhealthy dieting.

D: Our own research shows that women feel more positive towards clothes that are modelled on such models rather than on women with fuller figures. Also, the clothes hang much better on a thin model – designers want their work to be shown as well as possible, you know, and a thinner model is perfect for that. Many designers see themselves as artists, and you know, you wouldn't expect to see a Picasso in a gallery with the lights turned off, would you?

S: That's just so irresponsible. Fashion isn't art; it's a global industry and its imagery directly affects women's sense of self and identity, and at the moment the industry's creating unreasonable and dangerous expectations in women. Even more dangerous is the immediate effect this has on the models. It's widely recognised that models frequently ruin their health in order to suit the whims of the designers and the industry.

D: Well, on that point, the industry's taking steps to help models look after their health, for example you know, we make sure that healthy food is always available at shoots and shows, and some agencies are providing health check-ups, and I should say, not all thin models are unhealthy; many of the girls are naturally just built that way.

S: But that's just missing the point again – what's important is not providing a few carrots at a photoshoot. I mean, it's not that kind of shallow change that I'm talking about. What you need to do is change the whole approach of the industry towards body size.

M: Well, on that point about deeper changes, perhaps we should now consider the effect fashion, particularly contemporary fast fashion, has on the environment.

Lesson 5.4 Track 1.31

CEO, Sandra, Sean

CEO: First of all, I'll run through the feedback from the consultant's report, which basically divides into three main areas – our shops and their facilities, the product range and our key markets.
It seems that our stores are seen as dull and dated in appearance. Basically, they don't offer a pleasant shopping experience. For example, bookshops often have cafés inside them nowadays, whereas we don't even have seating areas for people to rest in. The changing rooms are small and scruffy, and there are long queues for those and the tills. Overall, shopping in our stores is not an uplifting or relaxing experience, and this is exacerbated by poor standards of customer service. Now, any comments?

SANDY: That all has a ring of truth, but I think we should be careful how we change things. Suppose we did have a café, wouldn't that just reduce our sales space? And also, it'd mean that we'd have to have food storage and preparation facilities. Most of our stores are in restricted high-street locations, I'm not sure how feasible that'd be.

CEO: Indeed, but we'll leave such discussion till later in the meeting. More importantly, is there anyone who disagrees with the consultant's findings so far?

S&S: No, not really.

CEO: Right. Moving onto our product range, on the positive side, our clothes are seen as good quality. The fabrics are good and the clothes are long lasting. However, they are not seen as up-to-date in terms of look and design, and it's not cheap, although this is balanced by the impression of quality.

SEAN: Can I just say something here?

CEO: Sure.

SEAN: Well, if we were to copy new designs by major designers, rather than use our own in-house designers, we'd certainly be more up-to-date. Mind you, we'd need to produce the clothes quickly then, otherwise we'd still be behind the times.

CEO: Well, I'm not sure we want to ditch our in-house designers just yet, although it's clear that they aren't designing the kind … right kind of thing. The other thing is that our overall range was described as having a little of everything, but nothing that's special. If you're looking for a winter coat, we'll certainly have a few, but not so many because we'll also have sportswear. At the moment, we cater for everyone; we aim our clothes at all ages and at a very general market. The consultants wonder if this market really exists any more; exactly who are our customers? Yes, Sandra?

SANDY: Just on that point, I was wondering if we might introduce an element of specialisation, rather than make a wholesale change.

CEO: How do you mean exactly?

SANDY: Well, if we had a special range, say one for kids, but still offered a wide general range for customers, we'd differentiate ourselves from other stores without losing our current customer base. There'd be a chance to market the special range and use this as a way to get people into our stores.

SEAN: Erm, Sandra, I think a special range is an interesting idea, but surely it'd be better to target one part of the market much more aggressively. Admittedly, that'd mean taking a big risk and possibly losing some of our traditional customers. But then, we're losing them anyway at the moment. We can't go on trying to be everything to everyone, because we just end up being nothing to anyone.

CEO: OK, save those thoughts for later, I've got just a couple more points to make. Currently, we don't offer any accessories such as handbags and jewellery and so people feel they can't get a complete outfit or find little things that are different to other stores. And, in general, our homeware range is severely limited. Right, that's it as far as the consultant's report is concerned. I'm most interested in how we position ourselves in the market, and then how we revamp our stores and product lines. So, I suggest we have a meeting next week to determine our recovery strategy. Obviously, this will cost the company money, and bank loans are not so easy to get these days, so we'll also be looking for ways to cut costs and save some money. Can everyone come with some ideas and we'll get things moving forward. Basically, we need to become a destination store, a store that people are actively choosing to go to and a store where they enjoy their shopping experience. Agreed?

S&S: Agreed.

Lesson 6.3 Track 2.1

A: How are you coping at the moment?

B: Well, to be honest, I had absolutely no idea I was going to get fired.

AUDIOSCRIPTS

It was a complete shock. Profits were good. We were beating the competition and there hadn't been any talk of takeovers or mergers, see? So it came out of the blue. They said the reason for the redundancy was technological advances.

A: Well in that case, try not to take it personally. The job was made redundant, not you.

B: It was just the way that they did it that made me angry. I had an interview and then they made me leave the building immediately. I wasn't allowed to clear my desk. They didn't even let me say goodbye to my staff. Apparently they'd even had all the locks changed. I mean what did they think we were going to do?

A: Well, don't let it get you down. Try to focus on moving forward rather than looking back. Try to use your time constructively. If you don't get a job straightaway you could do voluntary work to get experience in a new line of work. You could broaden or update your skills. There are so many courses out there. And if you're looking at a complete career change then you'll need to get new knowledge and skills to make that change.

Lesson 6.4 Track 2.3

Part 1

I'm going to talk about mobile phones. In my opinion, they're the modern technology that's brought the most benefit to mankind. I'll start by describing them, then talk about some of their uses. Next, I'll deal with some criticisms of mobile phones. Finally, I'll outline the many benefits they offer us.

What are mobile phones? Well, a mobile phone, which is also called a cell phone or hand phone, is a long-range, electronic device used for voice or data communication over a network of sites, known as call sites.

I think the facts speak for themselves, don't they? They're the most widely spread technology and the most common electronic device in the world. Let me give you an amazing statistic. The total number of mobile phone subscriptions is over 4.1 billion. Yes, 4.1 billion, that's the latest official figure.

What are the uses of mobile phones?

I'm sure you'd agree, mobile phones are an extraordinarily versatile piece of equipment. You can do so many things with them. As well as voice messaging, you can do text messaging, send and receive email, get access to the Internet, take and receive photos, take and watch short video recordings, play online games, listen to music, and so on. Even

while I'm talking, new functions are being added to mobile phones. It's incredible what this small electronic device can do.

I'd like to give you just one other striking example of the use of mobile phones. In the Philippines, in 1999, they launched the first commercial mobile payments system. It's not unusual in that country for workers' entire pay-check to be paid into their mobile phone account.

Lesson 6.4 Track 2.4

Part 2

So, what about the criticisms of mobile phones?

Some people, it's true, criticise mobile phones. For example, they say mobile phones are a social nuisance. They ring at the wrong times in cinemas, theatres and restaurants, they interrupt classes and upset passengers in trains. I accept that this happens, but almost every electronic device can upset people some of the time. However, that's a small price to pay for such immense benefits.

I accept too that mobile phones can distract people while they drive and cause accidents. However, many countries have already banned the use of mobile phones while driving. It's also true that a small minority of users do get an allergic reaction to the nickel surfaces of mobile phones. But I would stress that this problem affects only a tiny fraction of mobile phone users.

Finally, let me deal with the argument that the radiation from mobile phones is harmful to young people. The truth is, this is pure speculation. No studies so far have proved this to be the case.

Now, what about the enormous benefits of mobile phones?

The strongest argument, surely, is that they are a key means for people of all ages to communicate with each other, quickly and easily. You can contact by mobile phone anyone almost anywhere, at any time. That's why they're so indispensable for everyone these days. If you don't believe me, think about how you feel if you lose your mobile phone? It's not a pleasant feeling, is it? It really upsets your life.

There are many other benefits from mobile phones. They've saved the lives of people who've been trapped in dangerous situations. They've helped the police check the locations of people involved in crimes. They've helped governments in some countries, for instance, Japan, to use the mobile phone networks to warn people quickly

of disasters, such as earthquakes, and so save many lives.

I hope I've convinced you that mobile phones have revolutionised our lives and brought us all much closer together. If you have a mobile phone, you'll never be isolated or forgotten. They are the supreme example of the application of modern technology.

Lesson 6.5 Track 2.6

Part 1

OK, everyone, let me start by giving you three golden rules for writing an impressive sales leaflet.

Firstly, the leaflet must grab the attention of your reader or target audience. In other words, it's got to be eye-catching.

Secondly, it has to make the reader interested in the product or service you're selling.

Finally, it should persuade the reader or potential customer to take action, for example, phone a number, fill in a card, place an order, attend a demonstration or visit a website.

Now, there's a well known structure for devising a sales leaflet and if you follow it, you can't really go wrong. You can remember it by the acronym, AIDA. The letters stand for: Attention; Interest; Desire; Action. A word or two about each.

Attention: You must capture the attention of the recipient of the leaflet, and the best way of doing this is probably to have an eye-catching headline, one that'll appeal strongly to your target audience. If your headline isn't effective, people won't bother to read the text of your message.

Interest: You've got to provide interesting information in the leaflet, things that are relevant to the reader, so that they'll keep on reading your message until the end of the leaflet.

Desire: You must show that your product or service meets a desire or need that the target audience already have. You want the reader to experience a desire for what you're offering them.

Now, Action: Your leaflet must contain a call for action, as I explained above. You want your customer to act right away – not put the leaflet away and forget about it.

So, follow the AIDA structure and you'll get good results. But, of course, writing an impressive leaflet is an art, a skill that needs practice.

Another point, you'll need to think carefully about the design of the sales leaflet. Here are a few tips:

Keep the design simple.

Use the minimum number of words for your message.

Use images to back up your message.

Use bullet points, headings, paragraphs, different fonts and italics to vary the look of the leaflet and to make it more 'punchy'.

Leave as much white space as possible. 'More is Less' when it comes to writing leaflets.

Finally, in a sales leaflet, which is a promotional tool, it's good to use words and phrases which have impact, memorable phrases or images which make people think and react positively. And don't be afraid to use humour if it's appropriate. Humour gets people on your side.

Lesson 6.5 Track 2.7

Part 2

A sales leaflet is a bit like a press release. You need to put as much key information as possible in the first paragraph, and the less important information can come towards the end of the text.

It's very important that the leaflet highlights the major benefits of the product or service. Make it clear how your product or service meets the needs or desire of the target audience. You've got to give the reader a convincing reason for buying the product or service. Is it because your product is better quality or cheaper than competitors'? Will it ... will it make the consumer's life easier, more convenient? Will it help to make the reader happier, healthier, more satisfied with their life?

It's good if you can provide proof for what you're claiming: for example, the results of some research, or if you can give the consumer a free trial, a demonstration or a money-back guarantee.

So that's it really. To summarise:

Offer a solution to a problem or say how you're meeting a desire or need of the consumer.

State clearly the benefits you're offering them.

Select two or three attractive, appealing features of your produce or service.

And ... present them clearly and simply.

OK. Any questions about writing a good sales leaflet?

Review Units 4–6 Track 2.8

Ivan, Jaya, Patty

I: Have you looked at last month's figures? We really need to do something to boost our sales. You know, we're one of the last independent shops in the High Street now – the big chain stores are taking over all the small shops. What can we do to avoid it? Jaya, what do you think?

J: Well, we're obviously struggling against the chains. The facts speak for themselves, don't they? We clearly can't compete against them with the clothes we sell at the moment, so we have to rethink what we're doing. Suppose we started to stock much cheaper clothes anyway, you know, sports and leisurewear, teenage fashion designs, that sort of thing? I think we're too upmarket. Don't you agree, Ivan?

I: I'm not sure, Jaya. The fact that we're in a very affluent part of the country means we should focus on people with money, I think. If people round here want cheap clothes, they'll go to the department stores in the shopping centre, or supermarkets. I was wondering if we'd do better to go more upmarket – focus on quite expensive classic clothes and drop the fashion items. One reason I favour this is that we know we can't compete on the fashion stuff – the big stores do that so much better. They can stock different ranges so they can have both the real designer clothes and cheaper copies. No, I think we should go for classic suits, cocktail dresses, maybe accessories as well – a lot of women in this area have high-powered jobs and need a wardrobe of good, classic clothes. You can see what I mean, can't you, Patty?

P: Well, yes, but actually, I think we should seriously consider selling the shop.

J: What?

P: Think about it – the strongest argument for changing our stock and keeping the business going is to make money, but we just aren't doing that, and we haven't done very well for over two years now. We need to increase our turnover by about 30 per cent, otherwise there's no point in continuing. We could easily sell to a chain store, and we'd all walk away with a reasonable lump sum.

I: I don't know, Patty. While I accept your arguments, I can't help feeling that there are other solutions. You know, if we were to stay open later, say, to about seven o'clock every evening, we'd catch people coming from the station on their way home from work. It'd mean that we'd all have to do a few extra hours until we could afford to take someone else on ...

J: I'm not sure about that, Ivan, we already do six days a week ...

Lesson 7.1 Track 2.9

Part 1

Good morning everyone. Our topic today is creativity - something I know many of you have been looking forward to. So what is creativity? Well, I think we can say that it is a mental process connected with the generation of new ideas or concepts. It's also a way of approaching issues, solving problems and exploiting opportunities. It has been studied in a variety of disciplines from business to psychology, from design to philosophy. However, there is no unified single definition of what it is, or a standardised measurement technique.

So, how do you spot a creative person? Well, creative people are constantly asking questions and challenging assumptions. They are able to make links easily and see relationships between things. They explore possibilities, are flexible and open to alternatives, and they reflect critically on ideas, actions and consequences. Creativity has also often been linked to genius, mental illness and humour, and while some argue it is a character trait people are born with, others claim it can be taught using simple techniques. Although the idea of creativity is these days generally associated with the arts – art and literature – it is also extremely important in the idea of innovation and invention, and therefore important in business, music, design, engineering and science as well. It seems that sometimes the term 'creativity' is preferred in the context of the arts, whereas the term 'innovation' is preferred in business, although the latter is considered to be both the generating and application of creative ideas. Within organisations, innovation is the term used to describe a process where new ideas are generated and then converted into commercial products and services.

Lesson 7.1 Track 2.10

Part 2

Finally, I'd like to take a look at the work of Graham Wallas in psychology and his pioneering theory which attempts to explain the creative process. This model is often the basis for many creative thinking training programmes available today. Wallas, working with Richard Smith, presented one of the first models of the creative process in their 1926 book, *Art of Thought*. Here they outlined a five-stage model. So, they argued that creative thinking proceeds through five phases. I'd like to take a brief look at each stage.

Firstly, there is the 'preparation' stage, where an individual does preparation work which focuses their mind on the problem and explores the limits of the problem. Secondly, they identified an 'incubation' stage, where the problem is brought into the unconscious mind but nothing seems to be happening. The idea is that a break from the problem may in fact aid the process. Next, there is the 'intimation' stage, where the creative person gets a feeling that a solution is on the way. Fourthly, there is the 'illumination' stage, sometimes called 'insight', where the idea develops from its preconscious processing into conscious awareness, or the moment when the new idea finally emerges. The final step is 'verification', where the idea is consciously verified, expanded and then applied. Since ideas or solutions don't always work out in practice, this final stage is crucial to the success of any project: it's the 'checking it out' phase. Now, are there any questions before we move on to look at some …

Lesson 7.2 Track 2.11

Jonathan, Professor Kotov, Dr. Petrakis, Professor Hasan

J: Welcome to the last programme in the series *Extraordinary People and Ideas* and the theme of tonight's programme concerns people who did extraordinary things and were later rediscovered. You all know our regular panellists. Professor Kotov would you like to begin?

PK: Certainly, Jonathan. As an economist, I'm biased, but I'm a great fan of John Maynard Keynes, and he is so topical at the moment. Keynes was the first economist to come up with an answer to what happened in the Great Depression of 1929.
    If the goal of **many economists** is to secure full natural employment without inflation, then Keynes' interventionist policies hold up well. In simple terms, Keynes said that government spending, on **many things** such as construction and transport, was the key to managing the economy. This means that in an economic downturn, governments should spend a lot more, not cut, in order to stimulate the economy. So, in general, by adjusting government spending properly, a government should be able to set consumption and investment and government spending at just the

right level to produce full natural employment without inflation. Keynes' theories lost their popularity when Monetarism became the flavour of the 90s … when the state was cut back and most things were privatised. Competition became the deciding factor, really.
    And I suppose **all of this** contributed to out-of-control banking and finance sectors creating the credit crunch, as they were driven by the pursuit of profits for shareholders … and without **any consideration** of the wider impact on communities and society as a whole … And this is where a re-evaluation of Keynesian policies, whereby society's needs are seen as an organic whole, began. Keynes went out of fashion but now he's back and it will be interesting to see whether the financial community will re-embrace **some of his ideas**.

J: Thank you Professor Kotov. And I'd now like to bring in Dr Petrakis

DP: Well, Jonathan, as I said last week, I think the greatest thinker of **all time** was **either Aristotle or Karl Marx** … but … as today's programme is about people whose ideas or works have been rediscovered, I'm going to talk about Aristotle. His works had largely been lost in the West and were rediscovered in Arabic translation in the 12th century. Within a few years his ideas had spread across Europe contributing to the intellectual renaissance. Aristotle spent his whole life trying to understand and explain the truth about the world around him.
    He was the student of Plato and Plato was interested in what peoples' lives ought to be, but Aristotle thought more about what they were actually like and about how to solve **some of the problems** that people find in their lives. He looked at the facts of the real world that he could see and then tried to work out new ideas from those facts. You could say that Logic began with Aristotle. What was really impressive about him was his vast intellectual range covering most of the sciences and **many of the arts**. He wrote on **many subjects** including physics, poetry, theatre, philosophy, music, public speaking, politics, government, ethics, biology and zoology. I think it is true to say he is **one of the most important founding figures** in Western philosophy. It's fascinating as so much of Western civilisation was actually re-introduced to the West via Islamic cultural thinkers, philosophers and scientists. Fortunately, **some of the knowledge** of the Greeks was preserved by the Arabs in Alexandria

and reintroduced to the West via Moorish Spain. Our modern concepts of maths, science and medicine were heavily influenced by Islamic thinkers and they contributed massively to the expansion of classical Greek thought.

J: Thank you Dr Petrakis. It's over to you, Professor Hasan

PH: I'm going to carry on the Islamic theme of Dr Petrakis. For me, Ibn Battuta is another person who did extraordinary things and who was later re-discovered. During the 14th century, Battuta travelled around 75,000 miles across **all of the Muslim world** in search of knowledge. In some ways, he was the pioneer of globalisation. In order to share the learning and research which was so highly valued by Islamic culture, the Sultan of Morocco wanted Battuta's extraordinary journey recorded, and so a court secretary was appointed to write down Battuta's travel journal. This was called *The Rihla*. This remarkable journal gives us a first hand account of life in the Muslim world describing the conditions of the lands Battuta visited. *The Rihla* was lost till the 19th century when the journal was rediscovered in Algeria. In 2009 the film *Journey to Mecca: In the footsteps of Ibn Battuta* appeared and Battuta became more famous in the Western world. The film, which is beautifully narrated by Ben Kingsley, tells the story of Battuta's journey from Tangier to Mecca to perform the Hajj. This is the first time that a film crew has been admitted to the grand Mosque in Mecca. The film tells the remarkable story of a curious and inquisitive man who was eager to learn more about the world he lived in. In the film we experience the Hajj as Battuta did over 700 years ago.. and then in recognition of its timelessness the film moves to the Hajj as it is still performed today, by millions of pilgrims. For me it contains some of the most incredible and moving footage ever presented. Battuta's legacy is **one of the most extraordinary travel journals** ever recorded and, luckily for us, it was rediscovered …

Lesson 7.4 Track 2.12

Director of JBUP, Mayor, Manuela

JBUP: We've done a thorough analysis of the city's problems, Mr Alves, and also conducted a survey to get the opinions of members of your community.

MAYOR: Thank you for your hard work. Please go ahead and let me know what you've found.

JBUP: There are quite a few things that need changing, we think. Everyone seems to agree, there are not enough green spaces in the city, not enough trees, plants and vegetation, and that's one reason why there's a pollution problem here.

MAYOR: I see, go on please.

JBUP: You've also got a problem with your downtown shopping district. There are too many cars there, constant traffic jams and a lot of accidents with pedestrians. The whole area's overcrowded – something needs to be done about it.

MAYOR: You're right, of course. It's a nightmare for many people when they do their shopping there. I know you're worried about this, Manuela.

MANUELA: I am. Very worried. The number of traffic jams per month has increased by almost 20 per cent in the last three years.

JBUP: There another transport problem: your inter-city transport system. There are too many small buses and taxis, and they simply can't cope with the number of people wanting to come into the city or cross it. The trains need modernising, they're often late, and the stations are, well, let's say, not very well maintained. Also, people in the survey told us it's dangerous to walk in the streets later in the evening.

MANUELA: All that's true. Also there is a lot of petty crime on the buses because of the overcrowding. We've got to find an answer to that.

MAYOR: Well, transport is one of our greatest problems. No doubt about it.

JBUP: There are other things we could mention – the flooding after heavy rain, especially at the edge of the city, and the large number of children who live on the streets. They're certainly a social problem. We need to get them off the streets and into schools or jobs. And there are other problems mentioned in our report.

MAYOR: Well, thanks for highlighting some of the problems. Could we talk first about the lack of green space in our city?

Lesson 7.4 Track 2.13

Director of JBUP, Mayor, Christina, Fabio

M: We've talked in our council meetings about the need for green spaces and lack of trees and come up with an idea. I would like to know what you think of it.

J: OK, go ahead.

M: Well, we think the neighbourhoods in the city should be given trees

to plant. There are areas for development where they could do this and it would be possible to plant trees at the side of the roads in many cases. We have estimated we'll need to distribute at least half a million trees, maybe even more. They would really improve the environment in so many ways. What do you think?

J: Sounds like a great idea. What do you think, Christina?

C: I like the idea a lot. It's a very creative solution to an environmental problem. I can't see why it wouldn't work. How about you, Fabio? Do you think it's a good idea?

F: I don't know, I'm not too keen on this one, I think there'll be some real problems with the scheme.

C: Oh, in what way?

F: Well, for a start, it would be a very expensive option – major investment. And I wonder who would look after the trees? It'd cost a lot of money to take care of them. Also, the city wouldn't see the benefit of the tree planting for quite a long time. I'm not sure it's a good option.

M: Mmm, you've raised some important issues, Fabio. But, looking after the trees might not be such a big problem as you think. Our idea is that each neighbourhood in the city would be responsible for planting the trees and taking care of them. And the job could probably be done by unemployed youngsters, once they'd had a bit of training.

J: I must say, I think it's a really good suggestion, planting trees. It would involve the local communities – something you believe in – and it could have a big impact on the environment of the city in the long run. You can't change everything quickly, some of the projects must be for the long term. Fabio, you're still shaking your head.

F: I don't know, will it really work? I just don't think it's feasible. I think it relies too much on cooperation from the local community. And you can't depend on that. You could spend a lot of money and not get much in return.

M: I can't agree. You know, you have to trust local people and give them responsibility. I'm certain it will work. People will participate because they know it'll make their area more beautiful. It'll create jobs and get some people off the streets, and it will have a good effect on pollution.

J: I like the idea too. It's a good project in my opinion. I support it. And it may not cost as much money as you think. You could probably get a grant from a United Nations

environmental agency to help you finance it.

M: Mmm, that's an interesting thought. I will look into it.

Lesson 7.5 Track 2.14

The first question I'm sure you'd like me to answer is: what is critical thinking?

Well, when you read, critical thinking involves not just taking things at their face value. When you read critically, you should evaluate the writer's ideas and think about the implications and conclusions of what the writer is saying.

When you read an academic text, you need to approach the text critically. First, you should try to identify the argument and work out the writer's main line of reasoning. Next, try to analyse and criticise the argument. Has the writer given reasons for his or her views? Are the reasons valid? Is the argument presented in a logical and coherent fashion? Is the writer being objective or trying to persuade you by using emotive language?

Then, look at the evidence the writer gives you. That may be in the form of statistics, the results of a survey, opinions of influential writers with, er, references you can check or the findings of reports or experiments. When you look at the evidence, it's essential to evaluate it, and to decide whether it's weak or strong.

Now, after considering the evidence, study the writer's conclusions. Ask yourself if they're supported by the evidence. Has the writer given good reasons for the position he or she has taken? In some cases, you may feel there could be other explanations for the conclusions the writer has reached. For example, the writer may have been asked to present a particular point of view, in return for a payment.

Really, the key to critical thinking is to read actively and ask yourself questions all the time about what you're reading rather than just accepting, without questioning, the opinions or ideas of the writer.

Lesson 8.1 Track 2.15

1

'Well I have to make sure we hit the deadlines. There's a lot of emphasis on circulation figures these days, what with all the other media available. Although we do sometimes pay for feature stories from reliable sources, we have to be very careful because of the libel laws. It can cost a lot if someone decides to sue over something we've written. It's extremely gratifying when it all works and it's put to bed and we can start working on the next issue.'

2

'You really do have to be able to work under pressure especially when you have some breaking news on the evening bulletin and someone is screaming in your earpiece from the gallery. Sometimes I have to interview politicians, They're so evasive – beating around the bush. They never give a straight answer to questions and are always trying to put a spin on things. It's very competitive. We're constantly involved in ratings wars and we're all expendable. It seems there is more and more airtime given over to celebrity stories which is a bit frustrating.'

3

'Everyone is looking for a scoop, you know, that one really big story, or a real exclusive but mostly it's quite mundane stuff. When something new hits, it's good to be able to get a feature out of it. There's a lot of chequebook journalism around though in the popular press, and there are so many so-called press conferences which are anything but. It's just a prepared statement with no opportunities for questions. I think media bias is much worse in the broadcast media, though.'

4

'I've been posted all over the place. Last year, I spent six weeks with the army. The conflict got a lot of media coverage. I was filing reports at all hours. There are tight deadlines and sometimes you have to file copy under some difficult conditions. I've also had to do some live broadcasts, which can be a bit tricky sometimes. On the whole, though, it's a terrific way to make a living.'

5

'We get a bad press if you'll excuse the pun. I usually sell my stuff to the popular press, the red tops, the glossies, and there's a lot of online stuff now. So, you know, even some of the broadsheets are now getting in on the act. Sometimes it's really easy just to doorstep someone, but other times I have to stake places out for days just to get one shot. People will go mad for the right snap. People who go on and on about invasion of privacy make me sick. The celebs love the exposure. I have a few good sources who let me know who's in town – and then off I go. It's easy money. They're all fair game, these people.'

6

'The viewing figures are very important to the network, which I think is why there is a lot more infotainment around these days. These days everyone wants a sound bite rather than in-depth reporting. The audience are consumers and what they increasingly want is feel good news and human interest stuff – especially about celebrities. The marketing department has to be able to sell to our audience demographic. It's hard to take sometimes.'

Lesson 8.2 Track 2.16

I was delighted when you invited me to talk to you this afternoon about what I have learned in 35 years as a journalist and I'd like to congratulate you on receiving the 'Best Student Newspaper Award'.

First of all, I'm not going to apologise for being a journalist even though we are not flavour of the month. Journalists report what people want to read. It is the public who stop to look at a traffic accident, not journalists. I can't stand listening to complaints about sensationalist reporting from people who buy sensationalist papers.

I think the advice I can give those of you who want to go into journalism is best summed up in the words of Joseph Pulitzer. He said, 'Put it before them briefly so they will read it, clearly so they will appreciate it, picturesquely so they will remember it and, above all, accurately so they will be guided by its light'.

Many of you here today started writing stories and poems when you were very young. The crucial thing about a story is that other people must want to read it – and you don't want them to stop reading. A well-written introduction will encourage the reader to stay with you. Always treat the reader with respect and don't make them feel inadequate. Try to imagine who the reader is and put yourself in their place.

After giving you a few hopefully interesting stories from my career as a journalist, including my first attempts on our student newspaper, I'll be happy to answer any questions. Finally, I'll look at a current issue in journalism, namely invasion of privacy.

Lesson 8.4 Track 2.17

Sports Editor, Chief Editor

SE: We'd really like to run this story, Margaret. I don't think the asking price is high. What's 100,000 dollars when you think of the increased circulation we'll get if we publish the story? I mean, the coach is a household name, and no one's aware that he's unhappy at his present club. It'll be a huge story when we tell the readers that he's planning join another team. We've got to go for it.

CE: We need to think this one through, Dan. You're right, it could be a great story, but we've got to be very careful. If you don't get your facts right, he could take us to court and get substantial damages. And I don't want another court case.

SE: OK, but we have to take risks. That's how we've increased our circulation, you know that. I suppose the emails could be fake, but we could check them out. We can't miss this opportunity, Margaret, it'll make a terrific feature article. It's the kind of reporting our readers love.

CE: Hold on, Dan, there's a problem with this material. We have no idea how our source got the information. Maybe he did something illegal, and if that's the case, we could be in very hot water. I don't need to tell you, the coach is a popular guy, he's a legend in the sporting world, I … I don't think our readers will thank us for running the story. It's a very sensitive issue. If we get our facts wrong, it'll have a bad effect on our reputation. We wouldn't be able to say where we got our information from, so it would look like pure speculation on our part.

SE: OK, so you won't approve payment for the emails?

CE: No … no, sorry, we need to hold fire on this one. I've got a bad feeling about it. It could land us in court if the emails are not genuine. I think you ought to try to interview the coach. He might let slip that he's not happy with the performance of his team. Then you could sound him out, maybe suggest he'll be looking for a new job if the team performance doesn't improve.

SE: OK, I'll do that, but I'm really disappointed. I thought you'd support me.

CE: Well, sorry about that.

SE: OK, I'll try to get an interview with the coach. It won't be easy but I can probably persuade him to see me.

Lesson 8.5 Track 2.19

After you've written your introduction, (and that's the most important part of your article) you then write the body of the article. In the body, you give information about your topic in an objective way and include anecdotes to make your points, quotes, conversations with sources, and specific examples. Then you write a good conclusion. This summarises the angle you've taken and the main purpose of the article. It's good if you can end with a punchy sentence. Now, I'll give you my five top tips for writing feature articles:

One, focus on human interest, that's what people want to read about.

Two, be clear why you're writing the article. Is it to inform, persuade, appeal to emotions or entertain the reader?

Three, write in the active voice rather than in the passive. When you use the active voice, you describe what people do. This makes your text more lively.

Four, if you're writing a profile, concentrate on the person's personality and what's interesting about them. Give some background information, but don't make the article like a CV. It's good if you can describe the appearance of the person when you first met them at an interview.

And finally, five, use anecdotes and quotes to make your article lively and hold the attention of the reader.

Keep those points in mind and you won't go far wrong.

Lesson 9.1 Track 2.20

1

It's impossible to overstate the importance of privacy in English culture. Jeremy Paxman points out that: 'the importance of privacy informs the entire organisation of the country, from the assumptions on which laws are based, to the buildings in which the English live.'

Hover above any English town and you will see that the residential areas consist almost entirely of rows and rows of small boxes, each with its tiny patch of green. The English all want to live in their own private box with their own private little green bit.

I would add that a disproportionate number of our most influential social rules and maxims are concerned with the maintenance of privacy: we are taught to mind our own business, not to pry, to keep ourselves to ourselves, not to make a scene or a fuss or draw attention to ourselves, and never to wash our dirty linen in public.

2

English drivers are quite rightly renowned for their orderly, sensible, courteous conduct. My foreign informants noticed well-mannered customs and practices that most of us take for granted: that you never have to wait too long before someone lets you out of a side road or driveway, and that you are always thanked when you let someone else out; that all drivers stop for pedestrians at zebra crossings, even when the pedestrians are still standing waiting on the pavement and have not set foot on the crossing. (I met one tourist who found this so astonishing that he kept repeating the experiment, marvelling at the fact that he could

single-handedly bring streams of traffic to a deferential halt without the aid of red lights or stop-signs.)

3

In restaurants, as elsewhere, the English may moan and grumble to each other about poor service or bad food, but our inhibitions make it difficult for us to complain directly to the staff.

Most English people, faced with unappetising or even inedible food, are too embarrassed to complain at all. Complaining would be 'making a fuss' or 'drawing attention to oneself' in public – all forbidden by unwritten rules. They will not go back to that establishment, and will tell all their friends how awful it is, but the poor publican or restaurateur will never even know that there was anything amiss.

Some slightly braver souls will use method number two: the apologetic complaint, an English speciality. 'Excuse me, I'm terribly sorry, um, but, er, this soup seems to be rather, well, not very hot – a bit cold.' 'They look at the floor and mumble, as though they have done something wrong!' an experienced waiter told me.

4

… the most noticeable and important 'rule' about humour in English conversation is its dominance and pervasiveness.

In other cultures, there is a 'time and a place' for humour; it is a special, separate kind of talk. In English conversation, there is always an undercurrent of humour.

It must be said that many of my foreign informants found this aspect of Englishness frustrating rather than amusing: 'the problem with the English,' complained one American visitor, 'is that you never know when they are joking – you never know whether they are being serious or not'. This was a businessman, travelling with a female colleague from Holland. She considered the issue frowningly for a moment, and then concluded, somewhat tentatively, 'I think they are mostly joking, yes?'

The English may not always be joking, but they are always in a state of readiness for humour. We do not always say the opposite of what we mean, but we are always alert to the possibility of irony.

5

When asked to compare English working and business practices with those of other cultures, all my foreign and immigrant informants commented on the English sense of fair play, and specifically on our respect for the law and our relative freedom from

the corruption they felt was endemic and tacitly accepted (albeit in varying degrees) in other parts of the world. Many felt that we were not sufficiently aware or appreciative of this fact. 'You just take it for granted,' a Polish immigrant complained. 'You assume that people will play fair, and you are shocked and upset when they do not. In other countries there is not that assumption.'

Fair play, with its sporting overtones, suggests that everyone should be given an equal chance and that people should conduct themselves honourably, observe the rules and not cheat or shirk their responsibilities. At the same time, 'fair play' allows for differences in ability and accepts that there will be winners and losers – while maintaining that playing well and fairly is more important than winning.

Lesson 9.2 Track 2.21

Part 1

If we are to assess programs aimed at the punishment, and more positively, the rehabilitation of juveniles involved in anti-social behaviour, drug addiction and crime, we must first accept that teenagers are psychologically different to adults. Teenagers are not yet fully developed and, even when they have committed very serious crimes, adolescents have different needs to adult criminals. From this we can conclude that the juvenile justice system needs to take these differences into account, if we are to provide effective punishment and rehabilitation. The programs that are most effective will surely be those which do not violate the basic principles of adolescent development. If they do violate these principles, it can only lead to an ever deepening rejection of society and its laws by the teenagers in question.

Lesson 9.2 Track 2.22

Part 2

So, what are these particular psychological traits of the teenager?

Firstly, all teenagers, even law breakers, have a strong sense of fairness. They will be moralistic and intolerant of unfairness.

Secondly, they are looking for respect from the world and their peers.

Thirdly, they respond best to encouragement rather than punishment. Harsh punishment may temporarily alter behaviour, but their attitudes and deeper behaviour seldom change.

Fourthly, they reject imposed structure

and outside control. Teenagers do benefit from limits, like children, but, unlike children, they do need to have some kind of voice within that structure, or in the determination of that structure.

Also, whilst young people need help, advice and guidance, they will reject it when it comes from people or institutions that are felt to be unfair, disrespectful, punishing or that impose limits and structure.

Youths also have a need to feel competent at something and to achieve success, and, alongside this, they need, at times, to be in charge and to make their own choices.

In addition, there is also a need to belong, on equal terms, to groups and communities.

And finally, settled youths appreciate and value the strengths of their families.

Lesson 9.2 Track 2.23

While the wilderness camps are particularly strong with regard to counselling and therapy, the boot camps hardly address juveniles' psychological problems.

Because the boot camps principally operate on a punishment basis, the teenagers are quite likely to reject any advice or guidance that is offered by the adults there.

In a sense, boot camps partly meet teenagers' expectations of fairness, in that good behaviour is rewarded and bad behaviour is punished. However, as the teenagers utterly lack the chance to determine the structure and limits, they are fairly certain to see things as unfair.

It is extremely important that families are involved in the process, and this certainly occurs at wilderness camps, while it seems to be entirely absent at boot camps.

The suggestion that boot camps don't respond to the teenage desire for success is slightly unfair, as the physical military training offers plenty of challenges. However, wilderness camps are extremely focussed on success, from the building of a camp fire to the taking on of a leadership role.

The highly complex range of tasks and skills required at wilderness camps means teenagers are almost certain to feel that they belong to a group, get respect and to make their own choices. In contrast, the range of tasks at boot camps is rather limited and they completely lack chances for people to make their own choices.

Lesson 9.3 Track 2.24

Good morning and welcome to this meeting of the European Immigration Forum.

Let me begin with a little story. On January 1st 2009, at one minute past midnight, in a hospital in Barcelona, a baby was born – the first baby to be born in the region of Catalonia, and indeed in the whole of Spain, that year. Her parents had decided to call her Eulalia, the name of the patron saint of Barcelona. But the baby's parents were not originally from Barcelona – they were Uruguayan immigrants who had lived there for just four years. They chose the name in honour of the city that had welcomed them so warmly in that time. But Eulalia wasn't alone. Three other children were born in Catalonia on January 1st – all of them sons and daughters of immigrants. These births were highly symptomatic – a direct result – of what had happened in Spain in the preceding years.

My colleagues and I have been looking closely at the phenomenon of immigration to Spain in the early years of the new millennium, specifically from 2000 to 2008, and this afternoon I am going to present some of our findings.

At the risk of overloading you with statistics, I'll start with some of the key data. As you can see on the slide here, between 2000 and 2008, the population of Spain grew from 40.49 million to 46.15 million. Most of this increase was down to immigration. Approximately 8 out of every 10 new Spanish citizens were born outside Spain, and the total number of foreigners was roughly 5.2 million, about 11 per cent of the population.

Romanians formed the largest group, mainly as a result of a spectacular growth in their numbers following Romania's accession to the EU in 2007. This meant they'd overtaken Moroccans, who became the second biggest group.

Although, as the credit crunch of 2008 started to bite, the Spanish authorities took measures to slow the number of migrants arriving, there were forces pulling in the opposite direction.

One of these was the Law of Historic Memory, which came into force in December 2008. This law gave descendants of Spanish emigrants and exiles the right to become Spanish citizens. It offered large numbers of people in Latin-American countries such as Argentina, Chile, Mexico, Venezuela and Cuba, the grandchildren of those who fled Spain in the 1930s during the Civil War or during the dictatorship that followed, the opportunity to claim Spanish citizenship. I happened to be in Cuba on the day the law was enacted, and there were queues of people sleeping rough outside the Spanish Consulate in Havana to get the application forms for their Spanish passports. Estimates suggested that this law would add somewhere between 500,000 and 1 million people to the Spanish population – so between a 1 and 2 per cent increase.

During the period we investigated, however, there was little evidence that, in spite of the increase in their numbers, immigrants had made much impact on political life in the country. There were no members of the Spanish Congress or Senate from immigrant communities. There was, nevertheless, a feeling that things would change, largely as a result of the election of Barack Obama as US President.

We also found a strong correlation between economic circumstances and people's perceptions of immigration. The downturn in 2008 led to an increase in those who thought immigrants benefited their own countries more than their host countries – for example, through funds sent home – and racism also appeared to be on the increase …

Lesson 9.4 Track 2.25

Aidan, Brooke, Chien

A: So, let's look at the law concerning truancy. Obviously, we want to cut the levels of truancy, partly to reduce juvenile crime and also to improve the education of our country's lowest achievers. Having said that, this law is not solely about children. In a sense, it's more about making parents take responsibility for their children's education. Too many parents ignore their role in education, and particularly their role in discipline.
Now, although we're here to amend this law, I think that one of its current strengths is its clarity; there's no room for doubt and confusion. Basically, if your child doesn't go to school, and they don't have permission to be absent, then you will be punished. Also, the law applies to everyone, without exception.

B: That's all fair enough, but it's simply too inflexible as it stands. If a child's absent for only one day, then the parents will be punished. Surely this kind of punishment should be used only for serious repeat offenders?

A: Perhaps, but wouldn't it then be unwieldy and cumbersome as a law?

As I said, its current strength is its clarity and the strong message that it sends out.

B: Well, certainly it's important that the law sends out a strong message, but I still think there must be some built-in flexibility. People's lives are not straightforward. I mean, what if a child's being bullied at school, but can't tell anyone about it? In that case, missing a day in order to escape the bullying would then result in their parents being punished, which would only increase the child's sense of shame.

C: Well, obviously in that case, the punishment wouldn't apply.

B: You say that, but as it stands the law's very clear that the punishment's immediate and direct. I think we need to show that there's built-in flexibility and room for manoeuvre.

A: Well, whilst accepting that as a fair principle, we mustn't make it too complicated.

C: Can I just point out that there's another aspect we need to consider.

A: Oh, yes? What's that?

C: Well, the punishment, particularly the fines, may not be the best thing. I mean, I think that many truants come from poorer families, and many of these behavioural problems stem from this poverty. Surely, fines will only increase the level of poverty. And then, will wealthier families be concerned about fines? Admittedly, imprisonment would be deterrence, but, overall, I'm not sure that this particular punitive response is best. Perhaps parents and children should do some kind of community service, in the field of education – they could help out at schools for children with special needs, for example.

A: I see what you're saying, but one thing that I like about the current proposal is that it's easy to enforce. Community service would require special organisation and management. A fine's much more straightforward.

C: Well, I think there's more to say on that, but I think we should get some amendments agreed now; we know we've got to change this law in some ways. First of all, how can we ...

Lesson 9.4 Track 2.26

Aidan, Brooke, Chien

C: First of all, how can we build some flexibility into this law?

B: How about a three strikes and you're out kind of rule? You know, the first two times there's a warning, and the

third time leads to punishment of the parents.

C: And what about replacing imprisonment with community service – I think that'd be much more appropriate, and would still act as a deterrent.

A: I think I can agree to those suggestions; I think the law will still serve its original purpose. So, how shall we phrase it for the minister to look at? Let's see ... what about ... Parents are responsible for ensuring their children's attendance at school. When a child has been absent for three times without permission, the parents are liable to a fine or a community service sentence.

B: That's great.

C: Erm, hold on a minute.

A/B: What?

C: Well, when we say three times, do we mean in their whole school career, in a year, in a term?

A: Oh, good point. We'd better clarify that. Any thoughts?

Lesson 9.5 Track 2.28

Thanks for downloading this podcast. I'm going to be talking to you about literature reviews, what they are and how you should go about doing them. University students, especially at the higher levels, are often required to write a literature review. The term is potentially confusing, as it suggests reading Shakespeare or Tolstoy. In fact, a literature review is a survey of what has been published in a particular field – your field – be it astrophysics or business studies. It's a synthesis of what's known about a subject.

To carry out such a review obviously involves extensive reading, and by doing this you'll learn a great deal about the subject, and become – to some extent – an expert on that subject. As you prepare the literature review, you'll clarify your own ideas on the topics you read about, and form your own opinions about what specialists in the field have written. You'll be able to see how the subject – and the research on that subject – has developed over time. When you finish your reading, you'll be in a position to identify half a dozen key pieces of research on the subject and see how each piece has influenced the others.

Doing a literature review also helps to identify existing gaps in the knowledge about the subject, gaps that your research can fill. You can see how your work will follow on from the work of others, and how it might answer some unanswered questions. It's a bit like a jigsaw puzzle with one or two missing

pieces. When you've assembled it all, you can see where there's a gap to be filled.

As with any kind of synthesis, organisation is the key. Some students find it helpful to ...

Review Units 7–9 Track 2.29

1
Woman, Man
W: I should get my final results next week.
M: Oh. Do you think you've done well?
W: Well, I did OK in my coursework but the last exam was really tricky so I live in hope!
M: I'm sure they'll be fine!

2
Boy, Man
B: Dad, are you busy? Can I talk to you about something?
M: Yes, of course. I don't have to leave for another hour so I've got plenty of time.

3
Woman 1, 2
W1: Is everything OK?
W2: Not really. This steak is overcooked.
W1: Well, send it back then.
W2: No, it's OK. I don't want to cause any trouble.

4
Husband, Wife
H: Have you washed my white shirts? I want to wear one today.
W: No, I haven't had time. I was going to do it today.
H: Oh, that's annoying. I did mention it a couple of days ago.
W: I know, but I work too you know, and I do all the housework and cooking. Sometimes I think you don't appreciate everything I do in this house!

5
Employee, Manager
E: Dave, did you have a word with the sales director about my hours?
M: Yes, I did. She said that she needed you to work full-time, and that part-time is no good for the company.
E: Oh, that's really disappointing. I need some extra time for my studies.
M: I know, and if it were up to me, I'd help you. But it isn't my decision. I can't help you, I'm afraid.

6
Teacher, Student
T: Oh damn! Look what I've done!
S: Here, let me help you, Mrs. Graham.

7
Woman, Man
W: Look, why don't we talk to my parents about the money problem? I'm sure they'd be able to lend us some to help us out.

м: No! I really don't want other people to know that we've got money problems. It's private.

Review Units 7–9 Track 2.30

Andie, Jim, Steve, Fiona, Lewis

A: OK, now, you all know why we're meeting. Matt, our European correspondent, has come up with a story about a British Euro MP that's dynamite. If we print it, it could bring down the government in this country. Ultimately, whether we print it or not is Jim's decision, as he owns the paper, but Jim asked for all of you ... Well, Jim, you can explain.

J: Yeah, thanks Andie. I really want to get everyone's take on this. Obviously, I know the law, and the possible consequences if we run this story – we could be sued and the paper could go out of business. Having said that, it isn't solely about business. It's also about the integrity of the government. So, let's get everyone's opinion. Yeah, Steve.

S: That sounds like a great idea, Jim. I'm sure we all have different ideas. Personally, I think this story is so important that we have no choice. In fact, I'm incredibly excited about it. It will boost our circulation figures no end!

F: Now hang on a minute, Steve. You're right, of course, about the circulation, but as your legal representative I have to point out that we need to think this one through very carefully. If you don't get the facts straight, we could be taken to court. Also, I was talking to Matt last night, and he said that the politician who called him is willing to give her name to the story, but she's demanding a fee ...

J: That isn't a problem. You know I deplore chequebook journalism, but ...

F: No, no, it isn't that. I just don't think it's feasible because people will question the politician's motives if she gets a fee, and people find out, as they will. If she's revealing a cover-up and casting doubt on other politicians' morals, then she must be seen to be honourable herself.

L: I see what you're saying, Fiona, but the point is that she's very likely to lose her job once she comes into the open, and if that happens, well, of course she'll need some money to help her through.

A: You know, to be honest, I'm not too keen on this one, either. Can we trust this woman? Does she really have the country's interests at heart? Or is she giving us – selling us – this information for other reasons? It's

a very sensitive issue. You know that her husband used to be in the opposition before he left politics. The current government prides itself on its financial integrity, and if this scandal were to bring it down, then the opposition would form a government, and who knows, maybe her husband would be back in it.

J: You've all raised some good points. Thanks. It gives me plenty to think about. But, you know, while accepting all these views, we mustn't take a decision without having all the facts here. If we get our facts wrong, it'll have a bad effect on our reputation. I know there isn't much time before the deadline, but maybe I should go over and see Matt before we decide. I'll look into flights for this evening. Lewis, can you contact Matt and ...

Lesson 10.1 Track 3.1

1

It was OK, but, well, the music is rather dated, I mean, the musical is over 20 years old now, and it was always very much of its time, wasn't it? But, still, I was pretty impressed by the sets and it's such a lovely romantic story.

2

Astounding! What more can I say? It's probably the most inventive show I've ever seen, I mean, who'd've thought you could get a tune out of a chair leg? Great stuff. Well worth the cost of the ticket.

3

Goth music isn't really my kind of thing, but I guess they had a lot of energy. I'd really wanted to see the other band, but they weren't up to much really. So, a bit disappointing overall, I guess.

4

Well, it lived up to the hype, mainly cos those guys are so talented. You really can't go wrong when you're seeing people like that, I mean, they're legends really. The venue's good as well, not too big and a great atmosphere, although it took ages to get there. Top marks all round, I'd say.

5

Well, it could've been better. Mind you, his performance is certainly up there with the best, but, I don't know, in the end the production doesn't really hold up. Perhaps I'm too much of a fan of the original movie. They just didn't get the atmosphere of the New York docks over very well. But, that's not to say it's not worth seeing, just that it's not the best, and you can't always have that, can you?

Lesson 10.3 Track 3.2

Tyler, Mike and Josh

м: What was I getting at? Oh yeah, yeah, OK. So, um, yeah, I mean, with with television the way it is and the Internet being the way it is and everyone has access to information it's causing a lot of things like Attention Deficit Disorder, which is a problem afflicting many people, er, [like the three of us?] across the world. Yes, er, actually I read, er, a very interesting article on how, er, everyone's attention's being divided by the Internet and, I mean, you have so much information at your hands that it's, er, really difficult to retain information, you can look things up so quickly that, er, your focus isn't, er, well-concentrated in one specific area of study or research for very long. Er, I mean, you'll look something up and then find something else you didn't know and then you'll just look up something else and you go on these huge tangents like I am doing right now [yeah]. Er.

T: It's often, it's often fun just to sit there at about 1 o'clock in the morning while listening to a replay of this show, talking to Josh and you, well, you sometimes, cos you're ridiculous, I can't even get hold of you anymore. Er, and just kind of go on this, er, Internet, like, rampage [yeah] like you open one [yeah] you open one, like, to me the Internet is not, the Internet is good for society I believe, because you go and you search things [yeah] [it's mostly good, there are ups and downs] and you learn something else and that leads to another link and that leads to another link and you just keep going and when you started searching for, er, Madonna's left leg you end up [ha ha] looking at Rudy Guiliani's Presidential campaign [ha ha] it's unbelievable [ha ha].

м: That just sums up, er, a hot Saturday night for Tyler [ha ha]

J: It's, it's a good time for everyone.

м: I mean, you just go like from, er, from sea to shining sea on the Internet [ha ha]. [Yeah] well, yeah, I mean, I find that especially when you're cruising Wikipedia it's ridiculous you'll find something you don't know, look up the link to that then you'll find something in that article you don't know look up the article to that and then you'll go from topic to topic [right] and you'll lose complete focus.

T: Well, I mean, there's people who don't let their kids on the Internet and that's, kind of, like, despicable to me, like everything is today. Despicable. [Yep] But, I mean, why is the Internet such a bad thing? I mean, half these people who are banning [I can't] their kids from the Internet don't even know what's on there or how to use it [erm], same as the kids people who ban their kids from MSN don't even know what it is or how it works [yeah]. So, I mean, er, and I can understand it if it's, like, for disciplinary reasons but there are a lot of people. Same with television, I mean, there's a lot of people who say, you know, you you'll never watch television, their kids never watch television. Well. [yeah I know] there are educational things on television to watch. I mean, a lot of things I know I've either learnt from Internet or television. [I personally] Never a textbook. Never. [yeah]

M: I personally know, erm, a family that doesn't have a TV [um] they, they've grown up, their their kids have grown up without television whatsoever.

T: OK, well, it's a different thing if you don't like TV but I'm thinking about people who tell their kids you cannot watch TV cos it's bad for you. I disagree with that.

Lesson 10.4 Track 3.4

Tony, Robert

T: Hi! I'm Tony and I guess there's only one way to describe what I am, and that's a natural-born winner. That is, all my life I've come first in everything, you know, sports at school, my studies at uni, in my banking career, where I regularly out-bonus my colleagues. And as for surviving on the island, well, I reckon that won't be an issue, as I'm fit, strong and healthy – I play squash three times a week and I never take days off sick. But then again, that doesn't mean that I'm perfect. Just almost perfect! What I mean is, I don't suffer fools gladly, so I guess I can seem rude or impatient. Perhaps arrogant. But then again, is that really so bad? Oh, and before I forget, I'm single at the moment but that doesn't mean I'm not looking. Perhaps a little romance on International Island wouldn't be a bad thing, would it? Anyway, trying to win International Island will be a challenge that'll fire me up to even greater efforts, and it's a challenge I want to take on, and when I take something on, I come out on top. Always.

R: Hi. I'm Robert and I'm a builder,

which I reckon is one of the reasons I'd be a good person to have along on the island. If you're looking for a man who can, well, I'm that man. Stuck on an island without a toilet? I'll knock one up in under an hour. You could say that I'm more useful than an umbrella in the rain – and, as you can see, I've got my wits about me too. I like a laugh, and I like a good bit of banter, you know, if there's a chance for a joke, I'll make it, like a maid would a bed. Oh yes, and I guess I should tell you now – I'm absolutely terrified of spiders. Euurgh, even mentioning that word sends shivers down my spine. What else? Let me see … ah yes, I guess I should say that, by and large, I'm pretty laid back, you know, I'm a tolerant kind of guy, I don't get wound up much by people, I get along with most, that kind of thing. Mind you, I've got no time for laziness, especially when everyone needs to pull together to get things going. Oh yeah, and another thing is, I reckon my hobby'll come in pretty useful – I love fishing. So, if food is short, I can ease those hunger pangs. So, all in all, I reckon I'd be a great choice for International Island. I hope you choose me, the man who can.

Lesson 10.5 Track 3.6

Shanice, Students 1–6

S: Hi everyone, my name's Shanice and I'm your seminar leader today. Er … **we're going to be looking at the language of drama**. And trying to answer the question: how real is it? To start with, **I thought we should confirm what we mean by drama, so we're all clear about that. We're thinking about drama in quite a broad sense**. Obviously, we're including plays in the theatre, Pinter or Mamet or whatever. But we're also thinking about TV drama, stuff like *CSI*. Soap operas like *Eastenders*, *Coronation Street*. And of course screenplays of films … *Pulp Fiction* … etc. So those are the parameters of the discussion. **Is that alright?**

S1: **What about radio drama?**

S: Yeah, obviously that's part of it, too. OK? Hopefully, everybody's done the reading. And the conversation analysis task. Yeah? **Did everybody record a minute or two of conversation and try to transcribe it?**

S2: I did it, but I've left it at home.

S: Well, that should be OK. By the look of it, quite a few of us have got some data from that. OK, so, **first**,

we're going to look at the features of real conversation and **then** we can compare real conversation with the language of drama, and see how similar or different they are. Right, so, what are the features of real conversation? What did you find from your research? **Would anyone like to start?** (pause) Silence. No-one wants to be first! Jack, I know you spent some time on the task. **Do you want to kick off?**

S3: Yeah, I'm happy to do that. Well, in real conversation you get a lot of repetition. People say the same stuff again and again. But as well as the topic, they repeat the language, too. So you hear the same words and phrases over and over. Also, in real conversation, the sentences are usually very short. Much shorter than when we write …

S1: **Sorry, but can we really call them sentences, though?** I mean, aren't sentences something we only use in writing … you know … capital letters at the beginning …full stops at the end. Isn't speech more of a continuum?

S3: OK. Maybe 'sentences' is the wrong word. Perhaps I should've said 'utterances'. But it's true they tend to be relatively short.

S: **Right, what else?**

S2: The language is pretty informal. In the one I analysed, I noticed a lot of idioms, expressions, phrasal verbs… quite a bit of swearing, too. There's also the speaker's accent or dialect. I recorded a conversation with my Scottish flatmate. He's got a really strong accent. And he uses words like 'lass' and 'fitba'.

S1: Fitba. What's that?

S2: Football.

S1: Well, everyone's got an accent of some sort, haven't they? I mean, some people have got regional accents, some people have got class accents.

S3: **True. Something else we get in real conversation** is a lot of hesitations, false starts, fillers, overlaps, pauses …

S4: **Can you repeat that, please?** I'm taking a few notes.

S3 Yeah. Hesitations, overlaps, pauses, fillers, false starts … these are really common.

S: **Is everybody happy with these terms? Do we need to clarify anything before we go on? Yeah?**

S4: **What do we mean by fillers exactly?**

S3: Words like … er, well, you see, those kinds of words and phrases. Things we use when we don't know exactly what to say, and we're thinking … playing for time.

AUDIOSCRIPTS

s4: OK. Cheers.

s1: Er … I don't think it matters if conversation is like this, anyway.

s: **Sorry, what do you mean by that?**

s1: Well, conversation is only really for those people who are involved in it.

s: **Yes. Go on.**

s1: That's why we often can't understand other people's conversations. If we listen to them on the bus, for example. The participants can often understand each other because of shared background information, or from non-verbal behaviour. I think this has implications for dramatic language. You see, when we look closely at dramatic language, what we find is…

s: **OK, that's interesting … let's come back to that later** when we look at the language of drama …

s5: **Sorry, can I butt in here?**

s: **Go ahead, please.**

s5: Yeah. We're all talking about conversation as if it's all the same… you know… there's only one type … but it's well-known that men and women talk in different ways.

s2: Look, why ….

s: Let her finish, please.

s5: A lot of research has been done by people like Deborah Tannen. Men are always trying to compete with each other, even in conversation … you know, one guy tells a story, then another guy tries to tell a more interesting story, then a third bloke tries to beat them all and tell the best story of all.

s: **Does Tannen actually say that?**

s5: I don't know, but women don't talk like that. They way they talk is much more collaborative …they support each other.

s2: You're always coming out with this feminist stuff … Sorry, I don't know your name …

s5: Natasha.

s2: Yeah … well … I don't know why you can't look at any argument without turning it into a women's issue …

s5: Well, mainly, because men like you …

s: **Alright … wait a minute … hang on … I think Natasha's got a point, but maybe we can generalise, too.**

s1: Yeah. You're right. A lot of conversation IS co-operative … doesn't matter if you're a man or a woman … If we didn't co-operate, conversation couldn't happen. The way we take turns, for example …

s6: **Sorry, does anyone know why they're called soap operas?**

s: **Sorry, what?**

s6: Yeah, soap operas. Does anyone know why they're called that?

s: Right … that question is a bit out of the blue … **we don't want to get off track here … but does anyone know the answer?**

s1: I heard it's because when they first started in America, they were sponsored by soap manufacturers.

s: Right. Thanks. Er. **let's try to stay focussed here. We were talking about** how conversation is co-operative. Had you finished what you were going to say?

s1: Er …well … almost … except maybe to mention Grice's maxims.

s4: Sorry, whose maxims?

s1: Grice. Paul Grice. A linguist. Grice called it the co-operative principle.

s: **How many of us are familiar with this? Hands up.** 50/50. OK.

s1: Well, Grice claimed there are four maxims or rules of conversation. Basically, and I'm paraphrasing… we should be true, be brief, be relevant and be clear.

s: Alright. **I'm going to try to summarise what we've said so far.** We said that real conversation is repetitive, full of short utterances, false starts, pauses, hesitations. The speakers may have a particular accent or dialect. But perhaps this isn't important if … if the speakers can understand each other. We recognised that there might be some differences between the way men and women speak, but conversation is basically a co-operative activity.

Lesson 10.5 Track 3.7

Shanice, Students 1–6

s: Right, we're going to turn now to the language of drama. Let's compare what we know about real conversation with the way dramatists and scriptwriters use language. Yes, Jack, you've got your hand up.

s3: Well, I think the main point is that if characters in plays and films spoke like we do in conversation, it would be a terrible mess. The audience wouldn't be able to make any sense of it. And it would be almost impossible for the actors to pull it off. All those overlaps, for instance … Can you imagine? Loads of characters all talking at the same time?

s1: I guess what many modern dramatists are trying to do is to get as close as possible to real speech, but without the whole thing degenerating into that mess that you were talking about … so … it's an … an approximation of real speech.

s: Can we think of any good examples of this?

s3: Well, I think … er … Harold Pinter's a good example. You get a lot of

pauses in Pinter's dialogue. He's famous for his pauses. There's lots of repetition. It's often illogical. Like conversation.

s1: True. Pinter's got a great ear for dialogue. In one of the articles I found they call it the language of the bus-stop, the cafe and the living-room. But he's also shaped it; he's crafted it. It's got a rhythm. It's kind of poetry.

s3: Yes. I agree with that. But it's a very dark poetry.

s: Dark? Can you say a bit more about that?

s3: Yeah. Well, it's the way the language is used. Pinter's plays are often power struggles, fights over territory. The characters use language as a weapon. They often have battles with each other, linguistic battles.

s: Mmm. Good point.

s3: You don't know what the characters are thinking. But you have a feeling they're about to explode into violence. I haven't explained that very well.

s: Yes. I think we know what you mean. Ali, you've been very quiet today. Do you want to say anything?

s4 Well. I was just thinking that Pinter's had a big influence on the next generation of dramatists. People like Martin Crimp and Caryl Churchill. They've tried to take this imitation of real speech even further.

s: Why though? I mean, why do these dramatists want to use this demotic language – real speech – anyway? What's the point? What are they trying to achieve?

s3: Well, I think if you have real language, you, I mean, the audience identifies more with the situations and characters. They mean more to you.

s1: I think we could say the same thing about a lot of modern films. Think about Quentin Tarantino, for example. *Reservoir Dogs*. There's a kind of poetry about that language, too. And the characters often do explode into violence.

s: Good comparison, yeah.

s5: I'm not sure about that. I mean, how much do we identify with the characters in *Reservoir Dogs*? Although I know someone here who does.

s: Alright. Let's move on.

s6: Well, in all these cases, there's still a script, isn't there? There has to be a script of some sort, otherwise it'd all be a terrible mess. If it was like real conversation, people wouldn't be able to understand it.

s: Yes, I think that was the point someone was making earlier. Alright, I'm going to summarise what we've said so far …

AUDIOSCRIPTS

Lesson 11.2 Track 3.8

The, er, financial crisis ultimately led me to, er, lose my job. Erm, the industry that I worked in, er, banking was the primary sort of target, I suppose, or the primary cause and therefore the first area, erm, within the global economy that was affected by the entire process. Erm, the actual circumstances of me losing my job was er, rather surreal in the sense that, um, I was waking up to the ... to watching the TV or watching the news and saw that the company I'd worked for had gone pretty much into liquidation. Erm, the problem with these sorts of things is that it's erm ... and the way it affects you is ... the ramifications, as I said, um, were quite severe, you know, you've got things to pay, mortgages to pay, erm all the various other bills and things that you're responsible for ... erm, and losing your job, and losing your income source obviously affects that now. Erm, the company I worked for was ultimately bought by another bank and therefore some of the problems that are associated with redundancy were, were erm, removed for me. But obviously the embarrassment factor, which I think is the primary sort of concern when you do lose your job was very much apparent.

The colleagues that I worked with as well, erm, suffered in a very similar way. Erm, I was relatively lucky in the sense that I hadn't been at the company that I worked for, for particularly long and therefore was able to move quite quickly on to another job with another bank. But some of the guys that, erm, I'd actually worked with were relatively old, had been at the same company for a number of years and therefore, erm, did struggle.

Erm, I suppose the actual ... the main problem with losing your job as always, is ... and with the type of problems that were occurring in the economy at the time, in the sense of the ...it was a structural, erm, problem, it wasn't just isolated to the company I worked for, was that feeling that you're potentially not going to get another job for a significant period of time. Erm, I was lucky in the sense that I was able to find employment relatively quickly. Erm but, again, it's one of those Catch 22s in the sense that you do now have, erm, the stigma of sort of being made redundant, erm, on your CV.

In terms of the actual crisis itself, I suppose you could say that, erm, it couldn't have been avoided. Er, the circumstances that led up to it were more a crisis of confidence than anything else. There are a whole host of parameters and indicators that should have perhaps been more sort of warning ... or provided more warning I should say, erm, that something along this magnitude was going to occur, but, I think the problem was, until these things occur, erm, you know, people are a little bit unsure of the fact that er, ... not unsure. Are more *inclined* to believe that these things aren't ever gonna get as bad as they are – or as they do.

Lesson 11.4 Track 3.9

Neptune 1, Neptune 2, Kenneth, Ingrid
N1: Thanks for your interesting presentation. We'd like to ask you some questions now.
K: Go ahead.
N1: There are quite a few marine life-saving devices on the market. What's so special about your product?
K: Um, we think it's got a lot of advantages compared with competitors' products. It emits a very loud alarm signal, erm, it has a very wide coverage, a wide range, up to er four kilometers, and it constantly monitors the position of the person who's fallen overboard. The battery's rechargeable, that's a big advantage over our competitors, and the device is ultra-light and easy to attach. Oh yes, er one other very important point, the product will be sold at a very competitive price, the whole package will cost approximately $1,800 – that's less than most other devices on the market.
N1: Mmm, interesting. What about patents? Is the technology fully protected?
K: Yes, it is. We've taken out worldwide patents on the technology, the device and the receiver.
N1: Good, that's very reassuring. How many of the devices have you actually produced?
K: We've made four working prototypes. They've been tested here and in international waters. We've got written confirmation from several international marine associations that the device works and can do what we claim it does.
N1: Right, just four prototypes. So you're not really set up as a business yet.
K: No. That's why we've come to you. We need finance. The cost of bringing the product to the market and marketing it will be considerable. We have a couple of personal loans, but they're not nearly enough. Also we need advice and support.
N1: OK. Let's see if my colleague has any questions. Julia, over to you.

N2: Thanks. Erm, I've got two questions at this stage. Er, firstly, who would you say is your target consumer? Who do you think will buy your product?
K: I'll let Ingrid answer that. She's got some good ideas about how we should market our device. Go ahead, Ingrid.
I: OK, well, er, we'll aim at several segments in the market. Owners of sea-going private boats and yachts is one segment, sea rescue crews is another one, and um... of course there are the river boats. There could be plenty of demand from commercial companies hiring boats to inexperienced customers. Naval training boats, that's another segment that could be very profitable. Er, so our target consumer is really anyone who owns a boat and is concerned about their own security or that of their crew.
N2: Mmm, plenty of scope then for selling the product. A final question. Where do you think you'll be in five years time with this device?
I: Um ... It's early days now, of course, but we're both very ambitious and committed to the product. We think we'll have a multi-million dollar business in the future, selling and licensing our products all over the world. Our greatest asset is our ability to invent new products. We have other projects in the pipeline, We could talk about them later.

Lesson 11.4 Track 3.10

Neptune 1, Neptune 2, Kenneth, Ingrid,
N1: Let's talk about the agenda for this afternoon. I propose we discuss three specific areas: the amount of our investment in your business, the stake you can offer us and other projects you're working on. How about that?
K: Sounds OK to me.
I: Yeah, that's fine.
N1: OK, how much would you like us to invest?
K: We think we'll need $500,000 to market the product successfully, and for that we can offer you a stake of 15 per cent in the business.
N1: Well, I'm sorry, but that's not acceptable. Investing half a million for a 15 per cent stake wouldn't interest us.
I: If I can come in here, let me remind you of the benefits you'll get from investing in our device. Don't forget it's a state-of-the art product, and several marine associations have tested it and found that it works. Also ... Also, it's got an international

patent. MLSD will generate a lot of income for any investor. You'll get a very good return on your $500,000.

N2: We can't be sure of that. It's a risky investment. There are competing products on the market …

I: Ah but not with our advanced technology.

N1: Maybe. But we're not happy about the terms you offer. We're not prepared to invest in the project unless you improve your offer.

K: How about if we offered you a bigger stake, would you be willing to give us $500,000?

N1: We might consider it. What can offer us?

K: Supposing we give you a 20 per cent stake for the full amount. What do you say?

N1: I'm sorry. We were looking for a much higher stake.

K: Well, That's our final offer. It looks as if we can't make a deal.

N1: I'm afraid not. The numbers just don't add up for us.

K: OK, then, thank you for your time. I'm very sorry we couldn't reach an agreement.

N1: Well, that's too bad. We wish you the best of luck finding an investor. But, to be honest, you may find it difficult to get the terms you want.

I: We'll see. Thanks very much for meeting us.

Lesson 12.1 Track 3.11

1 In this story, the surface of a mysterious planet is in fact a huge organism. Humans have been studying it for about a hundred years but it is still an incomprehensible, alien form of life. Scientists orbiting the planet think that the organism is attempting to communicate with them, and they try to make contact with it. Kris Kelvin, a psychologist, arrives – to ascertain whether the research programme should be wound up, given its lack of progress. He finds a straggling crew, haunted by phantoms of people from their respective pasts. Then he, too, finds himself caught up in disturbing hallucinations.

2 An elite group of men rule the Republic of Gilead, formerly the USA. The society is rigidly hierarchical, with women subservient and generally confined to the home. The few women who are fertile are forced to bear children for childless high-class couples. Offred is one such woman. But she learns of an underground resistance

movement, one of whose members, Nick, helps her escape.

3 At the beginning of this post-apocalyptic tale, a meteor shower of dazzling beauty blinds virtually everyone. The main character, Bill, is spared because he's in hospital, his eyes covered in bandages. He's recovering from a sting caused by a mobile, genetically engineered, carnivorous plant. Once out of hospital, Bill, and the few remaining sighted people face a dilemma: should they try to protect the blind from the carnivorous plants, or should they flee and leave them to their grisly fate?

Lesson 12.2 Track 3.12

Today is something's birthday, something which we probably all use every day, but, I'm afraid that this isn't a happy day of celebration. This is a sad birthday, a birthday which would be better if it wasn't, because today's the birthday of the plastic bag. To be exact, it's 75 years since polyethylene was discovered, by cruel chance, by two scientists in the UK. Polyethylene, more commonly known as polythene, is the basic constituent of plastic bags. So, why shouldn't we celebrate its birthday? Allow me to explain.

First of all, polythene, and most other plastic, is made from oil, and it's all part of our dependence on this raw material, and that's a dependence which leads to pollution and the destruction of the natural environment. The oil industry's one of the most polluting industries that we have, and our excessive use of plastic only encourages that industry. We should aim for an oil-free society.

Secondly, plastic simply does not go away, or, at least, it takes an incredibly long time to do so, with some estimates that it takes 1,000 years for a plastic bag to decompose. This causes untold numbers of problems. Plastic waste takes up valuable space in our land-fill rubbish disposal sites, but more importantly, it has a direct effect on wildlife. Animals and birds eat plastic by mistake, or get caught up in plastic cables and bags, and suffocate to death. There are so many depressing images of dead birds that have been cut open to reveal guts that are filled with plastic. What right do we have to inflict this harm on animals? We share this world, and we need to share it responsibly.

This problem is no better exemplified than in the middle of the Pacific Ocean, where there is a floating island of plastic trash, but this island is twice the size of the state of Texas. That's right,

twice the size of Texas. This is only the most extreme example, as all of our oceans are teeming with plastic waste. Furthermore, some of this stuff slowly breaks down into tiny micro-particles which either are ingested by marine animals, animals that we then later eat, or gather on our beaches as plastic sand. So, we're actually eating plastic, and we'll soon be sunbathing on plastic beaches. We have done this to our lovely planet, and we need to stop.

So, stop using plastic bags, stop using coffee cups with plastic lids, stop buying over-packaged food. If we all do so, perhaps we'll no longer see the depressing and heartbreaking images of birds building nests for their young out of plastic, or turtles mistaking plastic bags for food as they look like jellyfish. This is all too sad, and it needs to stop.

Lesson 12.4 Track 3.13

Chair, Indira Patel, Bill Patterson, Molly Chang, David Perez

C: So, the first question is, do the panel agree that genetic engineering, in particular the genetic modification of plants and animals that we eat, should be halted due to the potential for unforeseen future dangers that it may cause for us and the planet? Well, certainly, this matter still raises a lot of controversy. GM foods are banned in many countries and the science is probably still relatively young. Indira Patel, what are your thoughts?

IP: Well, you won't be surprised to hear that I disagree with the basic tenet of the question, that is that this research should be halted. Genetic engineering may mean we can actually feed everyone on this planet, something we are significantly failing to do at the moment. Rice that requires less water; cows that produce higher yields of milk; potatoes that are resistant to disease. That's what genetic modification means, and I believe that is something we should strive for. How many more children do we want to see on our TV screens dying of starvation?

C: David, what do you have to say?

DP: Well, as Indira said, this, er, research certainly shouldn't be halted, although, although, I mean, that's not to say that it shouldn't be heavily controlled and carefully managed. Which is, which is really the situation we have now, and I think that if those safeguards continue, well, we, erm, we have little to, er, worry about, really.

C: OK, I imagine you might have a different view Bill. Am I right?

BP: What David said about current safeguards might sound reasonable, however he seems to be forgetting that not all countries engaged in GM food production have exactly the same standards as us. And don't forget, genetic engineering of food is really about business, not science and not academia. This means that profit is the driving force, and we all know that profit causes a blindness when it comes to potential dangers. Can we really trust scientists who are working for profit-driven multinationals?

IP: Hold on, hold on a minute. If I understand you correctly, you're saying that science-based businesses can't be trusted. That is patently absurd. You trust pharmaceutical companies, don't you? They're just as driven by profit as an agrochemical company. It would hardly be good for profit if they did produce something that was a danger to human society, would it?

C: Before you respond to Indira, Bill, could I just bring Molly in here?

BP: Well, I'd like to give an immediate answer actually.

C: I understand, but I think we should hear from Molly first. Molly?

MC: Thank you. First of all, could I just pick up on something that Indira said about feeding the world's population. She claimed that genetic engineering will enable us to feed the world, suggesting that that wasn't currently possible. Well, while it may be true that many millions of people are suffering from starvation, or poor diets, that isn't because there isn't enough food. It's because the world's food is divided unequally. We could feed everyone now, if there was the political and commercial will to do so. And I would predict that the current inequality would continue even if we had GM food. The whole thing is merely another attempt by big business to make bigger profits.

MC: And another thing, regarding Indira's argument that we trust pharmaceutical companies, so therefore we can trust agrochemical or bio-engineering firms, I'm not sure that that is a fair argument, and perhaps we should return to what the original question said, which was that there are unforeseen dangers. The problem is that we don't know what will happen once genetically engineered organisms co-exist with natural ones. Will they inter-breed to produce defective species, making the food situation even worse? Will one cause the extinction of the other? These kind of issues can't be answered in the lab, but they are real, fair and important questions. And so, can we really go on with this research?

Review Units 10–12 Track 3.15

Simon Armitage

Hi. This is the voice message board for *Public Opinion Counts* … and we'd like to hear your opinion. Our topic this week is the Modbury stand against plastic carrier bags. Tell us what you think after the tone.

S: Oh, er, hi … hello. Erm, my name's Simon Armitage, from Bristol, and my mobile number is 07944 675402. Erm … never done this before … Well, I think that what Modbury has done is good, I mean, we all take our lifestyle for granted but it can't, it can't go on forever. But I don't think Modbury really goes far enough. I mean, getting rid of plastic … plastic bags is all well and good, but what about other plas … plastic in general? We should look at other things too, like, bigger things, like, … erm, it's not only … there's also the bigger issue of packaging, the amount of packaging shops use, and we don't recycle this packaging, I mean, we can recycle all sorts of plastic but we don't. Too difficult, I suppose. Then there's the fact that supermarkets treat farmers so badly, they don't pay enough for their produce. Don't get me started on that! Erm … well, that's what I think anyway. I'd better go … I'd better stop now. Erm … hope to hear from you. Bye.

Review Units 10–12 Track 3.16

Presenter, Simon Armitage, Lucy Thompson, Graham Lister

P: OK, let's talk about packaging. If I could just pick up on something that Simon said in his voice message, about the amount of packaging that shops use. Simon.

S: Yes, I reckon that shops could do a lot more than just charge for plastic bags. They could reduce the packaging they use, I mean, look at a lot of the stuff that we buy in supermarkets – plastic wrappings in plastic boxes with a cardboard label …

L: Simon, you're right, but you haven't been to the shops in Modbury. It simply isn't the case that they use a lot of packaging. To be honest, the shopkeepers have really done well – they use paper now to wrap things or just put vegetables for example straight into our bags …

G: And that's where the problem lies!

By and large, these bags are made of unsustainable cotton – and think of the oil used in the process to make cotton. Is that any worse than plastic? Really, Lucy, it seems a little naïve that the people of Modbury think they're doing so much to help the environment.

L: No, Graham, we don't think that. We know what we're doing is very little, but at least it's a start. What Simon said about supermarkets is true – they should start to look more closely at the things they stock – is it really necessary to wrap bread in plastic?

S: Yeah, exactly. And as for the way they package vegetables – my local supermarket wraps individual peppers in plastic. I've complained, but they don't listen.

L: But Simon, they do sometimes. We have one small supermarket in Modbury, and they've started to change the way they do things. That's what I mean about starting small and …

Ian Lebeau studied Modern Languages at the University of Cambridge and Applied Linguistics at the University of Reading. He has nearly 30 years' experience in ELT – mainly in higher education – and has taught in Spain, Italy and Japan. He is currently Senior Lecturer in English as a Foreign Language at London Metropolitan University.

Gareth Rees studied Natural Sciences at the University of Cambridge. Having taught in Spain and China, he currently teaches at the University of the Arts London and is Course Leader for its Academic English courses in China. He also develops English language materials for the BBC World Service Learning English section and he makes films which appear in festivals and on British television.

David Falvey studied Politics, Philosophy and Economics at the University of Oxford and did his MA in TEFL at the University of Birmingham. He has lived in Africa and the Middle East and has teaching, training and managerial experience in the UK and Asia, including working as a teacher trainer at the British Council in Tokyo. He was, until recently, Head of the English Language Centre at London Metropolitan University. David is co-author of the successful business English course *Market Leader*.

Simon Kent studied History at the University of Sheffield. He has over 20 years' teaching experience including three years in Berlin at the time of German reunification. Simon is co-author of the successful business English course *Market Leader*. He is currently Senior Lecturer in English as a Foreign Language at London Metropolitan University.

David Cotton studied Economics at the University of Reading and French Language and Literature at the University of Toronto. He has over 40 years' teaching and training experience, and is co-author of the successful *Market Leader* and *Business Class* coursebooks. He has taught in Canada, France and England, and been visiting lecturer in many universities overseas. He is a frequent speaker at international conferences such as BESIG and IATEFL. He is currently visiting lecturer at London Metropolitan University.

Far left: Simon Kent
Centre left: David Falvey
Centre: Gareth Rees
Centre right: Ian Lebeau
Far right: David Cotton